"It's always important to stay conn[...]
Faithbook of Jesus will help twentysom[...]
nects with life, culture, and Scripture."

— LARRY OSBORNE, senior pastor, North Coast [...],
Vista, California

"In a world of transition and uncertainty, it's difficult to find a devotional that targets the unique issues young adults face. *Faithbook of Jesus* brings to the table Renee's fresh, funny, and much-needed voice."

— ANNE JACKSON, author of *Mad Church Disease*;
blogger, FlowerDust.net

"Any author who can quote *Good Will Hunting* while talking about Jesus has my attention. Renee Johnson does that while encouraging twentysomethings to grow in a new and fresh way. With an acknowledgment of a messy spirituality and a raw unfiltered style, Renee has written a devotional that should sit on the bedside of every twentysomething Christ follower you know."

— SHAWN WOOD, author of *200 Pomegranates and an Audience of One*
and *Wasabi Gospel*; experience pastor, Seacoast Church

"When I mentor a writer and speaker, I encourage her to make the Bible come alive so that the average person can be equipped and encouraged. In *Faithbook of Jesus*, Renee Johnson succeeds at this. Renee is a fresh voice, presenting solid truth in an exciting new way. If you enjoy Facebook, Twitter, or blogs, you will love Renee's clever writing style. Renee is a leader for her generation and will guide the reader into an exciting life-changing adventure with God."

— PAM FARREL, international speaker; relationship specialist;
author of *Men Are Like Waffles, Women Are Like Spaghetti*

"To a generation of people today, reality TV is real, text messaging is communication, and Facebook is friendship. The timeless, all-inspired Word of God can be seen as an outdated manual with little to offer the modern sojourner. It takes a creative, insightful, and dare I say younger writer like Renee Johnson to bridge the gap between the twentysomething, technically savvy, experiential generation and the ever-applicable, life-changing Word of God. Renee understands her generation. Her devotional will help her generation understand God's Word."

— CHICO GOFF, founding pastor, Mission Hills Church, San Marcos,
California; adjunct professor, Biola University

"This book is perfect for people like me who sometimes just need to get right to it with God throughout our busy days. It's uplifting and easy to keep up with daily. Renee's writing is relatable, not preachy, and her style will connect with readers at all levels of their faith walk."

—KERRI POMAROLLI, comedienne, speaker, and author

"Renee has a way of making the Word come alive and bringing it into your life through *Faithbook of Jesus*. Her passion and untamed faith pour off the pages. If you are looking for something to add to your daily time with God or are just looking for something to get you into the Word daily, this is the book for you!"

—KETRIC NEWELL, speaker; youth pastor, LifeChurch

"Renee Johnson's writing is both inspiring and informative! It is so refreshing to read a book that helps me break away from this noisy, busy world and become quiet enough to hear from the Lord."

—ALEX MCFARLAND, president, Southern Evangelical Seminary

"My dad always taught me the importance of presenting profound truths in a simple manner. Renee has mastered this principle. *Faithbook of Jesus* presents simple yet hard-hitting spiritual truths in a way that will challenge you to go deeper in your faith."

—SEAN MCDOWELL, speaker; educator;
author of *Apologetics for a New Generation*

"Renee Johnson's vibrant relationship with Jesus bubbles over as she loves, writes, and encourages others on their journey with God."

—ERIC BRYANT, navigator, Mosaic Church, Los Angeles, California;
author of *Peppermint-Filled Piñatas*; blogger, www.ericbryant.org

"This book is testimony to what a dream, passion, and persistence can accomplish. What started as an occasional blog has now become a book with a devotion for every day of the year. Renee presents biblical truth in a way that communicates to her own generation by often alluding to things that are a familiar part of most twentysomethings' worlds."

—NED MERVICH, twentysomethings pastor, North Coast Church

"Renee Johnson's passion for young adults is God-given and God-propelled. He has clearly entrusted her to spur young people into a lifelong love of God and His Word. Her life is a living testament to His mercy, and this book is just one more way she's doing all she can to fulfill His purpose in her life. Read this book if you want to find out what His glorious purpose is for you!"

—MICHAEL FRANZESE, author of *I'll Make You an Offer You Can't Refuse*

faithbook

of

jesus

CONNECTING WITH JESUS DAILY

RENEE JOHNSON

Devotional Diva

NAVPRESS

NAVPRESS●

NavPress is the publishing ministry of The Navigators, an international Christian organization and leader in personal spiritual development. NavPress is committed to helping people grow spiritually and enjoy lives of meaning and hope through personal and group resources that are biblically rooted, culturally relevant, and highly practical.

For a free catalog go to www.NavPress.com
or call 1.800.366.7788 in the United States or 1.800.839.4769 in Canada.

ACKNOWLEDGMENTS

To Jesus—you are my Husband, my Heavenly Father, my Healer, my Best Friend, my All-in-All. Even though I don't show it by my actions sometimes, you are my Everything. I owe you my life.

To my mom and dad and brother, Richard. Thanks for your love, prayers, and support over the past twentysomething years of my life. None of this would have been possible without you all.

Thank you, Mom, for showing me what it means to spend time with Jesus daily.

To my Aunt Mim, for being the best prayer warrior a girl could ever have.

To my mentors, Marcia, Pam, and Vickie. Thank you for cheerleading my dream.

To Chad, who made me join Twitter.

To my agent's roommate, Alyssa, who found me on Twitter.

To Rebekah C. and Rebekah G., for making my publishing dreams come true.

To Mike Miller, for granting me the pleasure of working with NavPress.

To my best friends, Jennifer, Amy, Monique, and Rachel. Your patient love walking me through ten painful years of suffering made me who I am today.

To my growth group at North Coast Church, for helping me through the painful process of writing a book and working full time.

To Scott Evans and everyone at Outreach, for allowing me to be the real me. To all the pastors, speakers, and comedians I have had the pleasure of working with on a daily basis.

THEM APPLES

*Now the serpent was more crafty than any of the wild animals the L*ORD *God had made. He said to the woman, "Did God really say, 'You must not eat from any tree in the garden'?"*

— GENESIS 3:1

Everyone likes apples. I just watched a three-minute YouTube video from the movie *Good Will Hunting*.[1] Will (Matt Damon) is famous for asking the question: "How do you like them apples?"

I looked up the origin of this phrase on Wikipedia but didn't find much — just a movie from 1974 called *Chinatown* and a few other movies, but nothing compared to Will's famous phrase.

It's no secret that apples have been the source of controversy since the beginning of man. Do you remember your first Sunday school story? God created Adam and Eve, and they lived happily ever after. Wait. No, they didn't.

They ate that stupid apple and got cast out of the Garden of Eden forever. Now the rest of creation has to suffer because they couldn't listen to the one thing God told them not to do. Eat an apple.

What amazes me even more is how we still fall into the same trap that Adam and Eve fell into that day. The Enemy is "more crafty," the Bible says. He knows how to deceive and make us disbelieve.

If you're hearing questions like "Did God really say that?" turn it back around and shove them apples back in the Devil's face.

66 99 Matt, 38, said, "How do you like them apples?"

  Dear Apple Jesus,
Sometimes you give us commands we don't like. Help us to trust that you have our best interests at heart and stay away from them dang apples. Amen.

When have you been tempted to do something you know God doesn't approve of? What happened? Please visit www.faithbookofjesus.com and click on "Community" to share.

To Read Further: Genesis 3:1-7

THROW IT OFF

Since we are surrounded by such a great cloud of witnesses, let us throw off everything that hinders and the sin that so easily entangles, and let us run with perseverance the race marked out for us.

— HEBREWS 12:1

What happens when a baby takes its first step? He or she stumbles and falls down, or looks for something to grab on to. Much like myself when I am learning how to walk in a new area of life; I am not very proficient.

Starting something new takes a willingness to throw off whatever is hindering me. That could be a relationship that I know I'm not supposed to be in, choosing how to spend my time, or even the way I spend my money.

Hannah Moore said, "Forgiveness is the economy of the heart . . . forgiveness saves the expense of anger, the cost of hatred, the waste of spirits."[2]

Today is the day to throw off whatever is bothering you—frustrating thoughts, negative emotions, or unrealistic demands on your time—as it says in Hebrews. Take those thoughts, crumple them up like a wad of paper, and throw them away.

Picture the wastebasket. Make the shot. Gone.

66 99 Brandon, 25, said if he knew he couldn't fail at trying something new, he "would own businesses, travel, and develop the largest music label and the largest network of commercial banks from the ground up."

 *Dear Jesus Who Makes All Things New,*
Thank you for looking at us as mature adults when we see ourselves as growing children. You know our limitations and you see us for who we will be—complete and whole. Help us to throw off whatever hinders us so that we can see ourselves as you see us. Amen.

What's your wastebasket story? I'd love to know how God helped you make the shot by throwing off whatever was hindering you from his best. Please visit www.faithbookofjesus.com and click on "Community" to share.

To Read Further: Hebrews 12:1-2

I GOT THE BLUES

And without faith it is impossible to please God, because anyone who comes to him must believe that he exists and that he rewards those who earnestly seek him.

— HEBREWS 11:6

It can be hard to confidently move forward and exercise faith when we are still learning how to walk. I feel tempted to shrink back from the first obstacle—which is usually due to stress or exhaustion at work, fear of being alone, or low self-esteem. That's when I start singin' the blues.

In his song "Don't Look Now but I've Got the Blues," B. B. King wrote that "troubles [are] everywhere." It's no different for you or me. Right now you could be experiencing a failed relationship, a lost college scholarship, your parents' divorce, or low funds to pay your rent because one of your jobs was cut due to the economy.

All of those things may make you want to grab a guitar and a microphone to sing the blues, but not so fast.

Let's learn to trust God. He can take care of our needs, and "without faith it is impossible to please God" (Hebrews 11:6).

66 99   Meghan, 24, said she prays when she feels like singing the blues. "I pray for healing, grace, mercy, understanding, wisdom, others, circumstances, life, my heart, ideas, creativity, courage, strength, patience, lots of things."

Dear Never-Got-the-Blues Jesus,
You see our strengths and weaknesses and carry us through times of depression and doubt. Help us to see that you've got a plan and that we can trust you instead of singing the blues. Amen.

What's your story of a time when you sang the blues? How did faith help you carry through? Please visit www.faithbookofjesus.com and click on "Community" to share.

To Read Further: Psalm 1

TRIALS PRODUCE FRUIT

He cuts off every branch in me that bears no fruit, while every branch that does bear fruit
he prunes so that it will be even more fruitful.
— JOHN 15:2

Do trials make you feel thirsty for more? Or do you just want out?

Learning what it's like to exercise faith in the midst of a trial is not easy. After I started reading through the Bible each day, I expected God to heal me right away. When he didn't, I was devastated.

I didn't want to develop more faith or be "pruned." I wanted to be back in school with the rest of my peers instead of nursing my health problems. With every trial there is a purpose, and what took me years to realize, I now wish to convey to you.

Jesus only prunes those he loves. If he didn't see potential in you or me, then he wouldn't cut off the branches that get in the way of our growth.

66 99 Virlu, 29, said that her times of "pruning" were over relationships "at least once or twice in my life (so far). . . . I am praying the next time is the last!"

Dear Jesus, the True Vine,
If we receive any encouragement today, let it come from you. Help us to realize that you prune only those you love. Help us to learn how to give grace to those in need. Give us the same love and purpose for one another. Amen.

What's your branch/vine story? Have you ever had a time in your life when God "pruned" you? Please visit www.faithbookofjesus.com and click on "Community" to share.

To Read Further: John 15:1-5

DESPERATE PRAYER LIVES

This, then, is how you should pray . . .
— MATTHEW 6:9

What do you consider praying? There can be many reasons why you pray, but the best reason of all is to talk with Jesus as you would your best friend. Here are four examples of how to know Jesus more personally today:

1. PRAY WITH PLEASE AND THANK YOU

"Do not be anxious about anything, but in everything, by prayer and petition, with thanksgiving, present your requests to God. And the peace of God, which transcends all understanding, will guard your hearts and your minds in Christ Jesus" (Philippians 4:6-7).

2. PRAY ABOUT ANYTHING

"And pray in the Spirit on all occasions with all kinds of prayers and requests. With this in mind, be alert and always keep on praying for all the saints" (Ephesians 6:18).

3. PRAY IN SECRET

"But when you pray, go into your room, close the door and pray to your Father, who is unseen. Then your Father, who sees what is done in secret, will reward you" (Matthew 6:6).

4. PRAY AS JESUS DID

"Our Father in heaven, hallowed be your name, your kingdom come, your will be done on earth as it is in heaven. Give us today our daily bread. Forgive us our debts, as we also have forgiven our debtors. And lead us not into temptation, but deliver us from the evil one" (Matthew 6:9-13).

66 99 Sheri, 23, said that prayer "is a place of quiet waiting on God. Other times it is requests for direction, healing of hurts, for Jesus to bring freedom to lives of friends, family, and for the many who do not know him."

Dear Teacher Jesus,
Thank you for the privilege of knowing you. Teach us how to pray. Give us prayer lives that are desperate for more of you each day. Amen.

What's your desperation story? Think about a time in your life when God answered the cries of your heart. Please visit www.faithbookofjesus.com and click on "Community" to share.

✗〇 To Read Further: Matthew 6:9-15

DISAPPOINTED MUCH?

Those who hope in me will not be disappointed.
— ISAIAH 49:23

What stresses you out? I stress when I don't get enough sleep and my schedule becomes too demanding. You'd think working with high-profile speakers and comedians (my dream job), graduating college, and moving out of my parent's house would keep me from disappointment. Wrong!

Every day, there are small disappointments that take my focus off Jesus—for instance, my singleness, my body image, and my bank account. I'm never satisfied. I'm sure you can relate. If I were to ask you to list five disappointments, I'll bet you could name them within five seconds.

The more consistent I am in spending time with Jesus daily, the less I let the day-to-day disappointments get to me. Having a daily routine with Jesus is just as important as getting to know your best friend. If you want to know more about your BFF, you spend time getting to know him or her.

Jesus promises us that those who wait for him will not be disappointed. Tell me then, what are we waiting for?

❝❞ Sheila, 24, said, "I stress about everything. . . . And what about when reading my Bible does not equal feeling better?"

 Dear Jesus Who Never Disappoints,
There are just some days that couldn't be any more stressful and full of disappointment. Show me what to do and how to pray when reading your Word doesn't make me feel any better about myself, my weight, my singleness, etc. I know that trusting in you will not put me to shame. Amen.

👥 Want to comment on your bad day? I know Sheila and I are not the only ones who sometimes feel that reading the Bible and praying aren't enough. Please visit www.faithbookofjesus.com and click on "Community" to share.

✖ To Read Further: John 16:33

GOD OF REFUGE

The LORD is my rock, my fortress, and my savior; my God is my rock, in whom I find protection. He is my shield, the power that saves me, and my place of safety.
— PSALM 18:2 (NLT)

When I picture a rock, I think of an immovable object. If Jesus is my rock, then why am I so easily moved?

It's easy to blame the economy. I can count more friends than I have fingers and toes who have lost their jobs, had a car repossessed, been kicked out of their apartments, or moved halfway across the country to get a new life.

The Israelites experienced something similar in Bible times. Cities of refuge were set up as places to flee for one's life (see Numbers 35). Don't you wish you had a place like that to go when you're short on rent, get in a fight with your girlfriend/boyfriend, or fail at a new career?

On the other hand, maybe you're not desperate. Maybe your life is going rather well, and you're in a position to help out your friends who are currently experiencing tough times.

Thankfully, we serve a God who is so big that he sent his Son Jesus to save us all—so that we could have eternal refuge through him.

66 99 Elisha, 23, said that in light of today's economy, what he fears most is "my friends having to move for work."

 Dear Jesus, the Eternal Refuge,
Thank you for being our refuge. Help us remember where to go when we feel lost, upset, or like we don't have any place else to go. Be our refuge and our comfort. Give us that time-out that we need to rest and reevaluate before we move on and take another step. Amen.

Have you been affected by today's economy? Would you like prayer? Please visit www.faithbookofjesus.com and click on "Community" to share.

To Read Further: John 3:15-16

BE SET FREE

Daughter, your faith has healed you. Go in peace and be freed from your suffering.
— MARK 5:34

There was a woman in the Bible who bled for more than thirteen years. She wanted to be set free. Amidst a crowd of people, instead of asking for help, she decided to touch the hem of Jesus' garment. When Jesus realized that healing power had gone out from him, he immediately asked who had touched him.

I wrote this poem for a friend who needed to feel Jesus' touch. Read it as if he is speaking directly to you today.

I can see behind the look in your eyes, something that goes much deeper
Than the smile on your face.
You long to be thought of as worthy.
The things you once thought would bring happiness and fulfillment
Have become your prison bars that separate you from your own freedom.
But there is a way out.
A man stands in front of you, with your freedom.
Will you notice him? Will you realize he is there? And cares for you like no other?
There is a way out. Put your hope in Him, and watch Him set you free.
Free from all the things that entangle you, disappoint you, and leave you insecure.
To the freedom you always wanted, thought you had, and can possess.
Will you choose to be set free?

❝❞ Thomas, 25, said, "It is okay to ask for help," when asked if there was anything else he could think of that would address the specific needs of twentysomethings.

Dear Jesus, Full of Healing Power,
I ask for your help. No matter if I am bold or timid—help me to have the faith to believe. I'm ready for a fresh start with you today. Amen.

Do you need a touch from Jesus? Please visit www.faithbookofjesus.com and click on "Community" to share.

To Read Further: Mark 5:24-35

(I'VE GOT) THE POWER

Let light shine out of darkness.
— 2 CORINTHIANS 4:6

Every time I hear the song "(I've Got) The Power," I think of the movie *Bruce Almighty* with Jim Carrey when he was walking on water. What struck me most from that movie was the fact that Bruce didn't know how much power he already had just by choosing to acknowledge the one who was in him giving him the power.

Jesus gave his power away so that I could have just enough light for my path—one day at a time. Psalm 119:105 says, "Your word is a lamp to my feet and a light for my path."

I try to make a habit of spending time in the Word for a few minutes in the morning before I start my day. "For God, who said, 'Let light shine out of darkness,' made his light shine in our hearts to give us the light of the knowledge of the glory of God in the face of Christ . . . to show that this all-surpassing power is from God and not from us" (2 Corinthians 4:6-7).

Why would I want to miss out on that power? Have we forgotten that Jesus has the power to light the dark places for us?

66 99 Kari, 24, said, "I think it's hard for twentysomethings to really have their 'quiet time' with God and time to read every day because of busy schedules, work, etc."

 Dear Power-Giving Jesus,
I need the kind of power that helps me remember who I am and whose I am. Shine forth your light on my path today to let me see just how blessed I already am. Amen.

Do you have a power story you'd like to share? Please visit www .faithbookofjesus.com and click on "Community" to share.

To Read Further: 2 Corinthians 4:7-12

CELEBRATE YOU

"Martha, Martha," the Lord answered, "you are worried and upset about many things."
— LUKE 10:41

One day Mary and Martha were getting ready for company. But not just any company—they were hosting Jesus and his crew. Martha found herself doing all the work alone. She was frustrated and said, "Lord, don't you care that my sister has left me to do the work by myself? Tell her to help me!" (Luke 10:40).

Jesus' next words to her are very interesting if you look at them from the perspective that Jesus was celebrating Martha. He challenged her by saying, "You are worried and upset about many things, but only one thing is needed" (verses 41-42).

What was that one thing? It wasn't an outward sign but an inward one. Yes, Jesus needed to eat and Martha was busy trying to make that happen, but Mary was just soaking up his very presence and being. When was the last time you got to enjoy that kind of time doing nothing? Jesus was trying to show Martha that she was already celebrated. No matter what she did or didn't do, her worth was not found in her work but at the feet of him who has the power to save from worry, fear, and a demanding spirit.

God wants us to celebrate life with him today by letting the worries of the world fade away.

❝❞ Ronald, 22, said what stresses him out most, like Martha, is "not taking breaks."

 Dear Celebration Jesus,
Please help me see that these trials are meant to make me the best version of me. Please forgive me when I blame those around me instead of focusing on this new thing you're doing—celebrating me. Thank you for forgiving me when I believe anything otherwise. Amen.

👥 If you've ever found your worth in your work instead of in who you are, tell your story by visiting www.faithbookofjesus.com. Click on "Community" to share.

✝ To Read Further: Luke 10:38-42

DO YOU FEEL LUCKY, PUNK?

If you remain in me and my words remain in you, ask whatever you wish,
and it will be given you.
— JOHN 15:7

What do we do when life deals us a devastating blow? Do we consider it pure joy?

No matter how big the trial, the test is developing our perseverance. Perseverance must have its perfect work so that we will be complete, not lacking in anything (see James 1:4).

"But what if I don't want it to have its perfect work?" you say. "What if I want everything to stay exactly the way it is?"

Jesus doesn't give us anything we can't handle—and if a trial is really disguised as a new beginning, then maybe the question isn't "do you feel lucky (punk)?" but "what can I learn from this trial before he takes it away?"

In the movie *Evan Almighty* the wife prays for her family to become closer, and through a series of unfortunate circumstances they were able to spend lots more time together. Now, their time together was spent building an ark as the laughingstock of the neighborhood, but nevertheless Jesus answered her prayers and they became a stronger family unit.

If you are struggling in the midst of a trial concerning your relationships, money, job, purpose, or health, I encourage you to ask Jesus if there is a lesson in the midst of your trial. He wants to bless you today.

❝❞ Carmen, 25, said, "I am a young mom of two. I often feel overwhelmed by all that is demanded of me as I try to be a great parent and wife."

 Dear Persevering Jesus,
Through whatever trials we face today, help us to remember there is a purpose and to look to you for strength. Please help us remember that you want us complete, not lacking in anything. Amen.

👥 How has Jesus taken your trial and turned it into a blessing? Please visit www .faithbookofjesus.com and click on "Community" to share.

⬄ To Read Further: James 1:2-8

TRY GIVING THANKS

I will give thanks to the LORD because of his righteousness and will sing praise to the name of the LORD Most High.
— PSALM 7:17

From the very beginning of the book of Psalms, David gives thanks. Of all people in the Bible, David knew what it meant to experience trials of every kind. He knew the purpose: One day he would be king of Israel. In the meantime, that didn't take away from the fact that everywhere he went, he was a walking dead man.

King Saul, the current king of Israel, had a hit out on David. Even though Saul had watched David defeat Goliath and save the Israelites from the Philistines and was soothed by David's skills on the harp, Saul knew that the Lord had rejected him as king and that David was to be next in line (see 1 Samuel 16:1).

So David hid. In mountains, caves, enemy towns, and any place that Saul's men wouldn't find him. For me, this means no BlackBerry service, portable laptop, cushy job, food to eat, or warm place to live. Can you imagine? And yet David still praised Jesus and still became the next king of Israel.

Today and every day start by giving thanks. The same God who spared David's life can and will spare yours too.

❝❞ Chris, 23, said if there was anything about the Christian walk that he would like to know more about it is "sanctification . . . something we don't talk about much anymore!"

  Dear King Jesus,
You are worthy of praise. You are the Alpha and the Omega, the Beginning and the End. Help see us through our trials from the moment they make us hide to the moment we begin walking in freedom again. By the power of your name we pray. Amen.

Do you have a praise story? Please visit www.faithbookofjesus.com and click on "Community" to share.

To Read Further: Psalm 30:12; 75:1

THE WAITING GAME

I waited patiently for the Lord to help me, and he turned to me and heard my cry.
— PSALM 40:1 (NLT)

One of my favorite devotional stories comes from *Streams in the Desert*. It is about a ten-year-old boy named George who was promised a stamp-collecting album for Christmas from his grandma. Christmas came and went, and no album. However, during the excitement of the holidays, little George told everyone that he had already received a stamp album. George's mom asked him if Grandma forgot, and George said, "Well, Mom, Grandma said, and that is the same as."[3]

Another month passed, and George decided to write a letter, thanking grandma for the stamp album. A week later, George received a letter in the mail from his grandma with thirty dollars because the stamp album that she ordered wasn't the right one and the new one wasn't in stock, so she sent George the money to buy himself one.

"Therefore I tell you, whatever you ask for in prayer, believe that you have received it, and it will be yours" (Mark 11:24).

"Only in returning to me and resting in me will you be saved. In quietness and confidence is your strength" (Isaiah 30:15, NLT).

66 99 Chris, 24, said, "How [do you] keep the Christian walk alive and active when you aren't living with parents telling you what to believe and to go to this church and to make this choice?"

 Dear Jesus Who Waits on Us,
Thank you for the story of the ten-year-old boy who waited. Help me to remember the same things, Jesus—that you are faithful and that you know just how long we need to wait. Put my mind at ease and allow me to rest while I wait on you. Amen.

When was the last time you waited for something and got it? Please visit www.faithbookofjesus.com and click on "Community" to share.

To Read Further: Isaiah 30:15; Mark 11:24

A NEW COMMAND

So now I am giving you a new commandment: Love each other. Just as I have loved you, you should love each other.

— JOHN 13:34 (NLT)

Whenever a new club opens in town, the owners make a VIP or exclusive guest list. Why, you may ask? The new owners are looking to attract a certain type of exclusive, high-paying customer.

When Jesus rolled into town with his entourage, he wasn't looking for some exclusive membership for the highest of society. Jesus said that he came to give a *new* commandment: to love everyone.

Non-exclusive—"If anyone would come after me, he must deny himself and take up his cross and follow me" (Matthew 16:24).

Everyone Included—"But you will receive power when the Holy Spirit comes on you; and you will be my witnesses in Jerusalem, and in all Judea and Samaria, and to the ends of the earth" (Acts 1:8).

Welcomes All—"Therefore go and make disciples of all nations, baptizing them in the name of the Father and of the Son and of the Holy Spirit" (Matthew 28:19).

❝❞ Emanuel, 24, said, "I want to know what it feels like to be forgiven for your sins [and not] judged."

 Dear New Jesus,
Thank you that you do not judge us where we are but instead include us in your nonexclusive club, where everyone is welcome to be a member. Help us to take that kind of love into the world today. Amen.

Do you have a story where someone included you and made you feel loved? Please visit www.faithbookofjesus.com and click on "Community" to share.

To Read Further: 1 John 4

OLD TESTAMENT PROPHECY

See, I will send my messenger, who will prepare the way before me.
— MALACHI 3:1

I don't have a degree in Old Testament theology, but what I do know is that Jesus fulfilled all 333 Old Testament prophecies.[4] There are eight prophecies about Christ in the Old Testament. Here they are:

First prophecy is Jesus was the seed of a woman (see Genesis 3:15). First prophecy fulfilled (see Galatians 4:4).

Second prophecy is Jesus was a descendent of Abraham (see Genesis 12:3). Second prophecy fulfilled (see Matthew 1:1).

Third prophecy is Jesus was born of the seed of Isaac (see Genesis 17:9). Third prophecy fulfilled (see Matthew 1:2).

Fourth prophecy is Jesus was born of the seed of Jacob (see Numbers 24:17). Fourth prophecy fulfilled (see Matthew 1:2).

Fifth prophecy is Jesus was from the tribe of Judah (see Genesis 49:10). Fifth prophecy fulfilled (see Luke 3:33).

Sixth prophecy is Jesus was the heir to the throne of David (see Isaiah 9:7). Sixth prophecy fulfilled (see Luke 1:32-33).

Seventh prophecy is his birthplace is Bethlehem (see Micah 5:2). Seventh prophecy fulfilled (see Luke 2:4-7).

Eighth prophecy is being born of a virgin (see Isaiah 7:14). Eighth prophecy fulfilled (see Luke 1:26-27,30-31).

I hope today's devotional will take you deeper into a better understanding of your faith. We won't always know everything about Jesus, but it's comforting to know that all the prophecies came true.

66 99 Sheri, 25, said, "My Old Testament knowledge is somewhat lacking in a few areas."

 Dear Prophetic Jesus,
You were a descendent of Abraham, from the tribe of Judah, born of a virgin in Bethlehem. We worship you because you are the One True God. Amen.

Do you want to know more about Old Testament prophecies? Please visit http://www.allabouttruth.org/old-testament-prophecy-concerning-the-messiah-faq.htm.

To Read Further: Genesis 3:15; Isaiah 9:7; Matthew 1:2

UNITY IN CHRIST

The body is a unit, though it is made up of many parts; and though all its parts are many, they form one body.
— 1 CORINTHIANS 12:12

Paul wrote in 1 Corinthians 12 that we are the body of Christ. Can you imagine? Brothers and sisters in the Lord living in China, India, Russia, the United States, or Korea. What about the United Kingdom, Malaysia, or the Caribbean? Europe. The Middle East. Africa. Japan. Australia. New Zealand. South America. Canada. Everywhere throughout the world there are people who are completely different yet all share something in common. We're all a part of the same body of Christ.

As someone living in the United States, it's hard to imagine what my "brother" is doing in South Korea or my "sister" in Uganda. Knowing that there are so many different cultures out there gives me hope to imagine just how big the family of Jesus is, and then imagine how awesome it will be when we celebrate diversity in heaven for eternity. We can also marvel in the fact that we are not alone.

66 99 Dana, 26, said, "Being single at this age is hard when most of your friends are married and everyone is saying you'll find someone someday, but you still sit home alone on the weekends."

 Dear Papa Jesus,
You are the one who made us beautiful on the individual level and beautiful together as one body. Help us to discover our part in the unit. Give us the ability to mix well with others, knowing that together we are representing you to the world. Thank you, Jesus. Amen.

Have you ever spent a summer in China or a week in Florida witnessing? Please visit www.faithbookofjesus.com and click on "Community" to share.

To Read Further: 1 Corinthians 12:12-27

REST ON

Come to me, all you who are weary and burdened, and I will give you rest.
— MATTHEW 11:28

Tough situations produce two different kinds of reactions: fright or flight. I usually tend toward fear (fright) when I feel weary and burdened.

To prove it to you, I read through some of my journal entries from 1996. "Jesus, my thoughts are all grumbled; I think my spirit's crumbled. I can't seem to think straight because all that I can do is wait, wait, wait. . . ."

I don't rest well. I will do everything I possibly can before giving up. I'll fix the problem. I'll push my burden on someone else. I'll ask my family and all my best friends for support—and then when it's the very last part of the day, when I'm so tired I'm about to fall asleep, then and only then will I give my problems to the Lord.

I guess it doesn't help that I was homeschooled. I taught myself everything I need to know—from English to mastering the piano to teaching math (I was once a math major). It's just easier for me to figure out a solution to my problems when my body is wired that way, instead of giving my problems to Jesus at the first sign of weariness and laying them at his feet.

Do you ever feel like that?

66 99 Arman, 23, said he becomes stressed by "my inability to say 'no' to others, ha-ha. I always get myself in a pickle by trying to help everyone other than myself."

 Dear Jesus We Can Rest On,
Thank you for your promises that tell us how to find rest. Please help us when we try to fix our problems and everyone else's problems on our own. Let us develop a devotional life that far exceeds any difficulty or burden because we already know how to rest on you. Amen.

How do you rest well? Please visit www.faithbookofjesus.com and click on "Community" to share.

To Read Further: Matthew 11:28-30

IF YOU'RE HAPPY AND YOU KNOW IT

Do not grieve, for the joy of the Lord is your strength.
— NEHEMIAH 8:10

I asked my friend Addison what her favorite Bible verse is, and she told me Nehemiah 8:10, which is our verse for today. I was shocked to hear this from my friend because Addison is eight years old. It reminds me of the song that says, "If you're happy and you know it, clap your hands."

Happiness is something we wear on our sleeves. Joy yields results. Nehemiah told his people, the Israelites, not to be sad because Jesus was going to fix their problem. You see, Nehemiah asked permission from an enemy king whom he was serving to leave and help his people rebuild their city wall. The entire book is actually quite fascinating. I encourage you to read through it.

There were many obstacles to building this enormous wall, and the Israelites didn't have any fancy tools or machinery. Instead, each man took care of the wall in front of his house. Nehemiah and the people chose not to look at their impossible circumstances with grief. They chose to sing with Jesus, "If you're joyful and you know it, clap your hands [one brick at a time]!"

Now, imagine your wall. Isn't it easier to have joy when there are no projects with impossible deadlines looming over your head? Instead of sinking down into the pit of anxiety or depression, choose joy.

❝❞   Dick, 24, said he handles fear this way: "Keep trying."

 Dear Joyful Jesus,
Thank you that what we have in you is more than a song. May we praise you for who you are, Jesus, and how you bring us joy no matter what circumstance, emotion, or pain we are facing today. Amen.

How do you sing a joyful song? Please visit www.faithbookofjesus.com and click on "Community" to share.

To Read Further: Nehemiah 8:10-18

SHOW ME THE CREDIT

Barak said to her, "If you go with me, I will go; but if you don't go with me, I won't go."
— JUDGES 4:8

Being in your twenties is a hard age sometimes because we don't have it all figured out yet. Do you have what it takes to finish college, get the job of your dreams, and find the love of your life?

Jael had what it takes. She is the woman who drove a tent peg into the temple of King Sisera. As a tentmaker, I'm sure her lifestyle was not always easy—so having a fugitive king asking for a place to hide and a drink of water was the perfect opportunity for her.

A few verses earlier in Judges 4, Deborah, Israel's prophetess, was telling Barak that he was to take his men and fight against Jabin's army. Because Barak was afraid, he asked Deborah to come with him into battle. Deborah said that she would go but that the credit of the battle would belong to a woman. The full blessing was supposed to belong to Barak, but because he did not believe, Jesus raised up someone else.

Do you ever feel that way in your own life? Scared to go after what you really want? Or that the credit belongs to someone smarter or prettier than you? Wherever you go, Jesus will go with you. Ask him to "show you the credit."

66 99 Alicia, 22, said she'd love to "change the world. . . . There's a lot of tough stuff facing the world today."

 Dear Jesus Warrior,
No matter if we're trying to get a new job, pursuing a new relationship, or wondering how to raise young children, help us to see that you're on our side. Show us the credit, Jesus; show us the credit! Amen.

How do you "show the credit"? Please visit www.faithbookofjesus.com and click on "Community" to share.

To Read Further: Judges 4–5

CAN YOU HANDLE THE GOOD NEWS?

How beautiful on the mountains are the feet of those who bring good news.
— ISAIAH 52:7

What does "good news" mean to you? Is it receiving a job promotion or popping the question to your fiancée? Or is good news about being forgiven? I've heard the word *evangelism* defined as "good news."

When I think of evangelism, I typically picture a guy standing on a soapbox preaching John 3:16. I also get scared and kind of upset all at the same time because it's *those* types of Christians who give a negative stereotype. They're loud, pushy, and aggressive when it comes to spreading the message of Jesus and the gospel—and I'm not like that.

Let's go back to the meaning of today's verse in Isaiah. Did you know that the modern-day printing press of fresh, hot news was a guy who would run into the heat of the battle to deliver (hopefully good) news?

In Ephesians 6:15, it says that runner's shoes are called the sandals of the gospel or the shoes of peace. They represent a readiness and willingness to respond to Jesus when he calls. Instead of thinking of Christianity as doom and gloom, think of it simply as good news.

I'm sure you can handle the good news.

66 99 Jamie, 24, said that she wants to know more about "background knowledge and general knowledge about the Bible and ancient cultures and history."

 Dear Good-News Jesus,
Help us have an answer for anyone who asks about the hope that we have, whether we're called to take that good news into our homes, twenty miles away, or two thousand miles away on the mission field. Amen.

Do you have a good-news story? Please visit www.faithbookofjesus.com and click on "Community" to share.

To Read Further: Acts 20:24; Ephesians 6:15

LIONS, TIGERS, AND BEARS, OH MY!

Be self-controlled and alert. Your enemy the devil prowls around like a roaring lion looking for someone to devour. Resist him, standing firm in the faith, because you know that your brothers throughout the world are undergoing the same kind of sufferings.
— 1 PETER 5:8-9

What if you lived in a foreign country that didn't allow Bibles? What would you do? For me, these verses would quickly become my favorite Bible passage for two reasons: the Enemy is real, and I'm not alone.

The Enemy is always looking for ways to devour us. It usually comes at a time when we are not expecting it, doesn't it? *I urge you to watch out.* The most crucial time is while we're waiting. Just as Jesus was led out into the desert to be tempted by the Enemy for forty days and nights, we too must be careful while we wait. We must not doubt the promises of Jesus; instead, we should immediately resist and stand firm.

Your Christian brothers and sisters are also suffering. This is not exactly a comforting thought, but knowing that you are not the only one being picked on for your faith helps. Do yourself a favor and lend a helping hand to a Christian brother or sister who just might be standing in front of a roaring lion today.

❝❞ Lauren, 28, said what breaks her heart is "the way we as people treat one another—so often in a selfish or unfriendly manner . . . in relation to other countries and the poor who don't even have the bare essentials to live, when others have so much."

 Dear Protector Jesus,
We come before your throne and beg you to help us with our lions, tigers, and bears. Give us the ability not only to resist but to stand firm. Deliver us out of harm today. Amen.

👥 What's your lion, tiger, or bear story? Please visit www.faithbookofjesus.com and click on "Community" to share.

✚ To Read Further: 1 Peter 5:8-10

BECAUSE YOU'RE WORTH IT

Your faith—of greater worth than gold, which perishes even though refined by fire—may be proved genuine and may result in praise, glory and honor when Jesus Christ is revealed.
— 1 PETER 1:7

It's the weirdest thing, showing someone his or her worth. Just as gold is refined in fire (yes, fire!), so are we. The best example of fire in the Bible, which shows three men actually being put into a fire, is from Daniel:

> Shadrach, Meshach and Abednego replied to the king, "O Nebuchadnezzar, we do not need to defend ourselves before you in this matter. If we are thrown into the blazing furnace, the God we serve is able to save us from it, and he will rescue us from your hand, O king. But even if he does not, we want you to know, O king, that we will not serve your gods or worship the image of gold you have set up." (3:16-18)

Maybe Jesus is allowing you to walk through the fire to prove his love and how much he truly values your life. Don't be scared; you're worth it. Sometimes we all need a good refining moment to show us that we're worth it. Do you know your worth?

❝❞ Megan, 23, said she struggles from "poor self-image, because when I was growing up, my father told me that I was worthless. This has always stuck with me, and I believe it has made a huge impact on how I see myself."

Dear Refiner Jesus,
Thank you for loving us enough to show us our worth. Help us realize today that these trials we go through are meant to refine us to be pure gold. Thank you for taking the time to make us into something beautiful. We love you. Amen.

Do you have a unique way of showing someone his or her worth? Please visit www.faithbookofjesus.com and click on "Community" to share.

To Read Further: Daniel 3

NEED TO VENT?

A fool gives full vent to his anger, but a wise man keeps himself under control.
— PROVERBS 29:11

When you are upset, who do you talk to? Do you talk to your mother, a best friend, or maybe a co-worker or three or four?

When I get upset, I talk to everyone. I'm not shy. I'll tell the clerk at the grocery store, the family dog, and my downstairs neighbors and then update my status on Facebook at least three times. But it doesn't make it right—especially when there are other people involved.

Last year, I went through a painful breakup with my roommates. It got to the point where it was separating our friendship. I was the one used to living with everything neat and organized. The two girls I lived with weren't the Suzie Homemaker type.

I thought I was being a good roommate by asking them to keep the common areas clean and to wash and put their dishes away (so I could cook), but I became a nag. It was tough to decipher between common sense and what I wanted.

After my roommates stopped listening to me, my venting turned into anger, which led to gossip and slander. I have since apologized to my old roommates and restored the friendships, but if you find yourself in a position where it's just too easy to vent, don't do it.

❝❞ Brian, 27, said, "My main fear is anger, adversity, and hostility. I don't like volatile forms of confrontation."

 Dear Jesus Who Listens,
Help us to learn how to channel our feelings of hurt to you. Only you truly know a person's heart, thoughts, and intentions. Thanks for letting us vent to you. You truly are the best listener in the world. We love you. Amen.

Reality television tells us it's okay to gossip and slander others. What do you think of today's verse? Please visit www.faithbookofjesus.com and click on "Community" to share.

To Read Further: Psalm 37:8; Proverbs 17:9

OUT OF CONTROL

For God is not a God of disorder but of peace.
— 1 CORINTHIANS 14:33

Life can sometimes catch us off guard and throw us into a tizzy. We spin around and around, hoping to catch our breath. Disorder happens every day. What frustrates me to no end is chaos. I love order and peace. I am the kind of person who has a place for everything, and if I can't find something — it's definitely lost.

I'm a visionary. I pioneer new paths when people could never see a way through. So, when disorder happens in my life, I try to find a way through. Or I go around. Create a detour. And if that doesn't work — I panic!

Larry Crabb wrote in his book *Soul Talk*, "It's becoming clear that our first order of business is not to pursue satisfaction, but to identify what's getting in the way of the deepest satisfaction available to the human soul."[5] Sometimes, Jesus just wants my attention. If I'm getting too good at meeting my own needs and taking Jesus for granted, I notice he allows disorder in my life so I must seek his help.

What gets in the way of you experiencing peace? Take a few minutes and ask Jesus. He will show you by giving you his peace.

6699 Andrew, 28, said his current disorder is "being unemployed; I fear being financially dependent on someone else."

 Dear Orderly Jesus,
Help us to be honest with where we are. Don't let us hide the kind of disorder that can lead to living a life out of control. Help us to pay attention to warning signs. Remove the blocks that stand in our way. Thanks for helping us stay the course and for your peace that surpasses all understanding. Amen.

What is your current state of disorder? Please visit www.faithbookofjesus.com and click on "Community" to share.

To Read Further: Colossians 3:15

GREEN MEANS GO

Then the LORD said to Moses, "Why are you crying out to me?
Tell the Israelites to move on."
— EXODUS 14:15

I asked this question before: "When faced with a difficult situation, what is your first reaction? Run or hide?"

The problem with pain is that when we experience it, all we can see is our problem. Unless you're Superman (or Jesus, of course), it feels impossible to move forward.

When I experience pain that keeps me from moving on, I find comfort in Exodus 14:15. When God told the Israelites to keep moving, they were in no position to do so. All they could see was water in front of them.

How can we move forward if there is something standing in our way? A broken marriage. Health problems. Strained finances. How then are we to move on in freedom?

Moses answered the people, "Do not be afraid. Stand firm and you will see the deliverance the LORD will bring you today. The Egyptians you see today you will never see again. The LORD will fight for you; you need only to be still."

Then the LORD said to Moses, "Why are you crying out to me? Tell the Israelites to move on. Raise your staff and stretch out your hand over the sea to divide the water so that the Israelites can go through the sea on dry ground." (Exodus 14:13-16)

No matter what you face today, green means go.

66 99 Chris, 30, said, "Making decisions is hard for me, trusting my instincts."

Dear Green-Light Jesus,
Please show us the road marked Freedom. Give us a way out of our pain. May the pain we're experiencing today never be seen tomorrow. In Jesus' name, amen.

What is your green-light story? Please visit www.faithbookofjesus.com and click on "Community" to share.

To Read Further: Exodus 14:10-15

NEW WINE

Neither do men pour new wine into old wineskins. If they do, the skins will burst, the wine will run out and the wineskins will be ruined. No, they pour new wine into new wineskins, and both are preserved.

— MATTHEW 9:17

When I'm faced with something new, whether it's a problem or a blessing (both can require extra energy), I sometimes find myself cracking under the pressure. This verse from Matthew is such a great word picture as I explore new possibilities in life. Think of it this way: How do I know it's time to buy a new pair of jeans? When I can no longer fit into the old pair.

When I decided to go back to school and finish my bachelor's degree, it required a new way of thinking. I knew I could no longer stay at my dead-end job, which didn't use any of my true strengths and talents. But I couldn't go after a new career unless I knew what I wanted to do. So, I made some sacrifices, took out student loans, and decided to sign up for Biola University's BOLD program, which is a bachelor's degree in organizational leadership. It was in that process that I found a new wineskin. I found the new me I had known always existed and only dreamed of becoming.

Ask Jesus to reveal to you if there is anything in your life that is holding you back from pursuing a whole new you.

❝❞ Suzanne, 27, said she wishes to pursue a "singing/songwriting/performing" career.

 Dear New-Wine Jesus,
Thank you for showing us the biblical way to grow. Take my old, used-to-be, has-been faith and replace it with a new and improved desire to pursue a whole new me—what you have promised each and every one of us. Amen.

👥 If you're struggling with or excited about a recent change in your life, please visit www.faithbookofjesus.com and click on "Community" to share.

🐟 To Read Further: Matthew 9:16-17

"RUN, FORREST, RUN"

I run in the path of your commands, for you have set my heart free.
— PSALM 119:32

Some people wait for their dreams to come true; I chase mine. Today's verse encourages us to chase after Jesus if we want to be free. Freedom feels better than staying put. Comfortable. (Yeah, I'm talking to you.) Life is not about being on easy street or staying put. That's not what Jesus meant for you or for me.

Most people resist change. It's easier to stay home than pursue your dreams. But this verse means something more than running toward what you desire. In Psalm 119 David spent a lot of time talking about the commandments of God. When we are obedient to Jesus and his will, we experience the kind of freedom that makes our hearts sing. Now, it doesn't mean that our lives are free from pain, strife, or worry, but it does mean that we're no longer living life in the slow lane.

Jesus has more in store for us than we could ever think or imagine. He will sometimes let our options run out or our water run low, or he may squeeze us out until we get a clue that there is something wrong with our lives.

You don't think Jesus knows you need that job? Those relationships? What's in your wallet? Once you and I are honest with Jesus about our destination, wait and watch as he intervenes. He has a funny way of using obedience to move us into bigger and better things. Don't just anticipate it. Expect it.

Ready? Set? Jump!

66 99 Margaret, 34, said she still wants "to start my own company; in this day of real time, I wish results would be instantaneous."

Dear Jesus in the Fast Lane,
Give us room to run. Enlarge our borders and may your hand be upon us as we run in the path of your commands. Amen.

How do you run? Please visit www.faithbookofjesus.com and click on "Community" to share.

To Read Further: 1 Chronicles 4:9-10

FLY LIKE AN EAGLE

Even youths grow tired and weary, and young men stumble and fall; but those who hope in the LORD will renew their strength. They will soar on wings like eagles; they will run and not grow weary, they will walk and not be faint.

— ISAIAH 40:30-31

Today, we're going to fly!

Why? Because being squeezed out of our comfort zone can be pretty scary. It's easy to buy into lies that tell us we can't keep going, so we retreat. We lose faith. Give up. Quit.

When an eagle encounters harsh winds in a storm, it stretches out its wings toward heaven and flies above. We need to know the truth of who we are in Jesus before we soar to the heights to be with him.

Neil Anderson said in his book *Living Free in Christ* that "understanding your identity in Christ is absolutely essential for your success at living a victorious Christian life!" Want to not stumble and fall? Believe that you are an accepted child of Jesus (see John 1:12; 15:15; 1 Corinthians 6:19-20; Colossians 2:10). Want to run and not grow weary? Believe that you are secure in Jesus (see Romans 8:1-2,28,31-39; 2 Corinthians 1:21-22; Philippians 1:6; Colossians 3:3). Want to walk and not faint? Believe that you are significant (see Matthew 5:13-14; John 15:16; Acts 1:8; 2 Corinthians 5:17-21; Ephesians 2:6).[6] Take a few of these verses and find a quiet spot where you can be alone with God today. Let him teach you how to fly.

66 99 Teresa, 25, wanted to know "how to pursue only God and not be so easily distracted by relationships (all types) . . . or [by] implementing my walk into relationships."

Dear Jesus Who Renews Our Strength,
Give us the grace and power to stretch out our feeble arms and legs and rise above our current challenges. Thanks for keeping us accountable and for proving to us that we have what it takes to fly like an eagle. Amen.

How do you find your identity? Please visit www.faithbookofjesus.com and click on "Community" to share.

To Read Further: 1 Timothy 4:12-13

SPIRIT FRUIT

The fruit of the Spirit is love, joy, peace, patience, kindness, goodness, faithfulness, gentleness and self-control.

— GALATIANS 5:22-23

Fruit grows on trees. Most of them do anyway; some of them grow on a vine. What does it take for fruit to grow? It takes water, soil, sustenance, sunlight, and pruning.

Practically speaking, what does that look like in our own lives? What is the water, soil, and sunlight in our lives? Trials. Jesus allows trials in our lives to help build our character and make us "sugar baby sweet" (a term my mom came up with to describe ripe watermelon).

We don't just become "loving" overnight. Joy comes out of an abundance of remaining in the vine. A harvest of peace grows when we submit our will to Jesus. The same goes for the other fruits of the Spirit.

It's not a matter of how ripe you are or want to be; Jesus is the one who ultimately allows the water, soil, sunlight, and pruning.

So, what exactly is Spirit fruit then? It's the right amount of trials, seasoned with some time in the Son (with him, of course), oxygen (that's the Holy Spirit), and sustenance (which is the Word of God).

❝❞ David, 31, said, "I have found that not everyone is called to be one, but we can have ministry to others in different ways, i.e., being [Spirit fruit] friends with others, helping those in need, sharing your faith with them, and inviting others to church."

Dear Jesus, the Gardener,
We ask you to make us into Spirit fruit, the kind that fully ripens to spread the knowledge of who you are to other people. Let others want the kind of love, joy, peace, (insert fruit here) that we have because we are rooted in you. Amen.

What kind of Spirit fruit are you? Please visit www.faithbookofjesus.com. Click on "Community" to share.

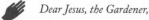 To Read Further: 1 Corinthians 13

THE END

You know with all your heart and soul that not one of all the good promises the L ORD your God gave you has failed. Every promise has been fulfilled; not one has failed.
— JOSHUA 23:14

When I fly, I prefer landings to takeoffs. Why? Because it means the flight is over. As with anything in life, landings symbolize a finale. The end.

Usually by the time the plane (or trial) ends, I'm so restless and ready to get off the plane that I forget to appreciate that Jesus helped me make it through the flight. Finished. Done. Do I ever stop to look back and see Jesus' faithfulness in my life?

I am living proof that Jesus can heal. I have been healed of acute eczema. There was a period of ten years when I did not have any skin on my feet, face, or hands. Through those years I learned how to have a daily quiet time. It is my desire that you will look back on your life and see all promises fulfilled.

When Joshua shared this verse with the Israelites, he reminded them that Jesus had been faithful just like he had promised: "Not one of all the good promises the L ORD your God gave you . . . *failed*. Every promise has been fulfilled" (Joshua 23:14, emphasis added).

66 99 Katie, 25, said, "I think twentysomethings often are obsessed with finding God's will for their life. . . . I need to learn to *rest* in the Lord . . . instead of focusing all my energy on my own life decisions: major, husband/wife, career, location, calling, etc."

 *Dear Faithful Jesus,*
We are confident that you will finish the work that you started in our lives. Thank you that you are faithful even when we aren't. Amen.

What story can you share about the faithfulness of Jesus? Please visit www .faithbookofjesus.com and click on "Community" to share.

To Read Further: 2 Timothy 2:8-13

ARE WE THERE YET?

God doesn't miss anything. He knows perfectly well all the love you've shown him by helping needy Christians, and that you keep at it. And now I want each of you to extend that same intensity toward a full-bodied hope, and keep at it till the finish.
— HEBREWS 6:10-11 (MSG)

Yesterday, we read that Jesus is faithful. Today, what happens when you feel cheated? Working hard with no results can be quite frustrating—especially when others achieve better results.

Watching others get what I've always wanted (marriage) or dreamed of (the ability to own my own home) makes me grow more impatient. As more time passes and my circumstances do not change, I begin to wonder. Like the saying goes, "Are we there yet?" The distance between faith and patience is trust. Do I trust God to fulfill what he promised?

My pastor Larry Osborne says, "Life is about progress, not perfection." I wish someone had told me that saying years ago. I feel I would've strived a little less toward my pursuit of becoming an adult, finding the perfect career, wanting a mate, and discovering my life's purpose.

66 99 Jaron, 20, said it best: "Being like Christ to everyone. Striving to buck the sin that creeps into relationships and just be a humble servant leader."

 Dear Watchful Jesus,
Thank you that you do not miss a thing. Give us the faith and patience we need as we learn to put our trust in you because it's the process of learning how to put our faith and trust in you that has rewards to last a lifetime—and that is where we truly want to be. Amen.

Do you have an "are we there yet" story? Please visit www.faithbookofjesus .com and click on "Community" to share.

To Read Further: Philippians 3:4-9

THE BEST KIND OF NIGHT-LIGHT

Your word is a lamp to my feet and a light for my path.
— PSALM 119:105

I love "aha" moments! To me, an "aha" is like a sudden burst of light near my feet when I'm trying to walk in the dark.

I think it's like that with our lives sometimes. It's easy to get comfortable in the dark, but it's even better when we can see. Sometimes, Jesus doesn't tell us the next step. He tests us to see what we're made of.

I love how "aha" moments help me understand the Bible in a new way. It could be through a worship service at church or praying with friends. Jesus can use anything in your life to light the way.

When I choose to trust Jesus, he lights up my path like those night-lights my mother used to put in the house so we wouldn't stub our little toes.

Do you want the kind of Christianity that goes the distance or the kind that gives up when the path gets too narrow and dark? To answer this question, read Matthew 7:7-8. You might just find another night-light for your path.

66 99 Kaylee, 20, said she believes that "worship . . . should be a continuous act, not just something done on Sunday morning."

Dear Light-of-the-World Jesus,
We are so lost without you. Thank you that you light our path each and every day. Help us to see that you are the best kind of night-light we could ever receive. Amen.

Have you had a darkness-to-light story? Please visit www.faithbookofjesus .com and click on "Community" to share.

To Read Further: Matthew 7:7-8

BROKEN RECORD

Once again the Israelites did evil in the eyes of the Lord, and because they did this evil the
Lord gave Eglon king of Moab power over Israel.
— JUDGES 3:12

I hate being the broken record. I hate asking people to pray for the same things over and over again. Why should I burden someone with my problems day in and day out?

Fortunately, I'm not alone. The Israelites sinned over and over again, and every time the Lord handed them over to their enemies. Sometimes I think I get mad and sin because I don't think Jesus can hear me. He can't (literally) talk back!

You would think reading through the Old Testament would give me a clue, but I'm just as stupid as they were.

The same broken record keeps playing over and over again in my head. It took me years after I graduated high school to understand Jesus' purpose for my life. I didn't know what I wanted to major in, what kind of job would make me happy, which roommates I should live with.

I eventually figured those things out, but not without a lot of time in prayer, asking Jesus to renew my mind so I could test and approve what his will really was for my life—his good, pleasing, and perfect will.

Now that I have found a new record, I will keep playing it over and over until Jesus says it's time to change.

❝❞ Natasha, 25, said she fears "settling my life dreams" and Sarah, 24, said, "Just show us what our purpose should be and why."

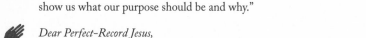 *Dear Perfect-Record Jesus,*
Thank you for stopping our broken records. Show us what our purpose is, even when we stumble and fall and make a mess for ourselves, which you have to clean up over and over again. Amen.

Do you have a broken-record story? Please visit www.faithbookofjesus.com and click on "Community" to share.

To Read Further: Judges 3:7-15

LIKE FATHER, LIKE SON

You have filled my heart with greater joy than when their grain and new wine abound.
— PSALM 4:7

I've seen alcohol make my twentysomething friends *very* excited—and David said that Jesus can make us even more joyful? That's amazing.

All of my life I've felt left out from the party scene. I grew up homeschooled. What homeschool girl gets invited to parties? Not that I would have gone, but I still wanted to feel included. There's something to be said for celebrating the hard work you've accomplished by grabbing dinner with friends and enjoying a glass of wine.

It's interesting that Solomon, David's son, said something similar to his father. He said, "A man can do nothing better than to eat and drink and find satisfaction in his work. This too, I see, is from the hand of God, for without him, who can eat or find enjoyment?" (Ecclesiastes 2:24-25).

What are you finding enjoyment in? Make plans to eat out this weekend with friends and enjoy the works of your hands. Don't forget to thank God for the food and drinks.

66 99 Richard, 25, when asked if there was anything else that would address the specific needs of real twentysomethings, said, "Drinking."

Dear Greater-Joy Jesus,
Thank you that we can celebrate at the end of a long day with food and drink. Help us to enjoy the works of our hands today. Amen.

What brings you great joy? Please visit www.faithbookofjesus.com and click on "Community" to share.

To Read Further: John 2:1-11; Philippians 4:4; 1 Timothy 6:6

NAGGED TO DEATH

With such nagging she prodded him day after day until he was tired to death.
— JUDGES 16:16

Have you ever met a woman who complains about everything? I'll bet if you meet her significant other, she is the one "wearing the pants" in the relationship. The story of Samson and Delilah is just that. Here we see Samson as the "perfect" man. He was handsome, muscular, with long hair, and a weakness for foreign women (see Judges 14:6-7). Sounds like a scene from a movie!

When Samson met Delilah, he fell in love (see 16:4). She became his life. He was living in enemy territory at the time, and once it became known that Samson loved Delilah, the Philistines convinced her (stupid woman) to find out the secret to Samson's strength.

This is a *spoiler*. Listen up. Not every woman nags. Samson may have been the most handsome and strong man in town, but the reason he was that way was because of the *Spirit of Jesus*. He chose the wrong woman, and he paid the price. Death.

Once Delilah discovered the reason behind Samson's strength, she called for the Philistines to attack. "[Samson] awoke from his sleep and thought, 'I'll go out as before and shake myself free.' But he did not know that the LORD had left him" (16:20). Ouch!

Today if you're feeling like Samson, don't let temptation be your downfall.

66 99 Steven, 22, said, "I just got married, and trying to figure out a career/lifestyle where I can provide well for my wife/future children but still do something meaningful stresses me out."

  Dear Nag-Free Jesus,
If you nagged us to death, imagine what kind of a world we'd live in. Thank you for free will. We can serve you with all that we are and were created to be without fear because your perfect love casts out all fear. Amen.

👥 Everyone has experienced an unhealthy relationship at some point. Were you the nagger or the nag-ee? Visit www.faithbookofjesus.com and click on "Community" to share.

✝ To Read Further: Proverbs 21:9,19; 1 John 4:18

THE YOUNG AND THE RESTLESS

I was young and now I am old, yet I have never seen the righteous forsaken or their children begging bread.
— PSALM 37:25

I love mentors! I can draw a lot of wisdom and strength from older, wiser people—especially the ones who have suffered.

In his best-selling book *Tuesdays with Morrie*, Mitch Albom wrote an incredible story of his visits with a dying man named Morrie. Mitch and Morrie talked every Tuesday for an hour or so about the meaning of life. I believe they came to the same conclusion as David did in Psalm 37:25. It's the kind of book that you pass along to your friends and family.

When life gets hard, it's important to seek out wise counsel. I cannot tell you how many conversations I've had with older women whom Jesus placed in my life at the times I needed them most—like when I went back to school to finish my bachelor's degree through Biola University. I was working and going to school full time, and I had a nervous breakdown. I couldn't handle the stress load on my own, and I needed to know that what I was doing was worth it. I'll never forget the day I felt young and restless. I didn't want to juggle life/work/school/homework/rent anymore. I wanted to give up and quit. My mentor told me that one day Biola would help me with my writing.

And wouldn't you know, two years later, she was right!

66 99 Jessica, 21, asked the question, "How do I maintain a really good relationship with Jesus after leaving college? I am a full-time student right now, but I'm excited to be a teacher."

 *Dear Mentor Jesus,*
You are the best mentor we could ever ask for. Help us spend time with you each day to understand what it is you want us to do and who you want us to be. Amen.

Do you have a mentor story? Please visit www.faithbookofjesus.com and click on "Community" to share.

To Read Further: Romans 12:2-3,16

PROFIT AND LOSS

If anyone else thinks he has reasons to put confidence in the flesh, I have more.
— PHILIPPIANS 3:4

One hindrance that can easily bring us down is our pride and confidence in what we can do in our own strength (or flesh). Paul talked about this confidence in Philippians 3:4. He said if anyone should boast, it should be him.

Paul was born of rank. He studied under the smartest teachers and knew more Scriptures than anyone else. But he said that whatever he once thought was his profit, he now considered loss for the sake of knowing Jesus as his personal Lord and Savior (see verse 7).

Is it wrong to put confidence in what you can do? Jesus has given us many choices. We can make decisions and goals and then go after them. But too often the line between self-reliance and healthy ambitions becomes blurred.

You might not know you're making selfish or prideful choices until something goes horrendously wrong, and you're faced with the realization that you weren't depending on Jesus like you thought you were. Instead of worrying which side of the fence you're on (profit or loss), live confidently in the One who has the power to change the outcome.

"Do not throw away your confidence; it will be richly rewarded. You need to persevere so that when you have done the will of God, you will receive what he has promised" (Hebrews 10:35-36).

66 99 Chris, 24, said this about confidence: "Having too much to do and not enough time to do it, or sometimes not having anything to do and too much time to fill, stresses me out."

 Dear Confident Jesus,
What a pleasure it is to put our hope and confidence in Someone greater than ourselves. Lead us and guide us when we don't know what we're doing or where we're going. Amen.

What makes you feel confident? Please visit www.faithbookofjesus.com and click on "Community" to share.

To Read Further: Philippians 3:1-11

MUCH AFRAID

For God did not give us a spirit of timidity, but a spirit of power, of love and of self-discipline.
— 2 TIMOTHY 1:7

In her book *Hinds' Feet on High Places*, Hannah Hurnard used an allegory to paint a beautiful story for us. The heroine of the story is named Much Afraid, and you can take a guess at what she's like.

How often do I act Much Afraid? I've struggled with anxiety since I was twelve. The verse above has been my favorite verse for more than fifteen years.

It's not easy being a twentysomething. There are lots of unknowns. Purpose and career keep me up at night sometimes. Wondering who I'm going to marry and where we're going to live wakes me up in the morning. Just thinking about the economy gives me an anxiety attack. Here are four ways we can take fear and lay it at Jesus' feet:

Rest in Jesus—"Come to me, all you who are weary and burdened, and I will give you rest" (Matthew 11:28).

Trust in Jesus—"Trust in the LORD with all your heart and lean not on your own understanding; in all your ways acknowledge him, and he will make your paths straight" (Proverbs 3:5-6).

Sonship in Jesus—"For you did not receive a spirit that makes you a slave again to fear, but you received the Spirit of sonship. And by him we cry, '*Abba*, Father'" (Romans 8:15).

Hope in Jesus—"Commit your way to the LORD; trust in him and he will do this" (Psalm 37:5).

❝❞ Leigh, 19, said in light of today's economy she fears "surviving—just trying to keep my head above water, settling for a full-time job here in America while my heart longs to go to the unreached."

Dear Abba Jesus,
Thank you for giving us a spirit of love, power, and self-discipline. Let this verse be a reminder each time we begin to fear. Amen.

How do you overcome fear? Please visit www.faithbookofjesus.com and click on "Community" to share.

To Read Further: Matthew 6:25-34

UNCONFESSED SIN

When I kept silent, my bones wasted away through my groaning all day long.
— PSALM 32:3

Imagine a rotting corpse for a moment. That's gross. Unconfessed sin eats away at your flesh. Disgusting, right? Horrific. David talks about this in Psalm 32.

Sometimes we hold things in. I know I'm guilty of that. I hold everything in until it catches up to me. "Then I acknowledged my sin to you [Jesus] and did not cover up my iniquity. I said, 'I will confess my transgressions to the LORD'—and you forgave the guilt of my sin" (verse 5). Unconfessed sin comes in all forms: the body bag of anger, the bitter route of strife, slander dripping with disdain, chewy morsels of gossip. The list can go on and on. What a release to be honest about our sin.

Let us bring our requests before God before it's too late. "Therefore let everyone who is godly pray to you while you may be found; surely when the mighty waters rise, they will not reach him" (verse 6).

Here is a simple prayer you can teach yourself if you're not sure how to confess your sins to Jesus: "Father, hallowed be your name, your kingdom come. Give us each day our daily bread. Forgive us our sins, for we also forgive everyone who sins against us. And lead us not into temptation" (Luke 11:2-4).

66 99 Timmy, 21, said, "I feel like prayer is still an area that I struggle with."

Dear Priest Jesus,
I confess my sins to you today. Don't let me hide them from you anymore. As far as the east is from the west, remove my transgressions from me today. Amen.

Do you ever struggle with confession? What helps you take your sins and nail them to the foot of the cross? Please visit www.faithbookofjesus.com and click on "Community" to share.

To Read Further: Psalm 24:4; Isaiah 1:18; Hebrews 4:16

GROWING IMPATIENT

One thing I ask of the Lord, this is what I seek: that I may dwell in the house of the Lord all the days of my life, to gaze upon the beauty of the Lord and to seek him in his temple.
— PSALM 27:4

What causes me to grow impatient is the inability to see beyond one thing: my problem. If it's sitting in traffic, the car in front of me always gets a piece of my mind. If it's my singleness, then it's the guy of the week who doesn't happen to like me back. There's always that one thing.

What one thing stands in your way? And how many of us don't have the patience to see things through in order to get what we really want? If we're honest with ourselves, living day to day from age twenty to twenty-nine can take an entire decade. I don't have ten years to wait for Mr. Right. I want Mr. Right Now!

We keep striving for what we want when *we* want it. We grasp for things that are almost within reach and force what we want before it's supposed to happen. Temporary satisfaction isn't as sweet as the blessing Jesus intended.

"This is what the Sovereign Lord, the Holy One of Israel, says: 'In repentance and rest is your salvation, in quietness and trust is your strength, but you would have none of it'" (Isaiah 30:15). Don't let impatience be a hindrance to the one thing that really matters: Jesus.

66 99 Erin, 21, said, "Psalm 27 is one thing I desire."

 Dear One and Only Jesus,
We desire one thing, and that is to see you, Jesus. Thanks for letting us stay at your place today. May we see the beauty of having a personal relationship with you. Amen.

What is one thing you desire? Please visit www.faithbookofjesus.com and click on "Community" to share.

To Read Further: Ecclesiastes 7:8; Habakkuk 2:3; Hebrews 6:12

AGAINST ALL HOPE

Against all hope, Abraham in hope believed and so became the father of many nations, just as it had been said to him, "So shall your offspring be."
— ROMANS 4:18

If I gave you a blank check and told you there were no conditions, that you could do whatever you wanted, what would you buy?

Abraham was given an unbelievable promise. Like a blank check, Jesus said that one day Abraham would be the father of nations—only he had to wait before cashing in his check.

Maegan, who is quoted below, asked how long she has to wait. She'd like to be in a significant relationship. If you are reading this and are between the ages of eighteen and thirty-five, I guarantee that you have waited or are still waiting for that question to be answered. "Jesus, when is it going to be my turn?"

The chick flick *27 Dresses* was so popular because women want a wedding. I don't think men fantasize about this as much as women do. However, when given a blank check, it's only a matter of time before we dream of how it could change our lives.

Go back to the Bible and look at how Abraham waited against all hope. Yes, he might have attended twenty-seven different baby showers before he held his son Isaac in his arms, but the laughter he brought made up for the years of waiting in an empty household.

66 99   Maegan, 25, is "wondering if I am ever going to have one! A significant other, that is!"

   Dear Right-On-Time Jesus,
Only you know the perfect time to deliver your great and precious promises in our lives. Help me realize that the date on the check is more important than the zeros in my bank account. Only you can buy me what really matters: hope! Amen.

What would be on your blank check? Please visit www.faithbookofjesus.com and click on "Community" to share.

To Read Further: Deuteronomy 4:29; Psalm 89

DON'T LEAVE HOME NAKED

So, chosen by God for this new life of love, dress in the wardrobe God picked out for you: compassion, kindness, humility, quiet strength, discipline.
— COLOSSIANS 3:12 (MSG)

Would you leave the house without putting on your clothes? I can just hear you laughing out loud. Think about it: In the same way we clothe ourselves in the physical, we also should dress in the wardrobe Jesus picked out for us to wear.

Here are five items that we should not leave home without:

Compassion—Be moved with compassion (see Matthew 9:36; 14:14; 18:27; Mark 1:41; 6:34).

Kindness—Be kind to one another (see 1 Corinthians 13:1; Ephesians 4:32; 1 Thessalonians 5:15).

Humility and Quiet Strength—Be humble, not proud (see Psalm 147:6; 149:4; Isaiah 26:5; 58:5; Romans 12:16).

Discipline—Be self-disciplined (see Psalm 38:1; 94:10,12; 2 Timothy 1:7; 2:5).

"And regardless of what else you put on, *wear love.* It's your basic, all-purpose garment. Never be without it" (Colossians 3:14, MSG, emphasis added).

❝❞ Rachel, 28, said that her purpose is "to use the spiritual gifts [wardrobe] that God gave me to glorify him."

 Dear Design-Label Jesus,
Don't let us leave home naked. Help us to remember each day to put on your brand and not just our favorite pair of jeans and flip-flops. Amen.

👥 What's your favorite article of clothing to wear? Please visit www.faithbookofjesus.com and click on "Community" to share.

⊂⊃ To Read Further: Matthew 9:36; Colossians 3:12; 2 Timothy 1:7

NO STRINGS ATTACHED

And she tied the scarlet cord in the window.
— JOSHUA 2:21

What do you think of when you see the word *kindness*? Do you think of someone being kind to you or of you showing someone kindness? Let's take a look at an example of kindness with strings attached.

In the book of Joshua, we are introduced to Rahab in the city of Jericho. She is a prostitute. Because she was a woman "in the know," the king sent his men to her home to investigate if the foreign men he assumed to be spies had been in her home.

Rahab hid these spies and, as part of her contingency plan to help them escape, just before helping them escape, she made a plea bargain for her life in return for her kindness.

The Israelite spies heard her plea and told her to leave a scarlet cord hanging from her window. This simple gesture ended up saving Rahab and her entire family when the city of Jericho fell into the hands of the Israelites as part of their new Promised Land.

Think about your life. Is there anyone you can think of who has been generous with his or her kindness toward you with no strings attached?

It might be time to return the favor with a scarlet cord of your own. Like Rahab, you never know who you might be saving.

❝❞ Erica, 27, said this about her relationships: "I hate to disappoint people."

✋ *Dear Jesus, Full of Kindness and Love,*
Because of Rahab's kindness, she saved her entire family—and because of your kindness, you sent your Son Jesus to die on the cross for our sins. Thank you for your incredible kindness and love today. Amen.

👥 What is one act of kindness that you would like to share? Please visit www .faithbookofjesus.com and click on "Community" to share.

✶ To Read Further: Joshua 2

HUMBLE CLOTHES

Humble yourselves before the Lord, and he will lift you up.
— JAMES 4:10

Because the spiritual clothing we wear is so important, I decided to spend just a few more days discovering what a spiritual wardrobe looks like so we can apply it to our everyday faith.

Today's question: What does it look like to wear humility? Not self-pity but the kind of humility that pleases Jesus.

First, let's look at what it doesn't look like: pride and arrogance. Everyone struggles with pride. In fact, I encounter pride at my job every day.

I work for a Christian speakers' bureau that represents top nationally known speakers such as Lee Strobel, Josh McDowell, and Kirk Cameron. Pastors from all over the United States inquire to book one of them for a Sunday service or an outreach event. When they find out the dollar amount it costs to book them, they all give me the same speech of how Christians shouldn't charge and how it should be free—instead, let them give a love offering. And don't even get me started on women speakers.

In the business of self, it's hard not to sell yourself because speakers are the product. Because of this line of work, my favorite person to look up to is Jesus. Every day he shows me how to give an appropriate response to these pastors.

"And being found in appearance as a man, he humbled himself and became obedient to death—even death on a cross!" (Philippians 2:8).

66 99   Karie, 23, said what stresses her out most is "money and people."

   Dear Humble Jesus,
Thanks for being our number one role model. Because of you, we have a perfect example of true humility. Help us to discern our thoughts and intentions. Lift us up today because we're depending on you and not our selfish pride. Amen.

How do you wear humility? Please visit www.faithbookofjesus.com and click on "Community" to share.

To Read Further: Deuteronomy 8:2; 2 Samuel 22:28; Matthew 11:29

SPIRITUAL HERO

Finally, be strong in the Lord and in his mighty power. Put on the full armor of God so that you can take your stand against the devil's schemes.

— EPHESIANS 6:10-11

If I were a superhero, I would be Superman. I love his cape, his cover ID (he's a writer/reporter for the *Daily Planet*), and how he gets the girl he's after.

In this world there is a physical realm and a spiritual realm. As things take place in the natural realm, most of us cannot see what is happening in the spiritual realm. For instance, Jesus has commanded the angels to take charge over us. He has gone ahead of us to prepare a place for us. A cloud of witnesses is rooting for us on the other side in heaven. And finally, Satan, an enemy of Jesus' chosen people (that's us), has been given permission to test us.

Want to be the spiritual hero of your life?

Stand firm then, with the *belt of truth* buckled around your waist, with the *breastplate of righteousness* in place, and with your *feet* fitted with the readiness that comes from the *gospel of peace*. In addition to all this, take up the *shield of faith*, with which you can extinguish all the flaming arrows of the evil one. Take the *helmet of salvation* and the *sword of the Spirit*, which is the word of God. (Ephesians 6:14-17, emphasis added)

"No weapon that is formed against you will prosper" (Isaiah 54:17, NASB).

66 99 Brian, 27, said if he were a superhero, he would "probably be Bruce Lee or Jet Li or perhaps Tony Jaa."

Dear Spiritual-Hero Jesus,
Thank you for the ability to meet the needs of others. Help us to put on the armor of God so that we can stand firm when trouble comes. Amen.

What would your superhero identity be? Please visit www.faithbookofjesus .com and click on "Community" to share.

To Read Further: Ephesians 6:10-18

EAT, SLEEP, AND WHISPER?

After the earthquake came a fire, but the LORD was not in the fire. And after the fire came a gentle whisper.

— 1 KINGS 19:12

When someone shouts at me, I'm usually not listening to what they're saying. At that point in the conversation, I've usually checked out—and started protecting my feelings and my ears.

When the noise in your life becomes too deafening, read Elijah's story in 1 Kings 19. We see that Elijah fled for his life because a wicked woman named Jezebel wanted to kill him. Why? Elijah had just called down fire from heaven. If anyone had reason to celebrate and have full assurance of faith, it was Elijah.

But "Elijah was afraid and ran for his life" (1 Kings 19:3). After he ran for an entire day, "he came to a broom tree, sat down under it and prayed that he might die. . . . Then he lay down under the tree and fell asleep" (verses 4-5).

Do you ever feel like that? Elijah couldn't hear Jesus' voice clearly because he was (1) tired and (2) defeated.

The worst is trying to listen to Jesus when we are the ones making all the noise. Sometimes, the best thing to do when we're stressed is to take a nap and eat something. Life always looks better when we've had enough sleep and have a full stomach.

66 99   Karis, 29, said, "I would love to hear God's voice more clearly."

   Dear Jesus Who Whispers,
Please forgive me for the times when I shout at you, when I'm wound up so tight that I can't hear you whisper to me. Like Elijah, please give me the space I need today to regain my strength and energy. Amen.

Have a great resting story? Please visit www.faithbookofjesus.com and click on "Community" to share.

To Read Further: 1 Kings 19

EXTRA GRACE REQUIRED

*Even fools are thought wise when they keep silent; with their mouths shut,
they seem intelligent.*
— PROVERBS 17:28 (NLT)

My pastor says that some people are "EGR," or "extra grace required." I'm sure he's not the one who came up with that expression, but it's true. I can't tell you how many times I've gotten upset at my roommates, co-workers, family, and friends. Here are three ways to say anything the biblical way:

1. **Everyone Listen** — "My dear brothers, take note of this: Everyone should be quick to listen, slow to speak and slow to become angry" (James 1:19).
2. **Rebuke Your Friends** — "If your brother sins against you, go and show him his fault, just between the two of you. If he listens to you, you have won your brother over. But if he will not listen, take one or two others along, so that 'every matter may be established by the testimony of two or three witnesses.' If he refuses to listen to them, tell it to the church; and if he refuses to listen even to the church, treat him as you would a pagan or a tax collector" (Mathew 18:15-17).
3. **Forgive Seventy-Seven Times Seven** — "Then Peter came to Jesus and asked, 'Lord, how many times shall I forgive my brother when he sins against me? Up to seven times?' Jesus answered, 'I tell you, not seven times, but seventy-seven times'" (Matthew 18:21-22).

When you find yourself unable to keep silent, remember it's okay to ask Jesus for extra grace.

66 99 Megan, 28, said she prays for extra grace "because I have a relationship with God and you communicate with those you have a relationship with."

 Dear Gracious Jesus,
When we encounter people who require extra grace, don't let us look like a fool.
When it becomes difficult to remain silent, help us to remember the truths listed above. Amen.

What's your "EGR" story? Please visit www.faithbookofjesus.com and click on "Community" to share.

To Read Further: Matthew 18:21-35

YOUR FEET

It is God who arms me with strength and makes my way perfect. He makes my feet like the feet of a deer; he enables me to stand on the heights.
— PSALM 18:32-33

A few days ago we looked at what superheroes wear. In Ephesians 6, Paul shared how to put on the armor of Jesus daily. I want to highlight a particular piece just in case you missed it.

Most women love shoes. I, myself, am more of a flip-flops person. The sandals of the gospel, or the shoes of peace, are important because they represent a readiness and willingness to respond to Jesus when he calls. Shoes protect your feet and keep you from slipping.

Here are a few examples of feet in the Bible:

- "How beautiful on the mountains are the *feet* of those who bring good news, who proclaim peace, who bring good tidings, who proclaim salvation, who say to Zion, 'Your God reigns!'" (Isaiah 52:7, emphasis added).
- "After that, he poured water into a basin and began to wash his disciples' *feet*, drying them with the towel that was wrapped around him" (John 13:5, emphasis added).
- "For he will command his angels concerning you to guard you in all your ways; they will lift you up in their hands, so that you will not strike your *foot* against a stone" (Psalm 91:11-12, emphasis added).
- "When I said, 'My *foot* is slipping,' your love, O Lord, supported me" (Psalm 94:18, emphasis added).

Stand firm today knowing that Jesus cares about you and your feet!

66 99 Andrew, 24, said his feet are firmly planted in "bringing glory to God. Right now, though, my purpose is being faithful in a meaningless job. How I will do that specifically is a work in progress."

Dear Foot-Supporter Jesus,
Thank you that we can bring the good news with us wherever we go — whether we're wearing a pair of Jimmy Choos or beach sandals. Amen.

What is your favorite pair of shoes? Please visit www.faithbookofjesus.com and click on "Community" to share.

To Read Further: John 13:1-17

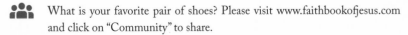

YOUR COVERING

He will cover you with his feathers, and under his wings you will find refuge; his faithfulness will be your shield and rampart.

— PSALM 91:4

When I think of a covering, I think of wrapping myself in my Egyptian-cotton blanket and lulling myself to sleep. It's soft, comforting, and shields me from the cold.

I don't know about you, but it seems like every day there are a number of things thrown at me—and it's all I can do just to stand there and protect myself. Work is never easy. Money is never enough.

It's important to remember that Jesus has it all covered.

In some churches I've been in, a covering is talked about and stressed as very important. What does that mean? In Psalm 91 we see that Jesus covered David and made himself available for protection—a shield even.

"In addition to all this, take up the shield of faith, with which you can extinguish all the flaming arrows of the evil one" (Ephesians 6:16).

Do you want to take cover from what life is throwing at you today? The Evil One likes to throw stuff at us all the time to get us to a place of unbelief, anger, frustration, discouragement, disappointment, bitterness, rage, malice, slander, hate, depression, worry, anxiety, fear, etc. Ask Jesus to be your covering today.

66 99 Amy, 21, said she wants to be a covering to others by starting "a club on my college that reaches out to international students."

 Dear Feather-Covering Jesus,
Never let me go—even when I feel like you're not holding on. Let all the worries and cares of this world fade away in your arms today. Amen.

Did you ever build a fort (covering) when you were a kid? Please visit www .faithbookofjesus.com and click on "Community" to share.

To Read Further: Psalm 91

NEW MERCIES

Because of the LORD's great love we are not consumed, for his compassions never fail. They are new every morning; great is your faithfulness.

— LAMENTATIONS 3:22-23

Every day there is a pesky new problem. Growing up, I can remember going through some pretty painful experiences. In high school, I used to struggle with extreme eczema. I lost the skin off my hands, feet, and face. This verse never became so real to me until I experienced a problem that wouldn't go away.

Do you ever feel like that? You don't learn something until you *have* to learn something! That's why Jesus' mercy is so important. Today's problems are enough for today, and Jesus will give us the strength and grace to handle today's problems today.

"But he said to me, 'My grace is sufficient for you, for my power is made perfect in weakness.' Therefore I will boast all the more gladly about my weaknesses, so that Christ's power may rest on me" (2 Corinthians 12:9).

I don't want to boast in my weakness; I want my strength back. It took years for Jesus to teach me patience and loving-kindness—and I'm still not completely there yet.

Every day there will be pesky new problems, situations that steal your joy and rob you of your peace. Allow Jesus and his mercy to heal you today.

66 99 Shawn, 25, said this about her daily walk with Jesus: "I am unfamiliar with any specific Bible verses, and I am unfamiliar with a Christian walk."

Dear Merciful Jesus,
I pray for those who believe in you—and who still need to know you and your mercy every day. Thank you for putting this verse in the Bible and for giving us hope for the new day. Amen.

What do "new mercies" mean to you? Please visit www.faithbookofjesus.com and click on "Community" to share.

To Read Further: Lamentations 3:22-26

I SUCK WITHOUT JESUS

I messed up my life—and let me tell you, it wasn't worth it. But God stepped in and saved me from certain death. I'm alive again! Once more I see the light!
— JOB 33:27-28 (MSG)

I suck without Jesus. I can tell if I'm not reading the Bible every day. And others can tell when I stop praying.

I made it a habit ten years ago to read a little bit of the Word every day because I so desperately need his help.

Today's verse came from a daily e-mail I receive. It stopped me dead in my tracks because I knew I had sinned. I had gone out with this guy whom I knew I shouldn't. He never made any mention of Jesus. Nothing in his heart encouraged me in spiritual matters. Because I had built up my relationship with Jesus by receiving those daily e-mails, I knew what I needed to do. I asked Jesus to forgive me and help me once again wait patiently for the right guy he has for me.

I'll be the first to admit that I'm one of those "extra grace required" people. If you find yourself in the same position, be encouraged that you're not alone. Jesus is here to offer his strength.

I suck without Jesus. Do you?

66 99 Alexandra, 24, said, "Shame and forgiveness are things that kill twentysome-things too early on. If we could learn these things now, it would save us from a lifetime of heartache!"

 Dear Jesus Who Doesn't Suck,
Thank you that you don't suck! You forgive my sins, and you don't give me what I deserve (in a good way). Thank you for constantly helping me out of the messes I make. Amen.

What is your life like without Jesus? Visit www.faithbookofjesus.com and click on "Community" to share.

To Read Further: Job 33:27-30

LOVES YOU

But God demonstrates his own love for us in this: While we were still sinners,
Christ died for us.
— ROMANS 5:8

If you would've told me a few years ago that Jesus loved me, I would have given you a dirty look and said "whatever" or "yeah, right!" I've heard that phrase my whole life, but it didn't mean anything. It took me until I was about twenty-four to understand that Jesus really loves me. It wasn't anything I did, said, accomplished, or didn't do that caused Jesus to love me. The hardest part for me was accepting Jesus' love because I always felt like he was holding back from me. I wanted to be healed. I wanted so badly to be in a relationship—and still do—but that didn't change the fact that "Jesus loved me!"

Do you want to get to know your best friend and live in a loving relationship with your spouse? You become their best friend and learn to love them. Do you want to know Jesus and his love for you? Get rid of your preconceived notions, attempts at organized religion, all duty and obligation, and learn to love him because he cares for you.

When was the last time you accepted Jesus' love?

The good news about accepting Jesus' love for us is that "while we were still sinners, Christ died for us" (Romans 5:8).

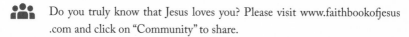 Amy, 30, said, "I'm not really a career-minded person. If I could pursue anything right now, I would want to start a family."

 Dear Jesus Who Loves Me,
We don't ever want to go back to the way things were before we knew you loved us unconditionally. Thank you for loving us. Let your love in our life be evident to all. Amen.

Do you truly know that Jesus loves you? Please visit www.faithbookofjesus .com and click on "Community" to share.

 To Read Further: Psalm 55:22; 1 Peter 5:7

SUNDAY SABBATH

Bear in mind that the LORD has given you the Sabbath; that is why on the sixth day he gives you bread for two days. Everyone is to stay where he is on the seventh day; no one is to go out.

— EXODUS 16:29

You might be wondering why I decided to write Friday's note on the Sabbath. Why not post it for the weekend? The original Sabbath started at sundown, Friday evening.

In the Hebrew language, Sabbath or *Shabbat* means "to cease work."[7] I love this verse. "No one is to go out." That meant one of two things: (1) The Israelites loved their football games, or (2) they rested well.

I have a feeling it was probably the second one. No, but seriously, the Israelites camped in the desert more than forty years, and they needed help to rest. If anyone tried to gather manna (bread from heaven) on the Sabbath, he wouldn't find any because there was none on the ground.

Jesus knew that resting well was not going to be easy, especially during those forty years waiting for their Promised Land. I can't imagine being forced to be stuck in the same place for forty years.

Before we turn on the TV to watch the game or our favorite show on our next Sabbath day off, let's not forget our Sunday Sabbath. Spending just ten minutes with Jesus is all we need.

66 99 Nathan, 27, said he is "currently unemployed. I would just love to have a job I enjoyed that paid enough for me to live off of."

 *Dear Sabbath Jesus,*
I love your mandatory day offs. You are the best boss ever! Help us to take our Sunday Sabbaths every week—even if it's just spending ten minutes with you. Amen.

What was the most exciting day off from work you ever had? Please visit www.faithbookofjesus.com and click on "Community" to share.

To Read Further: Exodus 16; 20:10-11

I HAVE A DREAM

Joseph had a dream, and when he told it to his brothers, they hated him all the more.
— GENESIS 37:5

One of my favorite Bible characters is Joseph. He was a dreamer, and so am I. Every time he had a dream, he would tell his brothers, and they hated him for it. Israel, their father, loved Joseph more than any of his other sons and even made him a special colorful robe.

One of the questions I wrote in the survey I conducted for this book was "If you could do anything without failing, what would you do?" Half of the people said they'd love to be able to support a family, and the other half said they'd be a rock star! Jesus knows some of us can dream big dreams—that's why they're called dreams.

The next time Joseph went to visit his brothers, they said, "Here comes that dreamer!... Come now, let's kill him and throw him into one of these cisterns and say that a ferocious animal devoured him. Then we'll see what comes of his dreams" (Genesis 37:19-20).

Joseph was not killed, but instead his brothers sold him into slavery. His slavery led him to Egypt, where he became second in command next to Pharaoh.

Later in the story Joseph said to his brothers, "Do not be distressed and do not be angry with yourselves for selling me here, because it was to save lives that God sent me ahead of you" (45:5).

Let Joseph be an example to you. Adversity doesn't have to kill your dreams.

❝❞ Christina, 24, said it's tough "trying to work with judgmental and/or selfishly opinionated people. Also, the ugly way that Christians rate each other on the holiness scale—especially when we call some of the more spiritually wise 'rock stars.'"

Dear Jesus Who Fulfills Dreams,
No matter what kind of adversity we face today, help us know that you do not kill dreams. We may not understand where you are leading us, but we can trust you to fulfill our dreams and our destiny. Amen.

Have you ever had a dream fulfilled? Please visit www.faithbookofjesus.com and click on "Community" to share.

To Read Further: Genesis 45

LOVE NOTES

How beautiful you are, my darling! Oh, how beautiful! Your eyes are doves. How handsome you are, my lover! Oh, how charming! And our bed is verdant.
— SONG OF SONGS 1:15-16

Have you ever written a love note in class, on the bathroom mirror, or in an e-mail? Significant relationships are the number one issue for most twentysomethings, whether single, in a relationship, or "it's complicated."

Jesus talks a lot about his love relationship with us:

- I miss you and want you all to myself; I'm actually jealous that you spend all this time away from me. (See Exodus 34:14.)
- I am moved with compassion for you and want to touch you and heal you. Won't you let me? (See Matthew 14:14.)
- I will be faithful to you and make you mine even if you are not faithful to me. (See Hosea 2:19.)
- I want to bless you and give you gifts. Don't you believe me? (See Matthew 7:11.)

Since Jesus has left us plenty of examples in Scripture about how loving he is, we should take note and spread the love. Is there a person whom God is putting on your heart? Pray for him or her. Is there something you can do for that person? Do it! Is there an act of service by which you could pour your love on someone? Express your love in this way today. Don't wait.

❝❞ Rachel, 20, said she'd like to know "how to balance the present worldview of feminism with the biblical worldview of wives submitting to their husbands in a healthy, relationship-building way."

 Dear Loving Jesus,
I enjoy reading your love notes every day in the Bible, and today is no exception. Help me take an example from you today. Amen.

Have you ever written a love note? Please visit www.faithbookofjesus.com and click on "Community" to share.

To Read Further: Song of Songs 1–8

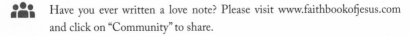

OTHER GODS

You shall have no other gods before me.
— EXODUS 20:3

Maybe you're off having a love affair with this world. I don't mean to shock you, but some of my friends have slept with married men. Others have made way more money than is necessary, and it's become their god. The first of the Ten Commandments says not to have any other gods before Jesus. Here are two ways to determine if you have an idol in your life:

Your Time — How you spend your time — whether it be on a significant relationship, your career, or a certain degree — can become a god in your life's pursuit.

Your Money — If I were to look at your checkbook, I'd see what is most important to you, good or bad.

It's not wrong to have relationships, money, or a career. But if we place them before Jesus, that becomes sin. Take a few minutes today and ask him if there is anything hindering your time and money. If you're short on time, pray on your way to work. If you're short on pay, ask! Jesus blesses those who continue to put him first.

❝❞ Tamara, 28, said, "I'm a wife and mother first, but I'm also a marketing coordinator for a design and marketing firm, a doula, and a small-business manager for my husband's music studio. I don't wish for anything else. My plate is full, and I'm content with it."

 Dear One and Only Jesus,
It can be hard not to put time and money before you — especially when some of us are so blessed. Show us how to place our time and money second to you today. Amen.

Have you allowed other things to become gods in your life? Please visit www .faithbookofjesus.com and click on "Community" to share.

To Read Further: 2 Corinthians 10:5-8

WORSHIP IS WORTH-SHIP

You are worthy, our Lord and God, to receive glory and honor and power, for you created all things, and by your will they were created and have their being.

— REVELATION 4:11

Worship is a natural, built-in response Jesus has given us to show worth. Whenever we are excited about something, we sing. We're all practicing here on earth for when we get to heaven, where we'll worship God with mind, heart, body, and soul.

My pastor Chris Brown said he hopes that worship in heaven won't be like one giant choir forever singing on a puffy white cloud because, if so, he wouldn't want to go! I agree. I grew up in a Baptist church with hymnbooks, wooden pews, and uncomfortable lacy dresses. Thank Jesus that true worship is so much more than that.

What or whom do you worship? It's important to give Jesus worth through worship: singing to him, praising his name, proclaiming all the good things that he has done for you. Also, living your life for Jesus is considered your spiritual act of worship (see Romans 12:1).

David wrote in Psalm 27, "One thing I ask of the LORD, this is what I seek: that I may dwell in the house of the LORD all the days of my life, to gaze upon the beauty of the LORD and to seek him in his temple" (verse 4).

That's worship in its purest form.

66 99 Karis, 21, said her purpose is "to live my life to the fullest and please God in everything I do."

 Dear Worthy-of-Praise Jesus,
You are worthy! You are worthy! You are worthy! Help us to say it over and over until it becomes a reality in our lives. Amen.

How do you worship Jesus? Please visit www.faithbookofjesus.com and click on "Community" to share.

To Read Further: Hebrews 3:2-4

PEOPLE PLEASER

In God, whose word I praise, in God I trust; I will not be afraid. What can mortal man do to me?

— PSALM 56:4

Pleasing people is a part of life. The list could include parents, teachers, friends, pastors, co-workers, bosses, lovers, mates, and children. Here are three reasons we sometimes please these types of people.

Sometimes we please people because Jesus requires it. Submitting to authority is key. Children submitting to parents and slaves to their masters (which in today's standards are workers and bosses) are examples of submitting to authority (see Ephesians 6:1-9).

We also please people because we can't say "no." What better way to inch our way into the inner circle than saying "yes" to every invitation to every party? Meanwhile our grades, sleep, attitudes, and thoughts become warped. Feeling compelled to say "yes" to everyone's desires is quite draining. The requests may not be evil, bad, or wrong, but they are time-consuming. It's tough to set boundaries (see 1 Corinthians 15:33).

Lastly, we do things to please others because it's the only way to reach them. Every once in a while, people come across our path that need saving. I'm sure you've met one before, whether you're saving Grace or some guy named Tom (see Galatians 6:1-2).

Don't let pleasing others become a drain. Ask Jesus to show you who should take your time today.

66 99   Amy, 29, said, "I am a people pleaser and cannot stand it when I think someone might be upset with me. I cannot function knowing that I have made someone mad. This is problematic because you can't please everyone all the time, and ultimately, I should only be concerned about pleasing Jesus."

Dear Jesus, My Delight,
Help us to please you first today. Push away the fear of saying "no" to others and replace it with sweet hope and confidence in you. Amen.

How do you please others? Please visit www.faithbookofjesus.com and click on "Community" to share.

To Read Further: 1 Corinthians 15:33; Galatians 6:1-2; Ephesians 6:1-9

ROYAL CONTROL

For if you remain silent at this time, relief and deliverance for the Jews will arise from another place, but you and your father's family will perish. And who knows but that you have come to royal position for such a time as this?

— ESTHER 4:14

The easiest way to see what is controlling you is to look at your calendar and your bank account. We control what we eat, how much money we spend, and what we're going to wear. We also try to control bigger issues, such as when we're going to get married, when we'll buy a house, and when we'll settle down to have a family.

How much of planning and perfecting your life leaves room for the mystery of Jesus? It's easy to get on the fast track and completely forget about him. Life is going great . . . and then something terrible happens, as was the case with Esther. Did you know that Jesus is never mentioned once in the book of Esther?

Esther, a happy orphan, is kidnapped and forced into the king's harem. She gets one chance to please the king, and she succeeds. Esther is chosen as queen, and because of her bravery, she saves her people, the Israelites, from complete annihilation.

Do you feel you have royal control over your life? Controlling your life is not about avoiding only the bad situations. Jesus may be behind the scenes in your life, setting up his next big move. "And who knows but that you have come to royal position for such a time as this?" (Esther 4:14).

❝❞ Amanda, 26, said she wanted to read "anything from the book of Esther."

 Dear Jesus in Control,
Sometimes you don't make yourself completely known, as in the case of Esther. Even if we can't see you working in our lives today, use us as you did Esther. Amen.

👥 What's your royal story? Please visit www.faithbookofjesus.com and click on "Community" to share.

✕◯ To Read Further: Esther 1–10

PUT YOUR HANDS UP!

When Moses' hands grew tired, they took a stone and put it under him and he sat on it.
Aaron and Hur held his hands up—one on one side, one on the other—so that his hands
remained steady till sunset.
— EXODUS 17:12

Moses had to keep his hands raised to heaven during a battle in order for the Israelites to win. Jesus had commanded Moses to do this. Hours later when Moses' hand got tired and he couldn't lift them up anymore, Aaron and Hur helped him keep his hands up.

Some battles are fought and won standing still, some through blood and tears, and others by raising hands to heaven.

What in your life causes you to lift your hands to the sky? Usually, I put up my hands when I'm ready to quit! For instance, I was at work and I thought to myself, *I wish I had someone to help me lift up my hands.* I'm only as good as my last sale. Yes, I represent top nationally known speakers and comedians, but the pressure it brings can be frightening. Adding writing to my already full-time schedule is even scarier. I don't have time to go out with my friends anymore and ask for their help.

You might be stuck in a similar situation. The sooner we both put our hands up, the sooner Jesus can help us fight through to the end.

❝❞ Burt, 23, said, "What is going to happen when nobody's money is worth anything anymore? It will be a great time to share the gospel!"

 Dear Hands-Up Jesus,
Your pleasure and delight are not in the strength of our hands and legs but in those who fear you. Help us to put our hope (and hands) in your unfailing love today. Amen.

Who raises your hands for you? Please visit www.faithbookofjesus.com and click on "Community" to share.

To Read Further: Exodus 17:8-16; Psalm 147:10-11

THE HARBOR

But Jonah ran away from the LORD and headed for Tarshish. He went down to Joppa, where he found a ship bound for that port. After paying the fare, he went aboard and sailed for Tarshish to flee from the LORD.

— JONAH 1:3

Merriam-Webster's Dictionary defines *harbor* as "a place of security and comfort: refuge."[8] Jonah probably thought he was fleeing to the harbor for a place of refuge, but fleeing from Jesus? Come on, Jonah! Don't be stupid.

How easy is it for us to be like Jonah? Jesus told Jonah to "go to the great city of Nineveh and preach against it" because its wickedness had reached all the way up to heaven (Jonah 1:2). But Jonah ran away.

So Jesus caused a giant storm. You might know the story. Every Sunday school teacher has a flannelgraph with three pieces: Jonah, the boat, and the giant whale.

Jonah knew that Jesus wanted to save the city of Nineveh, but Jonah didn't want to go. He felt hard pressed against it. How did Nineveh, a city full of wicked people, deserve to be forgiven?

When we sit and stew in our place of comfort, we choose to harbor all sorts of sin in our life: anger, bitterness, unforgiveness, the feeling that people (or even Jesus) owe you. Where are you fleeing?

66 99 Stephanie, 20, said she would love to "lead a missionary team to go overseas full time."

 Dear Jesus, Our Harbor,
When we want to flee, help us to remember we should run toward your embrace instead of finding our own refuge or harbor. Thank you that you are a God who gives second and even third chances. Amen.

Do you have a harbor story? Please visit www.faithbookofjesus.com and click on "Community" to share.

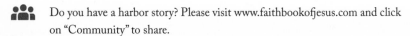 To Read Further: Jonah 1–4

I STILL LACK

When Jesus heard this, he said to him, "You still lack one thing. Sell everything you have and give to the poor, and you will have treasure in heaven. Then come, follow me."
— LUKE 18:22

Learning is a lifelong process. There will never be a day that you don't grow (physically, emotionally, or spiritually). We learn from others and ourselves. We learn from trials, situations, uncontrollable events, our pets; the list is as unique as you are.

Teachers. We've all had 'em. When I looked up the word *teacher* in the Bible, about 85 percent of the references were "teacher of the Law."

Jesus was a teacher. He had disciples, followers who yearned for his knowledge, people from the towns who came out to hear him speak, and religious leaders double-checking his accuracy of the Scriptures.

C. S. Lewis wrote in *Mere Christianity* that Jesus did not leave room for us to call him just a *Good Teacher*. Either Jesus was lying or he was right.

Jesus encountered a rich man who was interested in good and spiritual things. He asked Jesus what he must do. Jesus told the man to keep all the commandments, to which the man replied that he did. But the one thing he lacked, said Jesus, was to sell everything, give to the poor, and come and follow him. The rich man went away sad.

Only a good teacher knows his or her students. Jesus knew this man treasured his wealth more than anything else. What do you still lack?

66 99 Becca, 26, is "going back to school to become an elementary teacher and go back on the mission field, preferably Africa."

Dear Good-Teacher Jesus,
You want the best for us whether we're in the classroom or already in our careers. Examine our hearts and test our anxious ways to see if there is any offensive way within us and lead us in the way everlasting. Amen.

 Who was your favorite teacher and why? Please visit www.faithbookofjesus .com and click on "Community" to share.

To Read Further: Luke 18:18-30

TENT MEETINGS

Gather the entire assembly at the entrance to the Tent of Meeting.
— LEVITICUS 8:3

When I was reading my One-Year Bible, the phrase "Tent of Meeting" jumped out at me. It was like when you buy a new car, all you see on the road is your car—everywhere. It was like every few verses or so, starting in Exodus, I saw "Tent of Meeting." So I did a search. Sure enough, "Tent of Meeting" is mentioned more than 140 times in the Old Testament from Exodus all the way to 2 Chronicles.

Tent meetings today may look and feel like revival meetings. The tent meetings of old were tents where the Israelites would come to sacrifice animals to cleanse them from their sins.

We no longer need to sacrifice bulls or have priests relieve us of our sins. Jesus is our High Priest.

Therefore, since we have a great high priest who has gone through the heavens, Jesus the Son of God, let us hold firmly to the faith we profess. For we do not have a high priest who is unable to sympathize with our weaknesses, but we have one who has been tempted in every way, just as we are—yet was without sin. Let us then approach the throne of grace with confidence, so that we may receive mercy and find grace to help us in our time of need. (Hebrews 4:14-16)

Where is your Tent of Meeting? Do you meet regularly with friends at a coffee shop and discuss theology, or do you actively serve Jesus in your community?

❝❞ Mary, 23, said she worships Jesus by "serving others. I love it!"

 Dear High-Priest Jesus,
Thank you that you are a High Priest who can sympathize with whatever we may be experiencing today. May we approach the throne of grace with great boldness to receive the mercy and grace we need. Amen.

👥 Where is your Tent of Meeting? Please visit www.faithbookofjesus.com and click on "Community" to share.

✕◯ To Read Further: Exodus 27:21; 29:10-11; 2 Chronicles 5:5

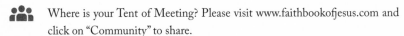

UNDERDOG MILLIONAIRE

For this is what the high and lofty One says — he who lives forever, whose name is holy: "I live in a high and holy place, but also with him who is contrite and lowly in spirit, to revive the spirit of the lowly and to revive the heart of the contrite."

— ISAIAH 57:15

I love that Jesus is so big that he has room for the underdog.

Do you ever wonder why movies that capture the spirit of the loser are popular in today's culture? Deep down we all feel inadequate. We all want to be winners but need someone to show us that we're made for so much more. Switchfoot sings about it; Rocky fights for it; and you and I both know that every Disney princess gets her man.

Jesus lives with the underdog. Wherever you're living, whether it's in an apartment with six roommates desperate to finish college, at home with your parents, or you're a newlywed trying to make ends meet, Jesus lives with you.

Jesus revives the underdog. 1 Peter 5:6-7 says, "Humble yourselves, therefore, under God's mighty hand, that he may lift you up in due time. Cast all your anxiety on him because he cares for you." Need strength for the day, or for the hour? Jesus in his mighty power promises to get us back on our feet. Knocked down? Jesus will pick you up again.

66 99 Hayley, 18, said in light of today's economy she wishes to "help all the people [underdogs] in need because more and more people are becoming dependent on government aid as the economy gets worse."

 Dear Former-Underdog Jesus,
I'm so glad you vouch for the underdog — me! When I feel like I can't get any lower, help me to see that what I have in you makes me richer than any millionaire on the planet. Amen.

Have you ever been the underdog? Please visit www.faithbookofjesus.com and click on "Community" to share.

To Read Further: Job 5:11; Psalm 138:6; Proverbs 29:23

WOULD YOU LIKE SOME JOY WITH THAT?

Consider it pure joy, my brothers, whenever you face trials of many kinds, because you know that the testing of your faith develops perseverance.

— JAMES 1:2-3

If I don't preface the above verses with two words — "testing time" — I have failed to set the stage for the proper response to trials. We should consider it joy when we face trials.

Wait, what? I would be lying if I said it's easy for me to respond to trials that way. Joy is not a natural reaction to pain. But isn't pain our body's natural defense to alert us to a problem so we can fix it and move on?

Trials produce perseverance. "Perseverance must finish its work so that you may be mature and complete, not lacking anything" (James 1:4). The answer to the question above is yes, trials make us stronger.

Trials test us. If we claim to be a Jesus follower, when trials come, they show what we're made of. We can talk all we want, but others will know if our faith is genuine by how we respond to trials.

Trials complete us. We can't grow to full maturity (not lacking anything) unless our faith is tested.

Finally, "If any of you lacks wisdom, he should ask God, who gives generously to all without finding fault, and it will be given to him" (verse 5).

Don't know how to consider it pure joy? Ask!

❝❞ Lory, 27, said in her relationships she has "the felt need to be the problem solver for everyone's issues."

🖐 *Dear Joyful Jesus,*
Trials are not easy — especially when they hurt. When we experience a trial threatening to rob us of our joy, help us to ask you for wisdom to make it through. Amen.

👥 How do you face trials with joy? Please visit www.faithbookofjesus.com and click on "Community" to share.

✝ To Read Further: James 1:1-8,17

MORE THAN ENOUGH

The eye never has enough of seeing, nor the ear its fill of hearing.
— ECCLESIASTES 1:8

My best friend Monique once asked me, "What happens when Jesus is not enough?" I was in the midst of writing this book and struggling to juggle a million things. Working, writing, hanging out, working out, my health—there just aren't enough hours in the day.

Writing more than three hundred devotionals sounds great in theory, but having to live each one out loud was painful. Revisiting all my favorite Bible verses was like being back in the hospital with no skin on my face and feet. My anxiety overwhelmed me.

I knew that Satan did not want me writing this book because guys were suddenly attracted to me. I thrived on the attention. I'm the Devotional Diva. Hello? But the guys I was meeting were *not* the kind of men Jesus had for me. (See Week 51 // Thursday • page 309 to read more about the kind of person Jesus has for you and wants you to be in return.)

I had to make a painful decision once again to allow Jesus to be enough before I made a stupid mistake I would regret. I know men and women have a tough time saying "no"—especially when it's something we so desperately want. I have been single for six years, which should be a living record or something.

Jesus doesn't care about records but about obedience and sacrifice. "The sacrifice you desire is a broken spirit. You will not reject a broken and repentant heart, O God" (Psalm 51:17, NLT).

 Chris, 37, said, "All I have in you [Jesus] is more than enough."

 Dear More-Than-Enough Jesus,
You are more than enough, even when my pride says differently. Your grace is sufficient for me, so I accept it gladly today and ask your grace to fall on my family and friends as well. Amen.

 Is Jesus more than enough for you? Please visit www.faithbookofjesus.com and click on "Community" to share.

To Read Further: Psalm 51

WE ARE COMMANDED

My command is this: Love each other as I have loved you. Greater love has no one than this, that he lay down his life for his friends.

— JOHN 15:12-13

Are you others-centered? Do you give to charity only at Christmastime, or do you help others daily?

"Now, most people *would not be willing* to die for an upright person, though someone might perhaps be willing to die for a person who is especially *good*" (Romans 5:7, NLT, emphasis added). What bothers me is how easy it is to help only those who are good. If Jesus laid down his life for us and commands us to love each other, what does that mean?

"But God showed his great love for us by sending Christ to die for us while we were still sinners" (Romans 5:8, NLT). Before judging someone, help him.

Jesus died for us while we were *still* sinners. It wasn't because any of us deserved it or because we did some important work that changed his heart. In fact, the Bible consistently shows—from Exodus to 1 Peter—that Jesus was moved with compassion for everyone, not just good people.

Jesus' legacy is very powerful: We are to help those who are hurting around us. Is there a person who needs your help? Pray for your brother or sister. Is there something beyond prayer you can offer? We are commanded, "Greater love has no one than this, that he lay down his life for his friends" (John 15:13).

66 99 Aaron, 27, said his favorite chapter in the Bible is "1 Corinthians 13—the love chapter. It is my favorite! I think that people miss the true meaning."

 Dear Compassionate Jesus,
You are a compassionate and gracious God, slow to anger, abounding in love and faithfulness. Thank you for modeling to us how we can love our brothers and sisters today. Amen.

How do you love others? Please visit www.faithbookofjesus.com and click on "Community" to share.

To Read Further: Exodus 34:5-7; Matthew 9:36; 1 Peter 3:8

LOVE ONE ANOTHER

Above all, love each other deeply, because love covers over a multitude of sins.
— 1 PETER 4:8

There's that command again. Love one another. Want to know how to really love your brother or sister today? Keep reading.

"Offer hospitality to one another without grumbling" (1 Peter 4:9). Without complaining or arguing, invite friends over for some grub.

I remember I was leading my first twentysomethings growth group when the economy had just tanked. More than 70 percent of my group lost their jobs, including my co-leader Donnie. It was in the middle of this dark time that every one of us came together to make sure that gas money, food, and rent were provided. Not one of us was evicted as we should've been, and everyone eventually found a new job.

"Each one should use whatever gift he has received to serve others, faithfully administering God's grace in its various forms" (verse 10). Going back to my growth group, everyone had a different skill set to provide. Some of us pitched in money; others pitched in free meals; and others helped with beefing up our résumés.

Jesus has given us different gifts. There are practical gifts like serving and hospitality, gifts of encouragement like mercy, grace, and compassion, and gifts of exhortation like prophecy, tongues, and teaching (see verse 11). Put your love into action today!

 Ashlie, 22, said regarding today's economy, "First of all, I don't think that the economy is as bad as people think it is. I know that I am taken care of by Jesus and my fiancé."

 Dear Loving Jesus,
Thank you for the ability to put our love into action today. What a great way to learn how to love others—by using our individual gifts to serve and help our brothers and sisters. Amen.

 Do you have a love-in-action story? Please visit www.faithbookofjesus.com and click on "Community" to share.

To Read Further: 1 Peter 4:7-11

LET'S GET DIRTY

"Then, Lord," Simon Peter replied, "not just my feet but my hands and my head as well!"
— JOHN 13:9

Imagine your pastor coming up to you and offering to change your oil in his best suit and tie. That's the significance of modern-day foot washing. Peter did not want Jesus touching his feet. But Jesus washed the disciples' feet because they were dirty.

Jesus got dirty. He wasn't afraid to roll up his sleeves and do a needed deep cleaning. But loudmouth Peter wasn't having it. "'No,' said Peter [to *Jesus*, mind you], 'you shall never wash my feet.' Jesus answered, 'Unless I wash you, you have no part with me'" (John 13:8).

Ouch! Peter and his big mouth again. He didn't want to get dirty, but Jesus' last statement caught him off guard, so he said not just his feet but his hands and head as well.

Do you want to play a part in the kingdom of Jesus? Get a little dirty. Service is highly underrated. We serve the self in today's culture, but just as Jesus made it easy for Peter to accept, we find ourselves in a similar situation.

Every church has an outreach program. Let's get dirty today by serving in the local soup kitchen, helping the homeless, or fixing up a neighborhood. Use the many skills God has given you to help others today.

❝❞ Ben, 33, said, "Twentysomethings who are connected and involved in serving others stay connected to a church and deepen their faith. If we can find ways to plug twentysomethings into service and also have some 'gatherings' where they receive, then we'll not only be able to help them stay involved but also help them foster their own spiritual maturity."

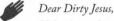 *Dear Dirty Jesus,*
If there's anything we can learn from you today, it's service. Help us find time in our busy schedules to get a little dirty and help others. Amen.

What's your dirt story? Please visit www.faithbookofjesus.com and click on "Community" to share.

To Read Further: John 13:12-17

LET'S TALK ABOUT SEX

For from within, out of men's hearts, come evil thoughts, sexual immorality,
theft, murder, adultery.
— MARK 7:21

I looked up the word *sex* in the *New International Version* of the Bible, and it appears at least fifty-six times. Most of the references are found in Leviticus about abstaining from weird sexual practices. However, Colossians 3:5 caught my attention. "Put to death . . . sexual immorality." Really?

I thought the New Testament was a loving, warm and fuzzy kind of testament. How did the "doom and gloom," "hell, fire, and brimstone" of the Old Testament make it into the New Testament? I know pastors preach a lot about loving others, but I found it particularly interesting to pair the last few devotionals of love with death.

I find when I am focusing on things that are pure, lovely, or admirable, I stay closer to Jesus (see Philippians 4:8). When I cheat my way through because I'm tired of waiting in my singleness, I find my road turns into a slippery slope—down to the pit.

Proverbs also warns us of how quickly sexual immorality ruins a person's life—even to the point of death. "For the lips of an adulteress drip honey, and her speech is smoother than oil; but in the end she is bitter as gall, sharp as a double-edged sword. Her feet go down to death; her steps lead straight to the grave" (Proverbs 5:3-5).

Before you make plans for the weekend, think quickly about where you're headed, and avoid the slippery slope.

66 99 Aaron, 27, said, "I think abstinence before marriage is the most important thing. We all fail at that on many levels, and shouldn't beat ourselves up, but we should strive for purity in this area."

Dear Put-to-Death Jesus,
Abstinence in today's world is a four-letter word. Staying the path of life instead of death can be quite scary. Protect the purity of our minds, hearts, and actions as we follow after you today. Amen.

How do you avoid the slippery slope of sexual immorality? Please visit www .faithbookofjesus.com and click on "Community" to share.

To Read Further: Proverbs 5

THIRTY, FLIRTY, AND THRIVING

"For my thoughts are not your thoughts, neither are your ways my ways," declares the
Lord. *"As the heavens are higher than the earth, so are my ways higher than your ways*
and my thoughts than your thoughts."

— ISAIAH 55:8-9

For those who are in their upper twenties, a "party" is not the same thing it is for those who have just turned twenty-one.

As a twenty-six-year-old who is flirty and thriving, not a day goes by that I don't love and hate my singleness. I love that I know my purpose in life, but I hate that I don't have someone to share it with. So I pray, "Jesus, when will your ways match mine?"

Did you see the movie *13 Going on 30*? Jenna, played by Jennifer Garner, wishes to be a thirtysomething and escape her teenage years because she's tired of waiting, too. She gets her wish and skips ahead to her thirties. She flirts. She thrives. And then she changes her mind and wants to go back!

Spoiler alert: At the end of the movie, she realizes she doesn't want a life led by her choices. Whether you're a young twentysomething who likes to party or a thirtysomething looking to settle down, trust Jesus. His ways are always better.

" " Amy, 29, said, "When you get into your twenties, people start moving from dating to marrying and having kids. I've heard a million times, 'When it's your time, God will bring you the right man,' but if you're nearing thirty and he still hasn't shown up, it's scary."

 Dear Single Jesus,
You lived a life of singleness to show us that it could be done. In fact, you didn't get into the heart of your ministry on this earth until you were thirty. Help us to trust you when your ways don't match up with our time line. Amen.

What's your "thirty, flirty, and thriving" story? Please visit www .faithbookofjesus.com and click on "Community" to share.

To Read Further: Isaiah 55:8-13

YES-MAN

Give your servant a discerning heart to govern your people and to distinguish between right and wrong. For who is able to govern this great people of yours?
— 1 KINGS 3:9

Solomon was given a huge responsibility—to govern the Lord's people, the Israelites. His father, David, was a man after Jesus' own heart. Assuming his role required big shoes and an even bigger heart, Solomon asked Jesus how to be a yes-man.

"Need wisdom?" Jesus asked. "Yes, please!" Solomon replied.

What about when our faith is tested? Do we act like Solomon and learn how to say "yes"?

Tamara, quoted below, said "no."

I wanted to know why. She said there are too many fluffy attempts at showing us how to say "yes," and what we really need is to be challenged. I totally agree with her. Solomon didn't want Jesus' fluff. He needed something real.

And so do we.

So Jesus said to him, "[Solomon,] since you have asked for this [wisdom] and not for long life or wealth for yourself, nor have asked for the death of your enemies but for discernment in administering justice, *I will do what you have asked.* I will give you a wise and discerning heart, so that there will never have been anyone like you, nor will there ever be" (1 Kings 3:11-12, emphasis added).

"Need something?" Jesus asks us. "Yes, please!" we respond.

❝❞ Tamara, 29, said, "No thanks! This has all been done before—over and over and over and over. Try pushing the boundaries a little further, and get us out of our comfort zone."

 Dear Yes-Man Jesus,
We need to be pushed out of our comfort zones sometimes. However, when we get there, what do we do? Help us to cry out for more wisdom, knowing you will answer us when we call. Amen.

👥 Are you a yes-man? Please visit www.faithbookofjesus.com and click on "Community" to share.

✦ To Read Further: 1 Kings 3

THE REAL WORLD

Do not throw away your confidence; it will be richly rewarded. You need to persevere so that when you have done the will of God, you will receive what he has promised.
— HEBREWS 10:35-36

It seems the only shows that cater to twentysomethings are reality shows like *The Real World*. Have you ever noticed that most media and TV shows are created for teenagers or for those in their mid-thirties with children?

For the twentysomething who doesn't know what he or she wants to be or do yet, it can be overwhelming. Stuck in the real world? You're not alone. There is a big transition from turning eighteen and graduating high school to becoming an adult.

Paul wrote in Hebrews that we should not throw away our confidence (see 10:35). We are tomorrow's leaders. We're so close to winning public office, publishing books, creating movies, and taking full financial responsibility.

If you are pressing through self-doubt, discouragement, or self-pity, keep persevering, for your faith will be richly rewarded. If you are experiencing sunny skies, then encourage a friend who is under the weather today. If you are neither sad nor happy, praise Jesus, for his plans are "to prosper you and not to harm you, plans to give you hope and a future" (Jeremiah 29:11).

❝❞ Christina, 25, said, "There's a crappy place between college and being married with kids. It's the middle twenties where society forgets you exist. Transitioning to the 'real world' after school is something not a lot of students are prepared for, especially where there are a lot of young families waiting to talk with you about parenting on the other side."

Dear Real Jesus,
Whether we have a case of the Mondays or a case of the twenties, help us to persevere and receive the crown, the prize, pass go, and collect our $200. Amen.

What's the title of your reality show? Please visit www.faithbookofjesus.com and click on "Community" to share.

To Read Further: Hebrews 10:32-39

THE CLOSER

But to Hannah he gave a double portion because he loved her,
and the LORD had closed her womb.
— 1 SAMUEL 1:5

Throughout the Bible there are places where Jesus "closed" a woman's womb. Why does Jesus withhold life? Sarah, the mother of all nations, bore Abraham only one child, Isaac. Rachel, the beloved wife of Jacob, bore only two sons and died giving birth to the second. And don't even get me started on Hannah!

It's a mystery to me why Jesus closes some doors and opens others.

As Christians, we have a responsibility to allow Jesus to use us, however he sees fit. We may not understand how and why, but who are we to say, "No, I don't accept this trial"? (Maybe it's so later on we can help others through the same trial.) Or we say, "I don't want to stay single and watch all of my other friends marry and have children" (when Jesus has clearly given you a life of love and service to others because of your singleness). Or this: "I don't like my workplace because I'm the only Christian." (Jesus may have put you there to have an influence.)

Try exercising faith in the midst of a closed door. Trust him. Oh, and Hannah? She gave birth to a son named Samuel.

66 99 Kari, 24, said, "My boyfriend being deployed halfway around the world in a war-torn country for an undetermined time frame stresses me out. Five-minute phone calls every few days that break up and have lags make it close to impossible to grow as a couple."

Dear Closer Jesus,
I don't understand why you close certain doors in my life, but help me to lean on you for my support, knowing that you have the power to change my circumstances when you see fit. Amen.

What doors have been closed for you? Please visit www.faithbookofjesus.com and click on "Community" to share.

To Read Further: Genesis 20:18; 29:31; Exodus 1:21; 1 Samuel 1

SPUR OTHERS ON

Let us consider how we may spur one another on toward love and good deeds.
— HEBREWS 10:24

It wasn't until last year that I understood my purpose. I always knew I enjoyed encouraging others who were experiencing painful times because I had been through some pretty painful times myself.

During my first marketing campaign I presented the verse above, along with my book proposal, to a couple of editors, agents, and publishers. I wanted Devotional Diva to be more than just a catchy name. I wanted them to know that I am the diva only because of how Jesus Christ set me free.

Later, after my literary agency signed me, my agent sent me a Christmas card, and this is what she wrote: "It's been such a joy getting to know you, and I'm so excited to be working with you as you expand your writing ministry to follow your calling to spur others forward. You've already been an encouragement to me with your infectious joy and passion for the Lord, and I can't wait to see what new opportunities he has waiting for you in 2009." One month later NavPress signed me. All those years of praying about writing a daily devotional came true.

What would you like your life verse to be? Could it be from Proverbs like this one: "Trust in the LORD with all your heart and lean not on your own understanding" (3:5)? Or this one: "Commit to the LORD whatever you do, and your plans will succeed" (16:3)?

66 99 Maggie, 21, said if failure wasn't an option, "I would write a book."

Dear Spur-Us-On Jesus,
It's such a joy and honor to serve the body of Christ because of what you've already done in my life. Teach me how to love others through good deeds today. Amen.

Do you have a story about spurring others on? Please visit www .faithbookofjesus.com and click on "Community" to share.

To Read Further: Hebrews 10:19-25

NO ONE IS PERFECT

Now David's son Absalom had a beautiful sister named Tamar. And Amnon, her half brother, fell desperately in love with her.

— 2 SAMUEL 13:1 (NLT)

You don't have to be perfect for Jesus to bless you. That would be impossible. No one in the Bible was perfect, except Jesus. David's story fascinates me. A little fame, and mistakes were made. What about Abraham, the "father of nations"? He slept with his wife's servant. Jacob, another hero of the faith, tricked his father-in-law, who had cheated him into marrying both his daughters. And Rahab was a prostitute.

David and his family had problems. One of his sons was so filled with lust for his sister that he had to have her. In fact, David's unruly children ran his house and eventually his kingdom after kicking him out of the palace. Does that discount that David was a man after God's own heart (see Acts 13:22)? Of course not.

Look at David's response when he was caught in the act of his own sin. Psalm 51:4 says, "Against you, you only, have I sinned and done what is evil in your sight, so that you are proved right when you speak and justified when you judge."

If you feel like you can't relate to the Bible and its characters, think again. No one is perfect but Jesus.

❝❞ Alair, 26, said, "I would like to see more in-depth devotionals about the prophets, both major and minor."

Dear Perfect Jesus,
Thank you for your perfect example of what it is like to be fully man and fully God. You walked on this earth and experienced the same feelings of frustration we experience daily. Help us through our hang-ups and remind us we don't have to be perfect, just men and women after your heart. Amen.

What's your less-than-perfect story? Please visit www.faithbookofjesus.com and click on "Community" to share.

To Read Further: Genesis 16:1-2; 31:20; Joshua 2:1; Psalm 51

CRUSHED

The LORD is close to the brokenhearted and saves those who are crushed in spirit.
— PSALM 34:18

I've had a few crushes in my lifetime. Crushing feats and disappointments. But rising through the ashes became my greatest accomplishment. I never thought I would graduate college, have a career, and make it past my twenty-fifth birthday. Now what?

My mom gave me a Bible when I was in the hospital. I chose to read through it for one year. During that year, Jesus took the crushed pieces of my life, showed me his scars and nail-pierced hands, and exchanged everything I had for his grace and mercy.

Living life with a crushed spirit is not fun. It's scary to think that everything you've worked so hard for, such as a career or a savings account, can be gone because of a trial. I've had to start over not once but three different times.

I'm still a work in progress. I've seen Jesus fix my problems. The worst part is the waiting. I know God can heal me, and when he chooses not to and makes me wait, I feel even more devastated. Why is it that a God who loves me doesn't heal me?

I'd like to tell you that Jesus fixes the crushed, broken pieces and relieves the overwhelmed-beyond-all-reason, but sometimes he doesn't. He doesn't promise us tomorrow. Jesus is our healer, but he doesn't promise us perfect health.

What crushes you? What leaves you feeling abandoned? Is it your circumstances, or is it the waiting period? No matter what, remember that "this is what the LORD says—he who created you . . .: 'Fear not, for I have redeemed you; I have summoned you by name; you are mine'" (Isaiah 43:1).

66 99 Katie, 24, said she is crushed in relationships "when communication breaks down or when there are areas of healthy boundaries pushed and not honored. So intimidating! I think it's because I fear confrontation, because I fear loss in that relationship."

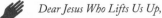 *Dear Jesus Who Lifts Us Up,*
Thank you for saving me over and over again when I was crushed. Lift up the spirits of those whose hearts may be broken and crushed under the weight of their disappointments. Amen.

Have you ever been crushed? Please visit www.faithbookofjesus.com and click on "Community" to share.

To Read Further: Psalm 34

NO DIFFERENCE

For all have sinned and fall short of the glory of God.
— ROMANS 3:23

Money cannot satisfy; it doesn't grow on trees. True love has its flaws. Our fancy cars break down; they need routine tune-ups. Houses can be broken into and our valuables stolen. Jobs don't guarantee a substantial income anymore, and a degree doesn't guarantee us a great job. We tear each other apart sometimes, for we all sin and fall short of the glory of God.

So how do we respond? This verse doesn't exactly leave us with hope. Paul's response to missing the mark (the literal meaning of *sin*) also comes from Romans 3. He wrote, "This righteousness from God comes *through faith in Jesus Christ to all who believe.* There is no difference" (verse 22, emphasis added).

The hope we have comes through faith in Jesus. That's what this book is all about. There is no difference whether you are connecting with Jesus daily, weekly, or monthly. The righteousness we receive comes through believing that Jesus is who he said he is and that he came to do what he said he'd do. That's faith.

So what's the difference? The difference is in your attitude—how you live, what you eat, how you speak, and how you interact with others. Is your faith living proof that Jesus lives?

"So don't worry about these things, saying, 'What will we eat? What will we drink? What will we wear?' These things dominate the thoughts of unbelievers, but your heavenly Father already knows all your needs. Seek the Kingdom of God above all else, and live righteously, and he will give you everything you need" (Matthew 6:31-33, NLT).

66 99 Kyle, 25, said he is worried about "not having enough consistent support to fund my ministry (I live and minister off support)."

Dear No-Difference Jesus,
Thank you that it doesn't make a difference if we never read another word; the important thing today is that we believe in you. Help us in our unbelief. Amen.

How do you make a difference? Please visit www.faithbookofjesus.com and click on "Community" to share.

To Read Further: Matthew 6:28-34

JUST DANCE

I will become even more undignified than this, and I will be humiliated in my own eyes.
— 2 SAMUEL 6:22

Tonight I was on the couch unwinding from a long day at work. I planned an epic devotional about David dancing shamelessly and thought about how we, too, can just dance.

Then my phone rang. My friend Emanuel burst into tears (he's a guy, so technically he *wasn't* crying). He went off about his life. He was unhappy. He felt drawn back into his old lifestyle of drinking and getting high. So we talked. We talked about how tough it is to have faith in Jesus after the initial feelings go away.

After I hung up the phone, my friend Tim texted me and said that his girlfriend broke up with him. I burst into his apartment (we're neighbors) and listened to him talk about his depression and the anxiety of being alone.

Suddenly, talking about David dancing before Jesus almost seemed stupid. But it's not. That's when we really need to dance. Too many worries, heartaches, and disappointments bring us down and keep us down, but the kind of joy that comes when we dance our inhibitions away will put us in a position to dance with others.

If we want to have a joy like David did, we need to get off our couch and start dancing. There are a lot of people out there who need our joy, not to mention our faith, hope, and love.

❝❞ Lisa, 24, said, "Girls find their identity in guys. Guys find their identity in accomplishments. We tell ourselves, 'If I only go out with this person, then I'll be happy. If we only get married, then I'll be happy. . . . If I only buy this house, in this neighborhood, then I'll be happy.' We need to find our fulfillment in Jesus Christ."

 Dear Dancing Jesus,
It's easy to tell someone to just dance and get over his or her problems (like an alcohol addiction or a recent break-up), but unless you change us from the inside out, we're not dancing today. Amen.

What makes you dance? Please visit www.faithbookofjesus.com and click on "Community" to share.

To Read Further: 2 Samuel 6

SHINE LIKE THE STARS

Those who are wise will shine like the brightness of the heavens, and those who lead many to righteousness, like the stars for ever and ever.

— DANIEL 12:3

Looking up at the velvet night sky, what do you see? I see the moon and the stars, and with the help of a telescope, clusters of stars and a comet.

What is it about a star that makes it shine so brightly? According to *Merriam-Webster's Dictionary*, a *star* is "a self-luminous gaseous spheroidal celestial body of great mass which produces energy by means of nuclear fusion reactions."[9]

When someone is filled with energy, that person produces joy and his or her physical gestures become more grandiose. The Bible says, "Those who are wise will shine like the brightness of the heavens, and those who lead many to righteousness, like the stars for ever and ever" (Daniel 12:3).

Showing light to the world doesn't happen naturally. A star doesn't shine alone, and we don't either. We need outside help. Let's ask Jesus today for more light. "I [Jesus] am the light of the world. Whoever follows me will never walk in darkness, but will have the light of life" (John 8:12). Shine forth with the light of Jesus in your life.

66 99   Whitney, 20, said, "Life is a process of pursuing some possible failure in which most turn out as failure, but what is failure anyway? Being perfect and flawless is not in our genetic makeup."

 Dear Light-of-the-World Jesus,
Infuse us with energy and strength to show others what the Christian life is all about. We can't shine without you. Thank you for being our light today. Amen.

How do you shine like a star? Please visit www.faithbookofjesus.com and click on "Community" to share.

To Read Further: Daniel 12:3; Philippians 2:14-18

YOU SMELL!

*Thanks be to God, who always leads us in triumphal procession in Christ and through us
spreads everywhere the fragrance of the knowledge of him.*
— 2 CORINTHIANS 2:14

Paul wrote to the Corinthians that Jesus leads in victory. He does not lead by fear,
discouragement, or failure.

Life is typically full of defeat, so I tend to think Jesus leads *through* fear, but this
is not true. "But thanks be to God, who *always* leads us in triumphal procession in
Christ" (2 Corinthians 2:14, emphasis added).

A triumphal procession means forward movement. Jesus does not leave you or me
stuck where we are. Through victory in Jesus, we always move forward. Through pain
of divorce, markets collapsing, job layoffs, and loneliness, we are not left alone. Praise
Jesus that he leads us on.

As we learn how to walk victoriously, we also smell. What? You heard me! You
smell. Paul also wrote to the Corinthians that through our victory we spread a fragrance of the knowledge that Jesus saves.

Remember the last crisis you went through? Who brought you through it? What
about your worst nightmare? Whatever is ruling your mind and your emotions is not
from Jesus. The enemy of this world is here to cause us to fear, and in our fear we sin.
Instead of cowering under the weight of failure, let's choose to stand up and smell for
Jesus.

I'm sure; are you?

66 99 Ana, 25, said, "I don't let fear consume me, and if I catch myself worrying over
something, then it just means I am not spending enough time with Jesus."

Dear Fragrant Jesus,
I want to live a victorious life! If I'm worrying about something today, it's because
I'm not spending enough time with you. Thanks for putting verses like this in the
Bible. Help me to see, as Ana did, that if I'm worried it's because I need to spend
more time with you. Amen.

Do you smell for Jesus? Please visit www.faithbookofjesus.com and click on
"Community" to share.

To Read Further: 2 Corinthians 2:14-16

JARS OF CLAY

But we have this treasure in jars of clay to show that this all-surpassing power is from God and not from us.

— 2 CORINTHIANS 4:7

Yesterday we smelled, and today we're clay pots. If you're wondering how many different things you can be, keep reading. Putting your faith in Jesus daily is what it's all about. Some of us need to realize that we smell, and others need to know that he can use cracked pots.

Everyone faces trials and tests that make them suffer. A pot is only made perfect through extreme heat in the oven. Paul said we show Jesus' power through our weaknesses.

Then Paul said one of my favorite lines in all of the New Testament: "We are hard pressed on every side, but not crushed; perplexed, but not in despair; persecuted, but not abandoned; struck down, but not destroyed" (2 Corinthians 4:8-9). We can thank Jesus for this. He does not leave us for dead.

And after we have suffered a little while, Jesus makes us "strong, firm and steadfast" (1 Peter 5:10).

Let the work of Jesus' hands mold and shape your life into a beautiful jar of clay. What a beautiful sight it is when his all-surpassing power is made clear through each one of us, cracked pots and all.

66 99 Ashley, 23, a fellow jar of clay, said she wants to know "how to truly rest and not be stressed out. How to be wise financially, stay pure, and have godly relationships."

Dear Potter Jesus,
As we step foot out the door, help us to remember that we aren't just any clay pot, but yours. You made us, and you desire to use us today. Amen.

What kind of jar are you? Please visit www.faithbookofjesus.com and click on "Community" to share.

To Read Further: 2 Corinthians 4:1-12

GIVE HIM PRAISE

I want to know Christ and the power of his resurrection and the fellowship of sharing in his sufferings, becoming like him in his death, and so, somehow, to attain to the resurrection from the dead.

— PHILIPPIANS 3:10-11

Living the resurrected life is a glorious sight to behold. The peace, grace, and strength I felt after going through a near-death experience was exhilarating. Of course, not everyone goes through a dying and rebirth process, but there is something special about a person who has suffered.

John Eldredge, one of my favorite authors, wrote in *Wild at Heart*, "I don't trust a man who hasn't suffered."[10] Suffering produces depth and beauty. There is an ugly side to suffering, but there is also beauty. After the rain comes the sun. After death comes life.

We know that the one who raised the Lord Jesus from the dead will also raise us with Jesus and present us with you in his presence. All this is for your benefit, so that the grace that is reaching more and more people may cause thanksgiving to overflow to the glory of God. (2 Corinthians 4:14-15)

Whether you've already put faith and trust in Jesus or you are checking out the Christian thing for the first time, I encourage you to ask Jesus to reveal himself to you. He will give you wisdom if you do not doubt (see James 1:5-6).

❝❞ Kari, 27, said, "I fear that some of my family members will act on decisions made in fear."

 Dear Resurrected Jesus,
Jesus, we believe in you today. Forgive us of our fear and the sins that keep us from you. Come into our hearts and resurrect our souls to live with you after death becomes life. Amen.

Have you seen beauty come from suffering? Please visit www .faithbookofjesus.com and click on "Community" to share.

To Read Further: Philippians 3:7-15

LETTER

With them they sent the following letter.
— ACTS 15:23

To all twentysomethings, and my brothers and sisters in Jesus Christ,

"Do not be surprised at the painful trial you are suffering, as though something strange were happening to you. But rejoice that you participate in the sufferings of Christ, so that you may be overjoyed when his glory is revealed" (1 Peter 4:12-13).

"For our light and momentary troubles are achieving for us an eternal glory that far outweighs them all. So we fix our eyes not on what is seen, but on what is unseen. For what is seen is temporary, but what is unseen is eternal" (2 Corinthians 4:17-18).

"Now if we are children, then we are heirs—heirs of God and co-heirs with Christ, if indeed we share in his sufferings in order that we may also share in his glory. I consider that our present sufferings are not worth comparing with the glory that will be revealed in us" (Romans 8:17-18).

"I have written to you briefly, encouraging you and testifying that this is the true grace of God. Stand fast in it" (1 Peter 5:12).

"Grace, mercy and peace from God the Father and from Jesus Christ, the Father's Son, will be with us in truth and love" (2 John 1:3).

—Peter, Paul, and John

66 99 Mandy, 25, said she is overwhelmed by "being overloaded with things to do and not seeing a way out or a light on the other side."

Dear Love-Letter Jesus,
For every situation and prayer under heaven, there is a verse to help us address our life. Thank you for people like Peter, Paul, and John, who are our source of encouragement for the day. Amen.

What verses would you put in your letter to fellow brothers and sisters in Christ? Please visit www.faithbookofjesus.com and click on "Community" to share.

To Read Further: Romans 8:17-18; 2 Corinthians 4:17-18; 1 Peter 4:12-13; 5:12; 2 John 1:3

YOU CAN RUN, BUT YOU CAN'T HIDE

I heard you in the garden, and I was afraid because I was naked; so I hid.
— GENESIS 3:10

The very first reaction to sin was fear. Adam and Eve had the perfect life in the Garden of Eden until they ate that stupid apple. Then God came strolling through the garden, and they hid.

Somehow this verse makes me feel more human. I don't feel so stupid anymore. No matter how many bad things I've done, Jesus is still there waiting for me.

What are you hiding? Could it be your fear of inadequacy, of not pleasing other people? Every person I surveyed said his or her biggest fear was being alone and not finding the right spouse.

We all strive for that perfect career, family life, bank account, etc. It can be easy to get carried away and think it's okay to do whatever it takes to pursue these things—even if it means cheating just a little. A bad apple still counts as sin.

God knows all things. He knew where Adam and Eve were hiding after they ate the apple, yet he asked them, "Where are you?" (Genesis 3:9).

Next time you run from your sins, stop and turn around. Let Jesus draw you back to himself because he loves you and desires a relationship with you.

66 99 Emily, 25, said her favorite Bible verse is "1 John 4:18—fear is a big thing for me and anything on accepting Jesus' love and grace!"

Dear Beloved Jesus,
I have to laugh at myself for how many times I run and hide from you as if you can't see my sin and how desperately I'm trying to cover it up. Forgive me when I am too afraid to admit my sins to you. Draw me back to yourself and lead me in the way everlasting. Amen.

What is your greatest fear? Please visit www.faithbookofjesus.com and click on "Community" to share.

To Read Further: Genesis 3:1-10

PUT TO DEATH

Put to death, therefore, whatever belongs to your earthly nature: sexual immorality,
impurity, lust, evil desires and greed, which is idolatry.

— COLOSSIANS 3:5

We are to put to death whatever belongs to our earthly nature. Why? Sin leads to idolatry.

Merriam-Webster's Dictionary defines *idolatry* as "the worship of a physical object as a god; attachment or devotion to something."[11] The first commandment clearly states we shall have no other gods before Jesus.

I once heard sin explained as a process of baby steps. My former pastor said we don't begin with sin—lust, anger, sex, or drugs—till we break down crying. No! But somehow every one of us ends up there. And guess what? A few Sundays later, my pastor was forced to leave the church because he had been unfaithful to his wife—numerous times.

Death is a serious matter. It's not to be taken lightly. Watch your thoughts and intentions. Eventually they could become the very steps you take to commit sinful acts that can separate you from your destiny.

Put sin to death. Be set free by the power of the cross and put these things to death: anger, rage, malice, slander, and filthy language (see Colossians 3:8).

66 99 Michelle, 20, said, "I feel the purpose of life is to honor and glorify God. That means every decision, action, and thought should reflect him."

Dear Death-to-Life Jesus,
Thanks to your shed blood on the cross, we ask for your help today to put to death anything that separates us from you. Come and bring us life by the power of your name. Amen.

How do you put sin to death? Please visit www.faithbookofjesus.com and click on "Community" to share.

To Read Further: Colossians 3:5-11

BIG BABY

Like newborn babies, crave pure spiritual milk, so that by it you may grow up in your
salvation, now that you have tasted that the Lord is good.
— 1 PETER 2:2-3

I've been through so much pain and depression from the Enemy. No matter how many times Jesus has healed me, I freak out every time. It's like I'm a big baby who doesn't remember who my dad is.

It reminds me of the classic story of the bully, his target, and an older brother. While the bully is picking on a boy, his big brother shows up. The bully backs off. The little boy is saved. Meanwhile, the little boy thinks that *he* showed up the bully and saved the day.

Now, if that little boy would drink his milk and continue to grow strong, he would eventually grow into a mature adult. And so should we.

Want spiritual authority in your life? Learn how to spend time with Jesus daily. Drink milk, the pure spiritual kind of milk. Open the Bible. Pray more. Seek wise council. Allow Jesus to meet your needs, and he will show you his purpose for your life in every circumstance.

Don't let sin and the Enemy control your life without your knowledge of what's happening. Ask Jesus to stand behind you. He's a good Father, and he'll always take care of you.

"Don't worry about anything; instead, pray about everything. Tell God what you need, and thank him for all he has done" (Philippians 4:6, NLT).

66 99 Jaclynn, 24, said her milk prayers are for "direction in knowing you are doing what God has called you to do."

 Dear Father Jesus,
We need milk to grow strong bones, and we need your spiritual milk each and every
day to teach us how to grow in our faith. Amen.

Do you crave pure spiritual milk? Please visit www.faithbookofjesus.com and click on "Community" to share.

To Read Further: 1 Peter 2:1-3

NOT YOUR AVERAGE CHRISTIAN

Many will say to me on that day, "Lord, Lord, did we not prophesy in your name, and in your name drive out demons and perform many miracles?"
— MATTHEW 7:22

Every time I register on a dating website, I select "Christian" as my religion. And to my surprise, so does everyone else. It's interesting how many guys claim "Christian" yet write inappropriate comments in their profile that have nothing to do with Jesus.

Most twentysomethings say they believe in God. What about *Jesus*? It's easy to claim to be a Christian, but what does that look like?

Vicky, quoted below, said, "I was never raised in church as a child, yet although no one told me what God was or anything of the sort, I still always believed someone was caring for me. I later learned that people called that 'God,' and much later learned that he was Jesus. I don't attend church, not even on Sundays. I listen to music other than gospel or Christian bands. I don't attend Bible studies. I don't dig deep into the Word every day. You get the picture. Yet although it may not seem that I have much devotion, I have been deeply moved and touched by Christ in my life."

I think the picture of the average Christian is changing. You don't always see twentysomethings in church much anymore, but that doesn't mean we're not out changing the world because of what Jesus has done in our lives.

❝❞ Vicky, 23, said, "I don't belong to a congregation at this point in my life. I have a deep gratitude and love for what Jesus has blessed me with and the wounds he has healed with his touch."

 *Dear Above-Average Jesus,*
Thank you, Jesus, for being ever-present in my life and healing wounds I thought would never fade. And thank you, Jesus, for the trials that I suffer through that bring me an understanding of what I have in you today. Amen.

👥 Have you been deeply touched by Christ in your life? Please visit www .faithbookofjesus.com and click on "Community" to share.

⟩◯ To Read Further: Matthew 7:21-23

COLOR-BLIND

Do not deprive the alien or the fatherless of justice, or take the cloak of the widow as a
pledge. Remember that you were slaves in Egypt and the LORD your God
redeemed you from there.

— DEUTERONOMY 24:17-18

Most people relate to Jesus based on their family life. If you're Caucasian, you've got at least one picture of Jesus holding a little lamb. You know the picture? He looks passive and has long, wavy brunette hair. If you're African American, you probably put up at least one black nativity set during Christmastime. And if you're Asian . . . Well, you get the picture. If you didn't know, Jesus is color-blind.

As followers of Jesus, we don't show preference. We're supposed to help everyone no matter their race or color. Every race has poor and fatherless people. That means Hispanics, Caucasians, African Americans, Asian Americans, Europeans, Middle Eastern people—we all need Jesus!

"For I was hungry and you gave me something to eat, I was thirsty and you gave me something to drink, I was a stranger and you invited me in, I needed clothes and you clothed me, I was sick and you looked after me, I was in prison and you came to visit me" (Matthew 25:35-36).

Jesus wants us to look beyond the color of skin and into the hearts and needs of people. "If you spend yourselves in behalf of the hungry and satisfy the needs of the oppressed, then your light will rise in the darkness, and your night will become like the noonday" (Isaiah 58:10).

66 99 Alex, 31, was once "involved with gangs. . . . My family moved to so many different places around California. It was a rough transition from nothing but Asians, Hispanics, and African Americans to Caucasians being the majority."

Dear Color-Blind Jesus,
Close our eyes to the prejudices of the day. Open our eyes to the needs of others around us regardless of race, shape, or size. Thank you for setting a standard of justice and for always redeeming us, your people. Amen.

What does Jesus look like to you? Please visit www.faithbookofjesus.com and click on "Community" to share.

To Read Further: Deuteronomy 24:17-22

LOSE YOUR SOUL

What good will it be for a man if he gains the whole world, yet forfeits his soul? Or what can a man give in exchange for his soul?
— MATTHEW 16:26

Have you ever wished you could go back and change your life? For instance, "My life would have been much easier if I had just done [fill in the blank]."

There was a time when I wanted to change my past. I fell in love and thought we would get married. When he broke my heart, I hated him. I regretted ever loving him, and it wasn't until a few years later that I forgave him.

Living life with regret sucks. But living with no discipline is even worse. The choices we make in our twenties will affect the rest of our lives. What good is it for you to gain everything you want if you have to forfeit your soul? Living the Christian life doesn't have to be boring or dull.

Have faith in Jesus and he'll show you the way. He guarantees a far greater reward. "And this world is fading away, along with everything that people crave. But anyone who does what pleases God will live forever" (1 John 2:17, NLT).

66 99 Tammy, 29, said, "I really get to experience the most exciting things now, more exciting than traveling, using drugs, partying, sex, money, and personal status. Jesus is so very miraculous, and I really wish I knew what I know now back in high school."

Dear Jesus, Lover of My Soul,
You long to have a personal relationship with us. You care about everything, from the socks we wear to the job we accept. Show us the way, so we can walk in it and be blessed today. Amen.

Have you ever felt like you lost your soul? Please visit www.faithbookofjesus.com and click on "Community" to share.

To Read Further: Matthew 16:24-28

WILL YOU MARRY ME?

I will be faithful to you and make you mine, and you will finally know me as the LORD.
— HOSEA 2:20 (NLT)

This is one of my favorite Bible verses. Jesus has been and is still restoring my heart. I am fortunate to have grown up in the church, and I came to know Christ at an early age. However, I have many wounds that have affected me greatly. Most of my hurts come from my health issues, and they still leave a sting in my heart. But God has made me his and has shown me compassion and tenderness in ways that I never experienced from my earthly dad.

All my life I've always wanted to be married. I've seen every one of my single friends get married before me, including my roommates. Yet, when I read this verse, I'm reminded that Jesus pursues my heart and makes me his daily. I am his bride; he calls me his wife.

I'm sure the void I have as a single person will exist even after I am married. I know everyone experiences some level of pain from living in a fallen world.

We are Jesus' bride, and believe me, he wants to go there with us because Jesus is love. He will pursue us and heal us in loving-kindness; then we will know the power of his redeeming love. Now that sounds like a proposal everyone should accept.

66 99 Rachel, 25, said, "This verse has been significant to me for several years and has been a reminder of God's redeeming love for me."

 Dear Fiancé Jesus,
Yes, I will marry you. I want to experience real love. I want to be your bride and finally know you as my husband. I want you. I need you. I love you. Show me I am yours. Amen.

What void does Jesus need to fill in your life? Please visit www .faithbookofjesus.com and click on "Community" to share.

To Read Further: Hosea 2:16-20

ALL ABOUT ME

I know, O LORD, that a man's life is not his own; it is not for man to direct his steps.
— JEREMIAH 10:23

It's such a relief to know that I'm not in total control of my destiny. I miss the mark every day. I fall short. I also do great things for the kingdom. But it's not all about me.

A few years ago, I created an Excel document and called it my life map. My life was going nowhere fast. My job sucked. I needed to finish my college degree. I was still living at home with my parents, and I felt helpless to change.

How on earth was I going to find the job of my dreams, afford the cost of living, move into a nice place, and marry Mr. Right all at the same time? But I was determined, so I made a spreadsheet. I wrote down all of my thoughts on the matter under three tabs: "Job," "Roommate," and "Future Husband." I invited Jesus into the entire process and asked for wisdom. Without his help, I would not have made it through.

The most important lesson I learned during that life-mapping process came through gaining life experience. The job I received was *much* better in real life than on paper. The roommates I lived with taught me about my pride and that it really wasn't all about me. And my future husband? Well, I'm still praying about that one.

❝❞ Arman, 23, said he feels his purpose is "to serve the Lord, be a good friend, be a good husband, a good father, and ultimately try my hardest to be an example of Christ."

🖐 *Dear All-About-You Jesus,*
Thank you for answering my prayers and for not leaving me stuck without hope. I cannot thank you enough for my job, my life, and the experiences I've gained along the way. I pray the same for those reading today. Amen.

👥 Is your life all about you? Please visit www.faithbookofjesus.com and click on "Community" to share.

🐟 To Read Further: Jeremiah 10:23-24

WHO AM I?

Who am I, O Sovereign LORD, and what is my family, that you have brought me this far?
— 2 SAMUEL 7:18

David is one of the most written-about men in the Bible. A man after God's own heart, he was the second king of Israel and was chosen by God through the prophet Samuel. In the above verse, David was talking with Nathan the prophet about his lament for God's house (which remained in a tent) while he got to live in a palace (see 2 Samuel 7:2).

During the night, the word of the Lord came to Nathan, and the very next day he told David everything. Humbled by the Lord's encouraging words (see 2 Samuel 7:8-16), David asked, "Who am I?" (verse 18).

David's response is the most common question people ask, including twenty-somethings. How do you find your identity in a world that's constantly changing? What if you don't even know who you are or what you want to be yet?

In my early twenties I thought I would never make something of myself. I never imagined having a job I enjoyed or friends who truly cared.

What about you? What makes you dream? What makes you laugh? What makes you cry? The Lord wants to do all these things and more for you if you'll honor him and put him first as David did.

66 99   Karianne, 20, said, "I am a student. I am satisfied for now, but I wish that I was a recording artist."

 Dear Knowing Jesus,
Thank you for David's example. May we find encouragement in you today even if we don't already know who we are or where we're going. Amen.

Can you relate to David's question: "Who am I?" Please visit www .faithbookofjesus.com and click on "Community" to share.

To Read Further: 2 Samuel 7:8-17

ONLY EXCEPTION

All the king's officials and the people of the royal provinces know that for any man or woman who approaches the king in the inner court without being summoned . . . he [or she must] be put to death. The only exception to this is for the king to extend the gold scepter to him and spare his life.

— ESTHER 4:11

When Jesus sets out to accomplish a task, he doesn't need us. If we are willing, he most certainly will use us, but if we are not willing, he can go elsewhere. We are not the only exception.

Queen Esther is known as a heroine of the Bible. She risked her life to save her people, the Israelites. What she did took great courage. What Jesus asks of us can sometimes take us by surprise as well. But Jesus doesn't ask us to do something he hasn't already given us the grace and strength to accomplish.

Esther went before the king without being summoned—which was punishable by death. She asked others to pray and fast that she would make it out alive. When the king extended his golden scepter and spared her life, he made her the only exception.

Did you know that God also made an exception by sending his only Son?

"For it is by grace you have been saved, through faith—and this not from yourselves, it is the gift of God—not by works, so that no one can boast. For we are God's workmanship, created in Christ Jesus to do good works, which God prepared in advance for us to do" (Ephesians 2:8-10).

66 99 Courtney, 26, said, "My favorite Bible verse is Ephesians 2:10."

Dear No-Exceptions Jesus,
Thank you for Esther's example to give us extra faith and hope. Whatever task or trial we are currently experiencing, we ask you to make an exception for us today. Amen.

Are you an exception? Please visit www.faithbookofjesus.com and click on "Community" to share.

To Read Further: Esther 4:1-14

WE WIN

Be thankful in all circumstances, for this is God's will for you who belong to Christ Jesus.
— 1 THESSALONIANS 5:18 (NLT)

Ever since I saw the movie *Big Daddy* with Adam Sandler, I play the "I win" game. Seriously, I am very competitive. I'm not an athlete, but I did cycle off more than eighty pounds that I gained from my health issues. I'm competitive at work, too. I want to make the most sales and book the most events. At church, I'm usually involved in four ministries because I know the outcome: I win!

Instead of writing another cheesy devotional on why you should *be* thankful in every circumstance, I chose instead to present thankfulness as an outcome versus a feeling. What Jesus did on the cross (he rose again on the third day!) has completely set us free from the power of sin and death. You win.

The choices we make still matter, but if you're experiencing a trial today that is keeping you from being thankful, think again. Whether you thank Jesus before, during, or after the trial, "you win!"

Let's choose thankfulness today even if it feels impossible (see Matthew 19:26). Whatever lies you believe about yourself today, tell yourself "I win" and move on. That's it.

❝❞ Rebecca, 26, said, "I fear being alone for the rest of my life, and I fear for the status of our country that the next generation is going to have to deal with, but I am thankful because I know that Jesus will provide."

Dear Victorious Jesus,
We win! I win! We all win! How exciting it is to think that our present trials are creating a much greater praise and glory on that day when Jesus Christ will be revealed to the whole world. Amen.

How do you choose thankfulness? Please visit www.faithbookofjesus.com and click on "Community" to share.

To Read Further: 1 Peter 1:3-9

MISSING OUT

Stay away from a foolish man, for you will not find knowledge on his lips.
— PROVERBS 14:7

Just imagine where you'd be right now if the Lord said "yes" to all your prayers. Like the time you prayed to marry this guy or that girl. If that were the case, I would have been married and divorced many times. That might be the reason I'm twenty-six and *still* single.

I always think I'm missing out. In fact, we can get ourselves into all kinds of trouble thinking we know what's best. Jesus knows when we're ready for a new opportunity, job, or relationship—even if we think that time is *now*. Here are a few verses to remind us we're not missing out:

"Let not my heart be drawn to what is evil, to take part in wicked deeds with men who are evildoers; let me not eat of their delicacies" (Psalm 141:4).

"There are six things the LORD hates, seven that are detestable to him: haughty eyes, a lying tongue, hands that shed innocent blood, a heart that devises wicked schemes, feet that are quick to rush into evil" (Proverbs 6:16-18).

"To man belong the plans of the heart, but from the LORD comes the reply of the tongue. . . . In his heart a man plans his course, but the LORD determines his steps" (Proverbs 16:1,9).

❝❞ Joshua, 25, said, "Missing out is not always a bad thing. The now is not as important as the later. A girl once told me that I was missing out while she was sitting topless in the hot tub."

 Dear All-Knowing Jesus,
Remind us daily that we're not missing out on anything you have in store for us.
Thank you that our lives are not our own, and it's not up to us to direct every step.
Amen.

Have you ever missed out on something? Please visit www.faithbookofjesus .com and click on "Community" to share.

To Read Further: Psalm 141:4; Proverbs 6:16-18; 14:7; 16:1,9

TEMPTING

No temptation has seized you except what is common to man. And God is faithful; he will not let you be tempted beyond what you can bear. But when you are tempted, he will also provide a way out so that you can stand up under it.

— 1 CORINTHIANS 10:13

Every day we are tempted in relationships, work, school, and finances. I could keep going, but you get the point. Once we take the bait and choose to believe that we're missing out, we walk into a trap. The Enemy offers an enticing temptation, and we respond, "Yes, please!" To the topless woman in the hot tub or naked people on the computer screen, it's easy to do what feels right in the moment.

The difference between temptation and trials should determine our reaction. Paul said to flee temptation and stand up to trials (see 1 Corinthians 10:18; 1 Timothy 6:9-11). How can you stand up to a topless woman when she's half naked? Run! (For a great Bible story on running from sin, check out the story of Joseph and Potiphar's wife in Genesis 39.)

Trials are meant to make us stronger. We need to stand up during them so we'll be complete and not lacking anything (see James 1:2-4). Paul wrote in 1 Peter that after we have suffered a little while, we will be strong (see 5:10). How can we grow if we don't encounter resistance?

Do you want to distinguish between temptations and trials? Get your shoes on and start running. At least you'll have a head start. And remember to stand strong.

❝❞ Tim, 24, said, "You know when something's tempting you, and you know when you should stand up to your problems instead of running from them."

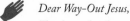 *Dear Way-Out Jesus,*
Thank you for always providing a way out of temptation. Whatever we are facing today, remind us to run for it. If it's a trial, help us to stand strong. Thank you for your strength and courage. Amen.

How would you describe the difference between trials and temptations? Please visit www.faithbookofjesus.com and click on "Community" to share.

To Read Further: 1 Corinthians 10:18; 1 Timothy 6:9-11

NEW LIFE, NOW WHAT?

Therefore, if anyone is in Christ, he is a new creation; the old has gone, the new has come!
— 2 CORINTHIANS 5:17

Most twentysomethings I know want to be better people. We want to know our purpose, that what we long for will one day be fulfilled in the area of relationships, career, or finances. But what exactly does new life in Jesus mean?

I'll tell you what it doesn't mean: perfection. Jesus said, "It is not the healthy who need a doctor, but the sick" (Matthew 9:12). As a literal "sick" person, I spent most of my life going from doctor to doctor asking for help. It was so difficult for me to wrap my head around why Jesus did not choose to heal me . . . right away.

Every day I'd read portions of Scripture. I even signed up for verses to be e-mailed to me daily in case I forgot to read my Bible. Ten years later, I finally got it. I no longer rely on my own strength, but Jesus and his strength. "My grace is sufficient for you, for my power is made perfect in weakness" (2 Corinthians 12:9).

New life does not happen overnight. Jesus doesn't use Band-Aids either. He will not leave us broken. He wants all of us to be fully healed. Yes, you! Yes, me!

66 99 Paul, 26, said, "Understanding obedience has been my big one. Not giving in to the ways of my past, not going back or looking back. Knowing that I get to start new. It's hard for me to understand what that means."

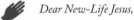 *Dear New-Life Jesus,*
Please encourage my friends and brothers and sisters in Christ to understand that you don't leave us hanging. Heal us today and give us new life in Christ. We love you, Lord. Amen.

Would you like a new life? Please visit www.faithbookofjesus.com and click on "Community" to share.

To Read Further: 2 Corinthians 5:17-20

GOOD TREE, BAD TREE

A good tree can't produce bad fruit, and a bad tree can't produce good fruit.
— LUKE 6:43 (NLT)

I'm a good tree who is waiting for my perfect tree-match. I know the world tells me that I have to kiss a lot of bad trees (or frogs) to meet my prince, but Jesus would disagree.

Knowledge is not found on the lips of a fool (see Proverbs 14:7). I'm not supposed to kiss every bad tree (or frog) that comes my way. It was easier when I was younger, but now that I'm almost thirty, I'm scared. I'm scared that no boy will ever resemble a good tree and that being a good tree in the midst of bad trees, I'll somehow mess up and miss out forever.

Luke wrote, "Each tree is recognized by its own fruit" (Luke 6:44).

How do you determine if that guy or girl you're dating is a bad tree? Look at his or her fruit. I can tell when I hang out with a bad tree. Instead of allowing the fruit of what Jesus is already doing in my life, such as love, peace, patience, and kindness, I choose instead to cuss, drink, kiss, etc. Bad trees bear bad fruit, and they can have a bad influence on you.

So, are you a good tree or a bad tree?

❝❞ Renee, 26, said, "I just gave up what I thought was the relationship of a life-time because I knew he wasn't a believer. And as much as it killed me, I knew I was making the right decision."

 Dear Good-Tree Jesus,
Help me hold tightly to your promises because as your child, who is loved and secure, I want to help encourage others to be the good tree they were created to be. Amen.

 What kind of fruit do you bear? Please visit www.faithbookofjesus.com and click on "Community" to share.

To Read Further: Luke 6:43-45

CRUCIFIED WITH CHRIST

I have been crucified with Christ and I no longer live, but Christ lives in me. The life I live in the body, I live by faith in the Son of God, who loved me and gave himself for me.
— GALATIANS 2:20

Although Jesus' death on the cross and victory over the grave are still very much alive today, the message of the cross in our lives isn't easily accepted and wildly popular among twentysomethings.

Do you want to die to your wants, desires, and dreams in order to follow Jesus? No thanks! Doesn't that leave us with nothing? That's what the Enemy wants us to believe. The Enemy's first lie is that we'll live a boring life with no fun if we follow Jesus.

The world will tell you it's okay to live however you want. But if you are living only for this world, then live it up — *because that's all you're going to get.*

Jesus said, "Enter through the narrow gate. For wide is the gate and broad is the road that leads to destruction, and many enter through it [actual land of nothing]. But small is the gate and narrow the road that leads to life, and only a few find it" (Matthew 7:13-14).

Jesus was crucified, murdered, and sent to the grave so that we could make it in this life. Want to find your life? Don't set your faith aside. Jesus wasn't crucified for nothing!

66 99 Shawna, 22, said, "Perhaps addressing the issue of 'success' in the world's (our culture's) terms compared to God's message about success or thriving" would be a good devotional.

 Dear Crucified Jesus,
Thank you for showing us another way to live. Because of your selfless act on the cross, we can put aside our selfish wants and desires and place our faith and trust in you today. Amen.

What does Jesus' death on the cross mean to you? Please visit www .faithbookofjesus.com and click on "Community" to share.

To Read Further: Galatians 2:17-21

WHEN, NOT IF

When the LORD your God brings you into the land he swore to your fathers.
— DEUTERONOMY 6:10

I love this verse because it doesn't say "if" but "when." Sometimes we say, "If I ever have a boyfriend, or if I ever make enough money, then I will be successful." But the proper response is to ask Jesus "when."

Here are three responses to take while waiting for "when" to happen. The first is surrender. There are desires I've longed for quite some time, and it's hard for me to understand that today is not the day. When a bunch of todays and tomorrows go by, I tend to get anxious. I take things into my own hands. I step out in what I feel is faith, but it's really a lack of trust that Jesus will do what he said he'll do (see Psalm 37:5).

The second response is playfulness. Sometimes, you just need to be around people who love you, like close family and friends. The Israelites were in good company for forty years wandering around in the desert. They knew what it was like to be stuck, but they were also in it together. Grab a friend and head to the movies, or go out for coffee and vent over a venti espresso.

The third response is a warning. When you're waiting for Jesus to fulfill his promises, you'll find temptations and trials around every turn. So buckle up and watch those guardrails of your heart (see Proverbs 4:23).

66 99 Darlene, 27, said, "When Jesus fulfills his promises in our lives, we will be pleased beyond comprehension."

 Dear Whenever Jesus,
Help us to see that you answer prayer and that we can trust you for our needs if we make your kingdom our primary concern. Help us to seek you first in all our ways so that you will make our paths straight. Amen.

Are you still waiting for something to happen? Please visit www .faithbookofjesus.com and click on "Community" to share.

To Read Further: Deuteronomy 6:10-18

THIRSTY?

O God, you are my God, earnestly I seek you; my soul thirsts for you, my body longs for you, in a dry and weary land where there is no water.

— PSALM 63:1

Have you noticed how the last few days before payday are the worst? Broke as a joke, you hope no one will notice or ask you to hang out until you've gotten paid. This is how I imagine David felt when he wrote this psalm.

Normally, I pray harder when my soul is broken. When I have nothing left to go on and I'm waiting for payday, I pour my heart out to Jesus. Imagine waiting days without water or weeks without a paycheck. No thanks.

Don't wait to spend time with Jesus. Open your Bible and start reading now. Earnestly search for Jesus today. Don't wait until you're broke (or hungry or thirsty).

Give your thoughts over to Jesus so he can carry them for you (see 1 Peter 5:7)—thoughts of your job, relationships and the one who got away, your hunger for more, or whatever it is that you desire today. Let Jesus' love pour into you as you seek him in this dry and weary land where there is no water. Only he can fill you up.

66 99 Alicia, 22, said she thinks about "student debt, things I can't control, confusing young men."

Dear Thirst-Quenching Jesus,
We pour our hearts and lives out to you today. May we not go thirsty because of your living water. Thank you for providing for our daily needs. Amen.

Do you need Jesus to fill you up? Please visit www.faithbookofjesus.com and click on "Community" to share.

To Read Further: Psalm 63:1-11

THE OTHER WOMAN

Jesus answered her, "If you knew the gift of God and who it is that asks you for a drink, you would have asked him and he would have given you living water."
— JOHN 4:10

This book connects you with Jesus daily. Today we see Jesus sharing his faith with others. That leads me to the question: "How do you share your faith with others?" Do you drag them to church or grab a beer with them down at the local pub?

In John 4 Jesus went to the local watering hole to grab a drink while his disciples went to find food. It was the middle of the day, and the women were home staying cool, except for *her*. She was the other woman.

Jesus spoke up and asked for some water. Back then, that was a pretty big deal. Jewish men never talked to women outside their race. Jewish rabbis *never* talked to women in public . . . ever. Jesus, the rabbi, asked the Samaritan (non-Jewish) woman for a drink of water at the well.

The woman was shell-shocked. Who was this man asking her for a drink of water? Instead of playing nice or churchy, Jesus got personal and told her "everything [she] ever did" (John 4:39). Because of Jesus' bold faith, many Samaritans believed that day.

What is holding you back from sharing with the other women or men around you?

66 99 Kristal, 28, said, "The only thing that continuously stresses me is when a family member acts in an unloving way, completely rude and lying to the rest of the family."

Dear Living-Water Jesus,
Show us what is hindering us from giving away the living water that you have so graciously given to us regardless of race, economics, or blood. May we reach out a hand and extend a glass of living water today. Amen.

What stops you from sharing your faith with someone else? Please visit www .faithbookofjesus.com and click on "Community" to share.

To Read Further: John 4:7-26,39-42

CONSIDER THE SOURCE

He became the source of eternal salvation for all who obey him.
— HEBREWS 5:9

Jesus is the source for everything. He became nothing so we could have everything. I'm not preaching the prosperity gospel that some people believe. Although we are rich beyond comprehension, it's not what we may expect or imagine.

Jesus is the source of all comfort. Blessed are you who are depressed, for you will be comforted (see Matthew 5:4). Don't fear or freak out; trust Jesus and put your faith in him (see John 14:1). The comfort we receive from Jesus we can use to encourage others (see 2 Corinthians 1:3-6).

Jesus is the source of our hope. Even if you feel there is no hope for you, there is (see Ruth 1:12). Your future as a wandering twentysomething may look confusing and hopeless, but we have hope (see 1 Chronicles 29:15-16). No one who puts his or her hope in Jesus will be put to shame (see Romans 10:11). We can put our hope in the Word of Jesus, which will not fail us (see Psalm 119:114,147). When we put our hope in Jesus, we gain new strength for the day (see Isaiah 40:31).

Jesus is the one source to follow. Following other people can lead us into a dangerous trap (see Proverbs 29:25) and cause us to do bad things (see Exodus 23:2). Following Jesus leads to many blessings (see Leviticus 25:18; Deuteronomy 7:11-13). The disciples followed Jesus, and we follow him still today (see Matthew 4:19-20; 28:19-20).

66 99 Andrew, 29, said, "Figure out how to be more like Jesus. All the other things—career, a spouse and family, etc.—will fall into place in God's time."

Dear Jesus, Our Source,
Thank you for being our source today. In a world full of empty promises and quick fixes, help us to take you up on your offer and put our hope and trust in you today. Amen.

Is Jesus your source? Please visit www.faithbookofjesus.com and click on "Community" to share.

To Read Further: 1 Chronicles 29:15-16; Matthew 5:4; 28:19-20

GET SMART

Show me your ways, O LORD, teach me your paths; guide me in your truth and teach me, for you are God my Savior, and my hope is in you all day long.

— PSALM 25:4-5

I don't know what the future holds. I search far and wide for what I'm looking for, and I dream a bit, too. Ultimately, Jesus knows and will show me if I ask him (see Proverbs 19:21; James 1:5).

While we're waiting, hoping, living, striving, and breathing, we should pray and search the Bible for answers. Don't just take my word for it. Read for yourself.

"Now the Bereans were of more noble character than the Thessalonians, for they received the message with great eagerness and examined the Scriptures every day to see if what Paul said was true" (Acts 17:11).

We don't become smart by *not* studying. Trials and tests will come our way, and if we're not prepared, we won't know what to do or how to act. Want to know what you should do at work or how to act toward a girlfriend who just broke up with you? Get smart. Search the Word.

66 99 Manny, 26, said, "I wonder what's on [girls'] minds, you know. Or if we are the only ones going crazy."

 Dear Smart Jesus,
I'm dumb sometimes. Okay, that's an understatement—I'm stupid. When I don't know what to do, I panic or try to take matters into my own hands. Help me to understand how to get smart by reading your Word and talking with you today. Amen.

Haw do you get smart? Please visit www.faithbookofjesus.com and click on "Community" to share.

To Read Further: Psalm 25

JUST KEEP SWIMMING

A furious squall came up, and the waves broke over the boat,
so that it was nearly swamped.
— MARK 4:37

Swimming in a pool or a peaceful stream is delightful. Swimming in the ocean is exhilarating. But swimming in a storm could be dangerous or deadly. The disciples were told by Jesus to cross over to the other side of the sea, and while they were "swimming," a storm came and overtook their boat.

How many times has Jesus led me into a storm?

I have been lost in the sea of life too many times to count. There have been times in my life when I wanted to die or thought I would die. What about you? Was there a time in your life when you felt blown and tossed by the wind, only to be left to drown? Just keep swimming....

I know it's not logical to keep swimming when you're drowning, but that's essentially what Jesus told the disciples when they woke him up on the lake that evening. They said, "Teacher, don't you care if we drown?" (Mark 4:38).

Never mind that Jesus slept through the storm. His reply? "Why are you so afraid? Do you still have no faith?" (verse 40).

Jesus doesn't lead us to the other side to let us drown because he's already swimming with us.

What's your faith look like today? Just keep swimming.

❝❞ Jennifer, 27, said she fears "not being able to feed my kids."

 Dear Swimmer Jesus,
Please help us to remember to keep swimming. Don't take us out into the middle of
a storm unless you intend to rescue us. Save us by your mighty power and strength
today. Amen.

What storm can Jesus help you out of today? Please visit www
.faithbookofjesus.com and click on "Community" to share.

To Read Further: Mark 4:35-41

YOUR VISION

Where there is no vision, the people perish.
— PROVERBS 29:18 (KJV)

Let's be honest. We all have a vision for our lives. Some of us aspire to be great spouses, parents, co-workers, and friends. Wherever you are at in achieving any or all of these things, it is difficult to dream if you have no vision. Wandering aimlessly in life is not fun. In fact, it is dangerous.

The New American Standard Bible says people who lack vision are "unrestrained." As a young twentysomething, I felt unrestrained daily. I felt like I was constantly reaching for something that didn't exist. I dreamed of becoming a writer and speaker, but how? One day I was happy being myself, and the next I was unfulfilled, lonely, and miserable.

The Message translates it this way: "If people can't see what God is doing, they stumble all over themselves; but when they attend to what he reveals, they are most blessed."

Jesus fulfilled my vision. I prayed for the past six years to write this book for my generation, and look at me now.

Do you want to be blessed today? Seek Jesus and give him your vision. Trust him to turn your vision into all your dreams coming true.

❝❞ Jaron, 20, said his vision is "to live a life [where my] main goal and purpose is to praise God and spread his fame to the whole earth."

 Dear Vision-Catcher Jesus,
Your Word and your Spirit teach us how to live and have vision. Please share with us daily how to dream and keep walking in our dreams until you've brought the vision to complete fruition. Thank you for answering our prayers daily. Amen.

What is your vision? Please visit www.faithbookofjesus.com and click on "Community" to share.

To Read Further: Joel 2:28-29

A PERFECT PEACE

You will keep in perfect peace all who trust in you, all whose thoughts are fixed on you!
— ISAIAH 26:3 (NLT)

I am not a peaceful person. By nature, I am a very driven person. Every day I search for the fastest way to satisfy my wants and needs. Why wait if you don't have to?

When I rely on myself, I'm never peaceful. I take Jesus at his Word when he said we can have perfect peace. Not a peace that fades or can be faked, but the real deal. Here is an acronym for this special kind of peace:

Persistent faith. Sticky situations and long-term trials don't need to rob us of the peace that surpasses all understanding (see Philippians 4:7).

Everyone wins. Have you noticed people who handle sickness or stress well? They are not only a testament that obtaining perfect peace is possible but they show others how it can be done.

Accept your trials. After Jesus invited the disciples into a storm, he calmed it. The same Jesus who leads you into trials can lead you out.

Change happens. Sometimes life happens. Living in the new normal takes adjustment; it's painful. But that doesn't mean we should feel sorry for ourselves. We should keep our peace in Jesus.

Encourage others. You might not be the only one in a bad situation. Find someone else to share life's joys and struggles with. You may find you can encourage others through your pain.

❝❞ Kate, 25, said she is peaceful when "I respect my husband and let him lead us, even when it would be easier to jump in and take over."

Dear Jesus of Peace,
Teach us how to fix our thoughts on you. Give us this peace you speak of that is perfect. Amen.

Do you have perfect peace? Please visit www.faithbookofjesus.com and click on "Community" to share.

To Read Further: Isaiah 26:3-4

BLESSED WITH A BURDEN

When I heard these things, I sat down and wept. For some days I mourned and fasted and prayed before the God of heaven.
— NEHEMIAH 1:4

Nehemiah was in Iran when he heard the news that Israel lay in ruins. He cried like a baby. There was nothing he could do but mourn for Israel. Once again, the wall had been broken down and its gates burned with fire (see Nehemiah 1:3).

Nehemiah began to ask for forgiveness on behalf of Israel and asked God for help. This little sentence explains his burden: "I was cupbearer to the king" (1:11).

If Nehemiah was found in low spirits by the king he served wine and spirits to, he could have been killed. Instead, the king showed favor. He said to Nehemiah, "What is it you want? . . . How long will your journey take, and when will you get back?" (2:4,6).

Nehemiah was able to take his burden and bless the Israelites. As a result, they rebuilt their wall in only fifty-two days, a seemingly impossible feat.

Sometimes we have an opportunity to bless others with our burdens. As Christians, we are commanded by Jesus to love and help one another. Don't let your burden or your position in life keep you from expressing what's really going on inside.

What burden are you blessed with today?

66 99   Brian, 21, said, "I am a student, but I want to become a missionary."

   Dear Blessed Jesus,
It's amazing how you've blessed each one of us in more ways than we can count. Don't let us grow tired or weary of waiting, for we will reap that blessing when the time is right. Amen.

What is your blessed burden? Please visit www.faithbookofjesus.com and click on "Community" to share.

To Read Further: Nehemiah 1:1-11

WHERE DOES YOUR HELP COME FROM?

I look up to the mountains — does my help come from there? My help comes from the LORD,
who made heaven and earth!
— PSALM 121:1-2 (NLT)

When I'm walking up a steep hill, I usually lean into the hill. I recently learned from my hairdresser, Kristi, that I won't get the full benefit of walking up a hill if I am leaning into it.

It's almost impossible to lean back when the incline is so steep. It's the same in life when troubles come: I want to lean into the most comfortable position and protect myself.

Every year the Israelites went up the mountain to make sacrifices to atone for their sins, and this song of ascents was a good reminder to themselves and to God to get them there safely as they climbed.

They said, "He will not let your foot slip — he who watches over you will not slumber; indeed, he who watches over Israel will neither slumber nor sleep" (Psalm 121:3-4).

How comforting is that? Jesus does not sleep. He knows when we are facing the wind and the steep problems in our life. He doesn't check out or take a nap. "The LORD watches over you . . . the LORD will keep you from all harm . . . the LORD will watch over your coming and going both now and forevermore" (verses 5,7-8).

66 99 Renna, 23, said that as a single mom, "Stress is an unfortunate term, mostly that I don't have enough help and feel there is no support for what I do."

Dear Helpful Jesus,
When we are leaning against the trials in our life, help us to remember where our help comes from — you! Wherever we are today, be the help and strength we need to make it through. Amen.

 Who do you run to for help? Please visit www.faithbookofjesus.com and click on "Community" to share.

To Read Further: Psalm 121

WASH YOUR HANDS

Who may ascend the hill of the LORD? Who may stand in his holy place? He who has clean hands and a pure heart, who does not lift up his soul to an idol or swear by what is false.
— PSALM 24:3-4

If your hand is stuck in the cookie jar, it means you're caught. I know how easy it is to get caught. Usually I'm looking for an excuse to go after what I want, and when the lid comes crashing down on my hand, I call out to Jesus and begin to pray.

Yesterday we read Psalm 121, which tells us where to find our help when we are facing insurmountable trials and a giant hill to climb. Today, we will look at reasons behind the trials some of us may be facing.

Some of you may be fighting an uphill battle because of poor choices. One more drink, one more sleeping partner, one more job to pay for your gambling addiction, or the desire to get what you want when you want it.

Your trials may not be from Jesus but instead are a direct result of living in sin. If that is true, Jesus said to wash your hands and come to him for help (see James 4:8). Allow him to forgive you and cleanse you.

Don't lean into pride; instead, lean toward Jesus. He will help you keep climbing that hill (regardless of whether you caused the hill in the first place).

Get clean and go, sin no more!

66 99 Sharon, 25, said, "I want the courage to know how to reach out more [for help]."

 Dear Clean-Hands Jesus,
You desire us to be clean, not living in sin. Unfortunately, it's not always easy to do the right thing, and we don't always know how to go about making right choices. Help us start today by washing our hands. Amen.

Are you fighting an uphill battle? Please visit www.faithbookofjesus.com and click on "Community" to share.

To Read Further: John 8:10-11

ANSWERED PRAYER

Do not be afraid, Daniel. Since the first day that you set your mind to gain understanding and to humble yourself before your God, your words were heard, and I have come in response to them.

— DANIEL 10:12

One of the most powerful answers to prayer happened in the book of Daniel. Daniel prayed and fasted for three weeks. He was under so much spiritual oppression that he almost died. When Daniel's prayers were finally answered, I'm sure he felt like it was almost too late.

When I'm waiting on my prayers to be answered, I usually fear the absolute worst. I think, *What if this happens or what if that happens?* And, just before I start to really panic, Jesus answers all of my prayers. It doesn't always happen exactly the way I expect, but my prayers are *always* answered.

Daniel's answer to prayer was *not* expected. The angel said, "The prince of the Persian kingdom resisted me twenty-one days. Then Michael, one of the chief princes, came to help me, because I was detained there with the king of Persia. Now I have come to explain to you what will happen to your people in the future, for the vision concerns a time yet to come" (10:13-14).

If you're waiting for an answer to prayer today, please know that Jesus already heard your prayer and has sent a messenger to help. Don't let the delay fool you. There is a spiritual battle taking place for your soul, and the good news is we already won.

66 99   David, 35, said he wanted to know about "ancient prayer and fasting practices and the daily office."

🖐   *Dear Answer–Man Jesus,*
You are faithful to answer our prayers. Every day you hear us and answer us. Strengthen us while we wait and help us to be strong and courageous even right now — today! Amen.

👥   How has Jesus answered your prayers? Please visit www.faithbookofjesus.com and click on "Community" to share.

🐟   To Read Further: Daniel 10:2-19

DON'T BE STUPID

Therefore do not be foolish, but understand what the Lord's will is.
— EPHESIANS 5:17

Don't be stupid. Yes, you. The Bible says not to be foolish because Jesus cares about our life. The choices we make can determine our future. Here are three common questions every twentysomething should ask: Who am I? What am I? and Why the heck does it matter?

Who are you? If you don't have an accurate understanding of who you are, I guarantee you're going to make some pretty stupid choices. If you're living to please other people, eventually you'll feel defeated and stop caring. If you're living above your means, the economy will catch up to you and take all your money. If you live for your boyfriend or girlfriend and then get dumped, suddenly the nightclubs will be screaming your name.

John Piper said, "When God is living in us, our desire to please Him is greater than our desire to please ourselves."

What are you? I decided to go back to school and get my bachelor's degree. It caused a lot of problems, so I asked for advice. I ended up meeting Vickie, who became my personal cheerleader, life coach, and mentor. She was the source of inspiration I needed to complete my dreams. My degree from Biola University ended up keeping me from being stupid, and it helped me become a published author.

Don't want to be a fool? Then pray this: "Since the day we heard about you, we have not stopped praying for you and asking God to fill you with the knowledge of his will through all spiritual wisdom and understanding" (Colossians 1:9).

66 99 Zak, 19, said, "I don't understand what [Jesus] wants me to do."

Dear Wise Jesus,
It's tough to act when I don't know what to do. Help me not to be stupid but to understand what you want me to do. Amen.

Do you need spiritual wisdom? Please visit www.faithbookofjesus.com and click on "Community" to share.

To Read Further: Ephesians 5:15-20

THE PURSUIT OF HAPPINESS

No servant can serve two masters. Either he will hate the one and love the other, or he will be devoted to the one and despise the other. You cannot serve both God and Money.
— LUKE 16:13

Jerry Bridges wrote in his book *The Discipline of Grace*, "Our involvement and cooperation with [Jesus] in His work is what I call the pursuit of holiness."[12]

You cannot pursue both personal happiness and Jesus' will. Why? Sooner or later you will hate one and love the other (see Luke 16:13; Matthew 6:24). Luke and Matthew were two disciples who stood by Jesus in his personal ministry. They left their own pursuits to follow Jesus.

When I asked twentysomethings about issues I should address in this book, the most common question I got via text messaging, online surveys, and personal conversations was "How do I know Jesus and his will?"

How do you know when your personal pursuit is based on your happiness or Jesus and his holiness? I can't answer this question for you. This is something you have to find out through the daily disciplines of reading the Bible, praying to Jesus, and surrounding yourself with wise counsel and truthful friends and family. But I can tell you, Jesus' will is the way to go!

66 99 Tisha, 25, said of her own pursuit, "I do not have a career of sorts. I am currently a part of a nonprofit that my husband started in which I am a full-time urban missionary in Portland or working with the poor and the homeless."

 Dear Holy Jesus,
Thank you for showing us there is another path. We don't have to follow our own wants, which can sometimes lead us astray. Thank you for giving us our heart's desire as we follow you. Amen.

Which path are you on? Please visit www.faithbookofjesus.com and click on "Community" to share.

To Read Further: Matthew 6:23-25; Luke 16:12-14

RETURN TO ME

Return to me, for I have redeemed you.
— ISAIAH 44:22

Throughout the Old Testament we see a common pattern. The Israelites were walking in pursuit of holiness, and then suddenly they were pursuing their own happiness. Rebellion against the Lord was so common that at least thirty Bible verses show the Israelites returning to Jesus (see the "Your Faith" section below).

I am just as guilty of this same sin. Every day I choose my own path and what suits me best. Thankfully, God the Father sent his only Son, Jesus, to die for our sins so that all of us could return to him. "But God demonstrates his own love for us in this: While we were still sinners, Christ died for us" (Romans 5:8).

That doesn't mean returning to him is easy. David wrote, "How long must I wrestle with my thoughts and every day have sorrow in my heart? How long will my enemy triumph over me?" (Psalm 13:2).

Don't let pride or self-pity keep you from returning to Jesus. Today, let's learn how to walk with Jesus in his pursuit instead of our personal happiness. "For the kind of sorrow God wants us to experience leads us away from sin [and our pursuit of happiness] and results in salvation [holiness]. There's no regret for that kind of sorrow. But worldly sorrow, which lacks repentance, results in spiritual death" (2 Corinthians 7:10, NLT).

66 99 Margaret Rose, 34, said, "I would invite someone to church if I knew I wouldn't get rejected. I wish they'd see the importance of it and come forward with an astounding 'Yes! I'd love to do that.'"

  Dear ROI Jesus,
When I have to return to you daily, even hourly, give me the courage to keep returning. My return on investment on this earth doesn't even compare to a lifetime spent with you in eternity. Amen.

How do you return to Jesus? Please visit www.faithbookofjesus.com and click on "Community" to share.

To Read Further: Numbers 10:35-36; Deuteronomy 4:30; 30:2; 2 Chronicles 30:9

A PSALM OF PRAISE

For God is the King of all the earth; sing to him a psalm of praise.
— PSALM 47:7

Want to have a dynamic prayer life? Pray the Psalms over your relationships, career, family, and health. Whatever is on your heart and mind, take the same prayers David wrote many years ago and let them become your psalm of praise to Jesus.

In the morning, Jesus, please hear me as I pray—and wait for you to answer (see Psalm 5:3). I will give you thanks; because of you I lack no good thing (see Psalm 7:17; 34:10).

You are a shield around me, Jesus. I lie down and sleep; I wake up in peace because you sustain me. Answer me when I call to you. Give me relief from my troubles. Be merciful to me and hear my prayers (see Psalm 3:3,5; 4:1).

Those who trust in you will never be forsaken. You even give us families so we won't be lonely. Encourage me today, Jesus (see Psalm 9:10; 68:6).

Your word is a lamp for my feet and a light for my path. Don't let me be drawn into evil. Today I will sing you a new song because you have set my heart free (see Psalm 119:105; 141:4; 144:9).

I love you, Jesus. Better is one day with you than a thousand elsewhere. You are my refuge and strength; you have delivered me from all my fears. Not to us, but to you, Jesus, belongs the glory, because of your love and faithfulness (see Psalm 18:1; 84:10; 46:1; 34:4; 115:1).

66 99 Frank, 31, said, "I just finished reading through the Psalms, and it has changed the way I pray."

Dear Jesus We Praise,
It's so awesome to take Scripture and directly apply it to our lives. Thank you for giving us David's example of how to take our faith and turn it into a song of praise back to you. Amen.

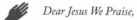 How do you praise Jesus? Please visit www.faithbookofjesus.com and click on "Community" to share.

To Read Further: Psalm 9:10; 34:1-3; 144:9-10

JUST ASK

So I say to you: Ask and it will be given to you; seek and you will find; knock and the door will be opened to you.

— LUKE 11:9

How can I read your mind if you don't tell me what you're thinking? If you don't tell Jesus what you want and need, how can he give it to you? Obviously, Jesus knows what you're thinking, but he waits for you to ask.

"So I say to you" points us to a parable found in Luke 11:5-13 where Jesus was teaching the disciples how to pray. Jesus told them about a man who was banging on his friend's door at midnight, asking for bread.

> Then the one inside answers, "Don't bother me. The door is already locked, and my children are with me in bed. I can't get up and give you anything." I tell you, though he will not get up and give him the bread because he is his friend, yet because of the man's boldness he will get up and give him as much as he needs. . . .
>
> Which of you fathers, if your son asks for a fish, will give him a snake instead? Or if he asks for an egg, will give him a scorpion? If you then, though you are evil, know how to give good gifts to your children, how much more will your Father in heaven give the Holy Spirit to those who ask him! (Luke 11:7-8,11-13)

What are you waiting for? Just ask Jesus.

❝❞ David, 31, said, "My wish has been granted. I'm a pilot."

✋ *Dear Jesus Who Answers Prayer,*
Thank you for letting us bother you over and over with our worries, cares, and concerns. I am so glad that you don't grow tired or weary and that your door is always open for answers to prayer. Amen.

👥 What are you asking Jesus for? Please visit www.faithbookofjesus.com and click on "Community" to share.

🐟 To Read Further: Luke 11:1-13

DO YOU REMEMBER?

There is a time for everything, and a season for every activity under heaven.
— ECCLESIASTES 3:1

There are times I remember all the wonderful things Jesus has done for me, but I confess there are also times I forget. Today, while I was listening to Pastor Chris Brown from North Coast Church on iTunes, he said something key to this devotional (see quote below).

I had been praying about how to convey the heart of Solomon when he wrote about remembering the times. Sometimes we remember, and sometimes we choose not to remember. A classic case of not remembering happened to the disciples when they were traveling on the road after the crucifixion of Jesus. It says in Luke 24:21 that "we had hoped." Somehow they had forgotten what Jesus told them over and over again—that he was going to die and rise again.

In this case, waiting does not equal "no." I know for me waiting is the hardest part because I tend to forget Jesus and his promises. I search and search and follow my heart. It never leads me to where I know I'm meant to end up because the heart can be deceitful (see Jeremiah 17:9).

Do you remember Jesus? There is still time. He isn't done with you yet. Wise King Solomon once said there is "a time to search and a time to give up, a time to keep and a time to throw away" (Ecclesiastes 3:6).

❝❞ Chris, 35, said, "Slow of heart is not a head problem but a heart problem. Do you remember?"

 *Dear Jesus Who Remembers,*
There is never a time or a season that you forget us, your children. Today, whatever we are facing, help us to remember how much you love us and that your love is enough. Amen.

Do you remember all that Jesus has done for you? Please visit www .faithbookofjesus.com and click on "Community" to share.

To Read Further: Ecclesiastes 3:1-8; Luke 24:13-35

I KNOW WHAT I WANT

You say, "I am allowed to do anything"—but not everything is good for you. And even though "I am allowed to do anything," I must not become a slave to anything.
— 1 CORINTHIANS 6:12 (NLT)

I am the type of person who knows what I want and goes after it. Relationships are the only area that I can't get what I want (so far). I've been successful in my career and writing—but not in my dating life. I find myself asking questions like, "Am I not skinny, pretty, or smart enough?"

The Corinthians' issues with sexual needs were similar to what we face today. The number of young couples cohabiting before marriage is on the rise. The way we treat the opposite sex is shameful. And the way we go after what we want is not always good.

Even though there is not a verse in the Bible that says you can't live with a person of the opposite sex, it does say to flee. "Run from sexual sin! No other sin so clearly affects the body as this one does. For sexual immorality is a sin against your own body" (1 Corinthians 6:18, NLT).

We all know what we want. We desire to be in a relationship, to be held and wanted by someone else. However, the way we get what we want can lead us into trouble. Honor Jesus with your body by staying away from sexual sin.

66 99 Richard, 25, said, "If [the relationship] was from Jesus, you wouldn't feel like crap after you give in to the temptation. Satan knows how to go after you with girls [or guys] and what plays to your emotions."

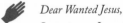

Dear Wanted Jesus,
I want you, Jesus. It's just not my natural reaction to run to you first instead of toward relationships of the opposite sex. I'm so glad Paul had the courage to show us how to stay sexually pure in the area of relationships. Please help me to remain pure today. Amen.

Do you know what you want? Please visit www.faithbookofjesus.com and click on "Community" to share.

To Read Further: 1 Corinthians 6:12-20

THE DARK NIGHT

My God, my God, why have you forsaken me? Why are you so far from saving me, so far from the words of my groaning?
— PSALM 22:1

Have you ever had a really bad day? Nothing in the world seems right, and you think you're dying? David wrote in Psalm 22, the darkest night of his life, that he was dying. He said to God, "Where the heck are you?"

I remember my mom used to tell me it's darkest before the dawn. David thought he wasn't going to make it, but he did. One chapter later he wrote the most beautiful and peaceful poem in the entire book of Psalms, which says, "The LORD is my shepherd, I shall not be in want" (23:1).

David wasn't exaggerating in Psalm 22. He was a hunted man. King Saul was not about to give up his throne to some young shepherd boy with no experience but herding sheep.

What changed? How do you turn your long dark night into the best day of your life? As David began praising and thanking God, God lifted his burdens and set him free.

Praise Jesus. Praise him in the morning. Praise him in the noonday. Praise him in the afternoon. Praise him in the evening, and praise him in the darkest night.

 Toni, 29, said, "Don't forget Psalm 23 comes after Psalm 22."

 Dear Darkness-to-Light Jesus,
When we are in our darkest night, it's okay to ask where the heck you are. Don't let us forget that you created the heavens and the earth, and nothing is too dark for you. Thank you for never leaving us or forsaking us. Amen.

 Have you ever asked Jesus, "Where the heck are you?" Please visit www.faithbookofjesus.com and click on "Community" to share.

To Read Further: Psalm 22:1-8; 23:1-6

FAST AND FURIOUS

I gave you milk, not solid food, for you were not yet ready for it. Indeed,
you are still not ready.
— 1 CORINTHIANS 3:2

One of my favorite movies is *The Fast and the Furious* (the original) with Vin Diesel and Paul Walker. Fast cars and furious attitudes. Did I mention fast cars? In the movie, Paul Walker plays Brian O'Conner, an undercover cop trying to infiltrate Dominic Toretto's street gang. He falls for Dom's sister Mia and fits into their clique by saving Dom from the police.

In one of the scenes, Dom's buddy races his car for a pink slip and loses. He put his car on the line because he expected to win. We should act like we expect to win, too. If we've put our faith in Jesus, we are fast and furious. Why live life in first gear?

But some of us aren't living as we should. Here we are with the best auto mechanic, Jesus, giving us the best car to race in, and we're not even racing it to its full potential.

Paul told the Corinthians that he gave them what they needed to win the race because they weren't quite ready to win—and some of us (just like the Corinthians) still aren't ready today.

You can't teach a baby how to drive a car, but when the baby grows up, he will eventually learn. Wherever you are in your walk with Christ, don't be afraid to learn how to drive. Live to your fullest potential. Win the race.

❝❞ Alex, 31, said, "It's like getting a Ferrari, but driving it in first gear."

 Dear Mechanic Jesus,
Some of us need to learn how to drive fast. We have so much potential in you if we can just learn how to use it. Teach us how to drive and how to be better followers of you, Jesus. Amen.

Are you living to win the race? Please visit www.faithbookofjesus.com and click on "Community" to share.

To Read Further: 1 Corinthians 3:1-9

SPIT GAME

So, because you are lukewarm—neither hot nor cold—I am about to spit you out of my mouth.
— REVELATION 3:16

A guy walks into a bar and sees a beautiful woman. He buys a drink and approaches her, hoping he's got game. Or let's reverse the story. A girl walks into a bar and sees a guy who catches her eye. She finds a way to flirt with him by playing with her hair and looking at him suggestively.

How many times have you walked into a bar hoping to spit some game? Maybe you brought a wingman or friend with you to help your odds. As a single twentysomething who's not much of a night owl, I've heard many stories and seen enough movies to know who's got game. Not me.

What kind of game do you have? Do you spit out Bible verses and encourage others daily, or do your words get you into trouble?

Jesus hates it when we act fake, but he knows we're human (see Matthew 26:41). He tells us to watch out so we don't fall into temptation. It's easy to be zealous for the Lord one minute and to be all into our girlfriend or car or shoes the next.

If you're not sure how to stay hot (yes, you!), ask Jesus. Seriously though, Jesus is our ultimate wingman. He wants us to succeed.

It's all or nothing. No wimpy faith. No weak game allowed. Get out there and spit some game.

❝❞ Emanuel, 25, said, "I'll be your wingman so you can get in there and spit your game!"

✋ *Dear Wingman Jesus,*
It's scary to be all in. Thank you for being our wingman and building our confidence so we can walk into the bar of life and spit some game. Amen.

👥 How do you spit game? Please visit www.faithbookofjesus.com and click on "Community" to share.

🐟 To Read Further: Revelation 3:15-16

HIDE-AND-SEEK

"Can anyone hide in secret places so that I cannot see him?" declares the LORD. "Do not I fill heaven and earth?" declares the LORD.

— JEREMIAH 23:24

I loved the childhood game hide-and-seek. It didn't require much skill. All I needed to do was run and hide. I made sure that I hid well so nobody would find me. If I were found, I ran to base before getting caught. Sometimes I stumbled from my dark hole or crevice in anticipation, and the other kids would already be on to the next game. I wanted to get credit for the best hiding spot, but instead I'd be tagged for the next game.

Going back to day one in the Bible, Adam and Eve hid from God when their sins were first discovered. They *hid*. It's just too easy to hide. I'm not sure if you are like me, but I don't like my sins exposed for all to see.

Sometimes we play hide-and-seek in life, too. We hide in work, relationships, or food when it's convenient. And when we're ready, then we seek after Jesus. He said, "Can anyone hide in secret places so that I cannot see him?" (Jeremiah 23:24). Jesus sees everything. There's nowhere we can go to hide from him (read the story of Jonah if you don't believe me). Even in our sin, Jesus waits for us.

"When Jesus spoke again to the people, he said, 'I am the light of the world. Whoever follows [seeks after] me will never walk [hide] in darkness, but will have the light of life'" (John 8:12).

66 99 Mark, 26, said of hide-and-seek: "Obedience to Christ isn't just [seeking God] on the good days or bringing glory to myself on bad days [hiding]."

Dear Find-Me Jesus,
I want to be found by you. There are a lot of things in this world that I should be hiding from instead of you. Help me bring all my worries and cares back to you today. Amen.

 Are you hiding from Jesus? Please visit www.faithbookofjesus.com and click on "Community" to share.

To Read Further: Jeremiah 23:23-24

SO LONG, FAREWELL

When the people saw that Moses was so long in coming down from the mountain, they gathered around Aaron and said, "Come, make us gods who will go before us. As for this fellow Moses who brought us up out of Egypt, we don't know what has happened to him."

— EXODUS 32:1

The Israelites had just committed the unthinkable. They had broken their covenant with God to worship an idol in the shape of a cow. Wow, really? Tell me they didn't do that.

After waiting for forty days with no leader, the Israelites got impatient and started partying, dancing, and singing (see Exodus 32:6,18-19). So long, God. Farewell, Moses. Hello, golden calf!

Moses was horrified when he saw this and broke the tablets of the Law. He burned the idol they had made, ground it to powder, mixed it in their water, and made the Israelites drink it (see verse 20). Go, Moses!

I'll admit I'm as stiff-necked as the Israelites were. *I don't like waiting for what I want.* I know just how far to test the limits before my roommate or my parents catch me.

Whenever I see something around me that sparkles like a golden calf, I just have to have it. And if you leave me alone for one second, I'll get it. But before you judge me (or agree with me), let's understand this: The calf was made up of gold jewelry. Each piece was relatively small but added up to the shape of a golden calf.

If you're struggling with the little things, confess them now before it's too late.

❝❞ Anne, 24, said, "Even though I have lived overseas in a very relational culture, I still struggle with being so darn independent."

 Dear Golden Jesus,
I always think I can get away with doing my own thing. I know it's not right to come clean only on Sundays. I want to lead a life that is pleasing to you at all times, not just when I feel somebody's watching me. Please help me to do that. Amen.

👥 Who or what is your golden calf? Please visit www.faithbookofjesus.com and click on "Community" to share.

✗○ To Read Further: Exodus 32:1-20

GIRLS RULE AND BOYS DROOL

While Jezebel was killing off the LORD's prophets, Obadiah had taken a hundred prophets and hidden them in two caves, fifty in each, and had supplied them with food and water.
— 1 KINGS 18:4

When I was in elementary school I used to go around with the girls and say, "Girls rule and boys drool!" Then we'd giggle and run off, and if they chased us, we'd yell at them to stay back because they had cooties.

The battle of the sexes can be a fun game to play even as an adult. At youth retreats and summer getaways, the girls' team always wins (okay, maybe not every time). Healthy competition is fun, especially when you have a fun group of people to play with.

The mightiest woman who ever ruled was named Jezebel. She was so powerful that she persuaded Ahab, the king of Israel, to do evil. He was more evil, in fact, than any other previous king of Israel (see 1 Kings 16:30). "He not only considered it trivial to commit the sins of Jeroboam son of Nebat, but he also married Jezebel daughter of Ethbaal king of the Sidonians, and began to serve Baal and worship him" (1 Kings 16:31).

Don't underestimate the power of a woman's influence. Women have more power than they realize. When a man stands by and lets a woman have too much power, it can be devastating to the relationship, but also to God. Once a man starts worshipping a woman, his heart is turned away from the ultimate ruler, Jesus.

Today, take a closer look at your relationships and ask yourself this question: "Who's ruling you?"

66 99 Christina, 24, said these things stress her out about relationships: "Trying to work with judgmental and/or selfishly opinionated people; also the ugly way that Christians rate each other on the holiness scale."

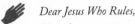 *Dear Jesus Who Rules,*
I love how you created women and men different yet equal. Help us to watch the way we treat each other. Let us look out for each other's best interests instead of our own selfishness. Amen.

Does Jesus rule in your life? Please visit www.faithbookofjesus.com and click on "Community" to share.

To Read Further: 1 Kings 18:21

THE QUESTION GAME

Let us not give up meeting together, as some are in the habit of doing, but let us encourage
one another—and all the more as you see the Day approaching.
— HEBREWS 10:25

One of my favorite games to play in a group setting is the question game. I first played the question game in a small-group Bible study in college. We took turns writing down questions we wanted anyone in our group to answer. Each person would write down up to ten questions (each on a separate piece of paper), fold them up, and place them in a basket. The basket was passed around the circle, and each person took a turn answering question after question until all the questions had been answered.

I have never had so much fun playing a game. Everyone can participate, and it doesn't require a skill set. What usually happens is once the first person reads the question, everyone else wants to jump in and offer his or her answer too. It really brings a group to life as everyone connects and laughs, defenses melt away, and people's hearts are open and ready to bond.

Paul wrote that we should not neglect meeting together. There's something special that happens when people of like minds get together and hang out. There might even be a neighbor, co-worker, or friend whom you could invite to the next hangout.

Reaching out to others is one of Jesus' specialties, and he passes the baton to you and me to encourage each other as we wait for his return. Who can you encourage today?

66 99   Richard, 26, said he wants "to use the gifts God has given me to bless him and others!"

   *Dear Reaching-Out Jesus,*
Thank you for showing us the importance of meeting together. Every day you make yourself available to us. Remind us to return the favor by playing games, having fun, and reaching out to each other. Amen.

Do you meet with others on a regular basis? Please visit www .faithbookofjesus.com and click on "Community" to share.

To Read Further: Acts 2:42-44

ALL FALL DOWN

If one falls down, his friend can help him up. But pity the man who falls and has no one to help him up!

— ECCLESIASTES 4:10

It's Monday. Are you feeling alone? Going to work after a long weekend is not fun. One of the perks of living with a roommate or with your family is having help to get you out the door every morning. I'm not a heavy sleeper, so if I hear my roommate getting ready for work, it reminds me to get out of bed and go to work myself.

Today's verse is a great reminder. Solomon was the richest person in the world. He had enough wealth and women to last him up to seven lifetimes, I'm sure. But all the wealth or women in the world couldn't satisfy his cravings. He needed a real friend to be there during good times and bad.

I love making myself available to my friends. Together we can try to figure out how to deal with our problems at work, home, or anything else we are facing. Sometimes, just getting out of the house helps.

When all falls down in your life (and it will), it's good to have someone there to help pick you up. Reach out a hand and help a friend up today.

66 99 Kaylee, 21, said, "Loyalty in any relationship is a huge thing, and when friends aren't loyal, that upsets me."

Dear Fall-On Jesus,
We all fall down. From the time we're infants to the time we die, things trip us up. Thank you for being our best friend and for showing us how to be a friend to those in need. Amen.

When was the last time you needed someone to pick you up? Please visit www.faithbookofjesus.com and click on "Community" to share.

To Read Further: Ecclesiastes 4:9-12

TEAMWORK GETS THE JOB DONE

Now the body is not made up of one part but of many. . . . If they were all one part, where would the body be? As it is, there are many parts, but one body:
— 1 CORINTHIANS 12:14,19-20

Have you seen those motivational posters that say things like "Teamwork," "Courage," or "Ambition"? They usually have some monstrously sized picture of a wave or of a person climbing a rock looking heroic.

Why do we even have posters like that in the first place? (Maybe it's because we were made for something much bigger than ourselves.) It is rare that a lone person accomplishes something great, but a team of people can accomplish a great feat.

We are reminded in 1 Corinthians that the body of Christ is made up of many individuals who together make up one body. So I can't say to you, "Since I'm not smart or pretty like you, I don't belong" (see 1 Corinthians 12:15). "The eye cannot say to the hand, 'I don't need you!' And the head cannot say to the feet, 'I don't need you!'" (verse 21).

There's room for everyone and every part. We don't need to fight for position. Jealousy, envy, and covetousness should not be found in the body of Christ. Competing is not necessary. There is room for everyone. We are all parts of a whole. It takes teamwork to get the job done.

66 99 Crystie, 44, said, "Hindsight makes me wish that I had not been so self-centered in my twenties. Lessons in how to make others feel important and how to have effective personal interaction would have been valuable."

Dear Team Jesus,
Thank you for giving each of us a special function. Show us what our roles are so together we can be a great team for Jesus. Amen.

What part do you play in the body of Christ? Please visit www .faithbookofjesus.com and click on "Community" to share.

To Read Further: 1 Corinthians 12:12-26

KNOW YOUR ROLE

Now about spiritual gifts, brothers, I do not want you to be ignorant. . . . There are different kinds of gifts, but the same Spirit. . . . Now to each one the manifestation of the Spirit is given for the common good.
— 1 CORINTHIANS 12:1,4,7

We can do more together as a team than we can do apart. But do you know your role? What gifts and talents do you bring to the team that could benefit everyone?

Some churches offer tests to help you figure out what your role is. Please visit one of the best surveys online to find out what your spiritual gifts are: http://therocksandiego.org/giftstest. Pastor Miles McPherson, former chaplain for the San Diego Chargers, now heads up a church full of twentysomethings. They use this test to help you identify your role and show where you can serve.

I took the test, and here is the breakdown of my gifts: Leader/Administrator, Prophet/Perceiver, Teacher, Exhorter/Encourager, Mercy/Compassion, Server, Giver. There are many things we can be good at, and taking a spiritual-gifts test is a great way to see how we can best serve the needs of those Jesus has placed around us.

To see how your answers line up with the Bible, read 1 Corinthians 12:8-11 and 1 Peter 4:9-11.

66 99 Heidi, 27, said her role right now is "to grow in stature with God and man. I am working very hard on becoming the kind of wife the husband I want would need."

 Dear Role-Giving Jesus,
You know just what roles to give each of us. Help us to love each other deeply and not be jealous or want someone else's role. We are each unique because of you, Jesus. Amen.

What is your role? Please visit www.faithbookofjesus.com and click on "Community" to share.

To Read Further: 1 Corinthians 12:8-11

THE BAD BOY

Do not be misled: "Bad company corrupts good character."
— 1 CORINTHIANS 15:33

In almost every group it's safe to assume there will be each of the following: leaders, followers, gossipers, micromanagers, and a bad boy (or girl).

One of the first verses I memorized growing up was 1 Corinthians 15:33. I'm sure it's because my parents wanted me to choose my friends wisely. To drive the point home, my mom would read a proverb to my brother and me every morning before we started school. I used to love hearing about the fool and the wise man. Here are just a few examples of what it means to choose your friends wisely:

A real friend. "A righteous man is cautious in friendship, but the way of the wicked leads them astray" (Proverbs 12:26). Anyone can pretend to be your friend at first, but a real friend remains through the good times and bad.

Mo' money, mo' problems. "The poor are shunned even by their neighbors, but the rich have many friends" (14:20). Sometimes people like you more because you have money. It's no secret that economic times have forced us to give up a lot of our hobbies, such as going to the movies or enjoying nice dinners out on the town. We should not be surprised when the people we spend our money on or with influence our behavior.

The bad boy. "Do not make friends with a hot-tempered man, do not associate with one easily angered" (22:24). This is why Paul echoed Solomon's advice: Stay away from the bad boy (or girl). Be careful who you wish for.

The older I get, the easier I find it to like the bad boy. It's as if society is saying I shouldn't be single in my twenties. I should be healthy and happy and have whatever I want. If you find yourself in the same position, ask Jesus to help you choose your friends wisely.

❝❞ Emily, 33 and single, said, "I'm always attracted to the bad boy."

 Dear Good-Boy Jesus,
You are good. Thank you for giving us a guidebook like Proverbs to show us how to choose our friends wisely. Help us to put the principles into practice each day. Amen.

How do you choose your friends? Please visit www.faithbookofjesus.com and click on "Community" to share.

To Read Further: Proverbs 12:26; 14:20; 22:24; 1 Corinthians 15:33

YOU TALKIN' TO ME?

*When the angel of the L*ORD *appeared to Gideon, he said, "The L*ORD *is with you,*
mighty warrior."
— JUDGES 6:12

We've already established that Jesus loves fighting for the underdog. We are the under-dogs. He died on a cross while we were still sinners (because he loved us) so that we could have power over death (see Romans 5:8).

Here we see Gideon, the least in his family, from the weakest tribe of Israel, hand-picked by God to save his people (see Judges 6:15).

We don't always know why Jesus picks us for specific tasks. Maybe he wants to help build our character or courage. Maybe Jesus wants to highlight our insecurities so that he can show himself strong in our weaknesses. Or maybe, just maybe, Jesus wants us to learn how to trust him.

Do you feel like a mighty warrior? If the answer is "no," "not really," or "yeah right," then you've come to the right place. Like Gideon, no Bible characters were chosen because they were perfect in strength or because Jesus loved them the most. Remember Rahab the prostitute or Matthew the tax collector?

"The LORD turned to [Gideon] and said, 'Go in the strength you have. . . . Am I not sending you?'" (Judges 6:14).

Is Jesus talkin' to you?

❝❞ David, 35, said, "I'm a youth pastor, although I wish I were a traveling speaker."

 Dear Talkin' Jesus,
What are you saying to me, to all of us? Thank you for not playing favorites. Help us
to remember Gideon when we don't feel up to the task or we feel inadequate because
of our circumstances. Amen.

 What is Jesus saying to you? Please visit www.faithbookofjesus.com and click on "Community" to share.

To Read Further: Judges 6:11-14

THE COMMITTED CHRISTIAN

I will walk among you and be your God, and you will be my people.
— LEVITICUS 26:12

Have you ever thought about the relationships you're committed to 100 percent? Ask yourself this question: "Do they bring me joy?" If you can be yourself around a person and are confident that he or she has your best interests at heart, then you've found a committed friend.

Joshua Harris, author of *I Kissed Dating Goodbye* and *Not Even a Hint*, wrote, "The joy of intimacy is the reward of commitment."[13] The joy of intimacy is a by-product of being committed to someone whom you love and cherish.

In the Old Testament, we read about a covenant God made between himself and his people, the Israelites. In Leviticus 26, God listed the benefits of following him and being committed to him and what will happen if you don't commit.

Jesus is 100 percent committed to us. He cannot be unfaithful to us, even though we sometimes are to him (see 2 Timothy 2:13). Do you desire to go deeper in your relationship with Jesus? If you haven't already made that commitment to him, I encourage you to get on your knees and ask Jesus to forgive you of your sins so you can become a committed follower of Christ.

Jesus has already pursued you; he longs to be with you. Try putting your name into today's verse: "I will walk among you, [your name], and be your God, and you, [your name], will be my people."

66 99   Shawn, 25, said, "I am unfamiliar with the Christian walk."

   Dear Confident Jesus,
I know a lot of us struggle with commitment issues because we're not quite sure who we are or what we want to be yet. Thank you for being 100 percent committed to us. Help us stay committed to you each and every day. Amen.

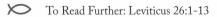   Are you committed to Jesus? Please visit www.faithbookofjesus.com and click on "Community" to share.

   To Read Further: Leviticus 26:1-13

ALL SCRIPTURE IS . . .

All Scripture is God-breathed and is useful for teaching, rebuking, correcting and training in righteousness, so that the man of God may be thoroughly equipped for every good work.
— 2 TIMOTHY 3:16-17

Sometimes I encounter a problem that isn't found in Scripture. For instance, "There's this boy . . ." and I don't know what to do. I run to all my friends instead of running to Jesus for wisdom; I seek out wisdom through every other means.

I have subscribed to daily Bible verses by e-mail for as long as I can remember. No matter what job I have, the first thing I do in the morning when I get to work is turn on my computer, write my Bible verses on a sticky note, and post it on my monitor.

No matter who I ask advice from, it never fails that my verse for the day will have something to do with my question about the boy—or whatever I'm seeking advice about. Some days it's scary and other days it makes me laugh that 2 Timothy 3:16-17 is *literally* true!

"*All Scripture is* inspired by God and is useful to teach us what is true and to make us realize what is wrong in our lives. It corrects us when we are wrong and teaches us to do what is right. God uses it to prepare and equip his people to do every good work" (2 Timothy 3:16-17, NLT, emphasis added).

❝❞ Karis, 21, said, "I need to be held accountable and have something to look forward to on a weekly basis or else I won't do it. I need to be put in a routine."

Dear Scripture-Texts Jesus,
We need help on a daily basis. Thank you that the Bible can literally help us with every area of life. Show us that today. Amen.

Where do you seek wisdom? Please visit www.faithbookofjesus.com and click on "Community" to share.

To Read Further: 2 Timothy 3:10-17

DENY YOURSELF

Then Jesus said to his disciples, "If anyone would come after me, he must deny himself and take up his cross and follow me."
— MATTHEW 16:24

Access denied! That's how I feel when it comes to relationships of the opposite sex. No matter what I do, I'm never successful at attracting the right guy. Maybe I stink. The verse above from Matthew always challenges me to rise above my selfishness and give it to Jesus.

Relationships are just one issue twentysomethings face that can get in the way of following Jesus. What about career and finances or identity and purpose? These seem to be the biggest problems I face daily.

Whenever I'm wrestling with denying myself, I usually take offense. I want to hold on to the problem instead of "taking up my cross." What does that mean anyway? Jesus was crucified, and we have to be too? That sounds like an awful statement.

"For God so loved the world that he gave his one and only Son, that whoever believes in him shall not perish but have eternal life. For God did not send his Son into the world to condemn the world, but to save the world through him" (John 3:16-17).

Whenever I'm feeling bitterness toward Jesus for making me deny myself, I find rest and comfort knowing that the cross symbolizes love and not torture. If we lay down our pride, we will find rest and peace in Jesus. That's the reason Jesus says to deny ourselves.

66 99 Stephanie, 20, said her needs as a twentysomething include "being content as a single [person], being fearless."

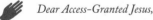 *Dear Access-Granted Jesus,*
When I am tempted to believe that you don't have my best interests at heart, help me remember that I have an all-access pass with permission granted. Help me to use it daily, hourly even! Amen.

How do you put Jesus first? Please visit www.faithbookofjesus.com and click on "Community" to share.

To Read Further: Matthew 16:24; Mark 8:34; Luke 9:23

THE DIFFERENCE BETWEEN

Once you were dead because of your disobedience and your many sins. You used to live in sin, just like the rest of the world, obeying the devil—the commander of the powers in the unseen world. He is the spirit at work in the hearts of those who refuse to obey God.
— EPHESIANS 2:1-2 (NLT)

How do you share your faith? This topic has been brought up repeatedly over the past few months when I mentioned to my close friends and family that I was writing this book.

So what is the best way to explain your faith to your non-Christian friends? And if you're reading this book and you're not quite sure what being a Christian is all about, I will try my best to clarify.

Today's verses say "used to" because there is a difference between life with and without Jesus. I think everyone would agree with me that there is good and bad in this world. Jesus calls the bad *sin*. If we are sinners, we cannot inherit the kingdom of Jesus. But if we confess our sins, he is faithful and just to forgive and cleanse us from all the bad (see 1 John 1:9).

Once you've put your faith in Jesus, he changes you. There is a difference between the old you and the new you. Even your friends and family can tell and smell the difference (see 2 Corinthians 2:15).

66 99 Aaron, 27, said, "I think it would be good to touch on the importance of all the things you mention, but also perhaps how to share Jesus with a nonbeliever."

Dear Faithbook Jesus,
Open our eyes to see how our faith in you changes us. It is my prayer that we will recognize the difference—and that difference is you! Amen.

What do you find is the most effective way of sharing your faith with others? Please visit www.faithbookofjesus.com and click on "Community" to share.

To Read Further: Ephesians 2:1-5

ARTSY FARTSY

See, I have chosen Bezalel son of Uri, the son of Hur, of the tribe of Judah, and I have filled him with the Spirit of God, with skill, ability and knowledge in all kinds of crafts — to make artistic designs for work in gold, silver and bronze, to cut and set stones, to work in wood, and to engage in all kinds of craftsmanship.

— EXODUS 31:2-5

When I was studying art, I found it interesting that the Bible talks about creativity and where it comes from. I should have guessed. You might not think so at first glance, but there is a Bible verse for literally everything. If you read the Bible daily, Jesus will find a way to speak directly to you.

In Exodus 31 the Israelites were building the Tent of Meeting, which was their church. It was very important to the Lord how the Tent was constructed and what went inside. So the Lord said to Moses, "Here's who I'm giving my creative Spirit to."

Jesus says we have every spiritual gift we need (see 2 Peter 1:3). That means we can pray about our creative needs, too. Whether you're decorating an apartment or designing media for your church, Jesus cares about the artsy things of life. What do you dream of creating? Does Jesus know? Have you asked him for help?

66 99 Linnea, 24, said, "I'm an administrative assistant of sorts. I really want to become a part of the culinary world! I love to cook for so many reasons. And being an office worker is just so unrewarding."

Dear Artsy Jesus,
It's so neat to see that you have given each of us different gifts. Inspire us today to create all kinds of work for your kingdom to show the world that you are the Master Inspirer of creative works. Amen.

What can you create for God? Please visit www.faithbookofjesus.com and click on "Community" to share.

To Read Further: Exodus 31:1-6

FOLLOW YOUR FAITH

May he give you the desire of your heart and make all your plans succeed.
— PSALM 20:4

Following your heart is a big load of crap. The heart is deceitful above all things and cannot be trusted (see Psalm 5:9; Proverbs 17:20; Jeremiah 9:8; 17:9; Hosea 10:2).

What is so evil about following our hearts? Well, does anyone watch *The Bachelor?* Jason Mesnick, a single dad, was one of ABC's recent bachelors on the hit television program.

I remember watching the four-hour season finale, which made me heartsick. Jason proposed to Melissa and sent Molly home. The episode ended with Jason, Ty, and Melissa jumping into the pool (fully clothed) wearing three of the biggest smiles on their faces. They had found happily ever after.

Then during *After the Final Rose* (the show after the finale), Jason told Melissa on camera that he had to follow his heart. His heart was with Molly. Seconds later a tearful Melissa left the stage and a hesitant but giggly Molly was kissing Jason. Say what?

I know I wasn't the only one in America asking myself, "Why am I watching this show again?" It's too easy to get wrapped up in the drama of life. Our emotions cannot always be trusted. Following your heart can deceive you. Look at Jason. Follow your faith instead of your heart, and you won't be put to shame (see Romans 10:11).

❝❞ Kari, 24, said, "It's a big adjustment going from college to a real job and life on your own. Then add marriage and kids and buying a house. It gets stressful."

Dear Heart Jesus,
You are the one who gives us the desires of our hearts and makes all of our plans suc-
ceed. What a huge relief to put our trust in you instead of ourselves. Show us how to
follow you when our hearts tell us one thing and our heads tell us another. Amen.

What does following your faith instead of your heart mean to you? Please visit www.faithbookofjesus.com and click on "Community" to share.

To Read Further: Psalm 20:1-4; 37:4

FREEDOM IN CHRIST

It is for freedom that Christ has set us free. Stand firm, then, and do not let yourselves be burdened again by a yoke of slavery.

— GALATIANS 5:1

It's amazing the kind of freedom we have in Jesus. He doesn't interfere with our decisions. We have free will to choose him or not.

On June 24, 1987, I got down on my little knees and asked Jesus to be my personal Lord and Savior. At that moment I felt free, changed even. Jesus took my stony heart of sin and replaced it with a new heart to love him and others (see Ezekiel 36:26).

Twenty-some years later I am still following Jesus. The same freedom I experienced on that day, I still experience today.

When, after four hundred years of slavery, the Israelites were released from Egypt, it took some time getting used to—just as I still process what freedom in Christ really means. It doesn't excuse their wishy-washy behavior in the desert (which caused them to wait and wander for forty years), but I can certainly see why they acted the way they did. Freedom in Christ and following your heart are two very different things. Sometimes they line up, and sometimes they conflict.

So how do we stand firm? We need to get out of whatever bondage we're in and rely on Christ and his freedom because it was for freedom that he set us free (see Galatians 5:1).

66 99 Andrew, 24, said, "The biggest challenge has been going from college, where I knew exactly who I was and what was expected of me, to postcollege, where everything seems up for grabs."

Dear Freedom-Giving Jesus,
When everything seems up for grabs and we don't know which way to turn, help us to rely on you. You've already given us all the freedom we need; now we need your wisdom in figuring things out. Amen.

What does freedom in Christ mean to you? Please visit www .faithbookofjesus.com and click on "Community" to share.

To Read Further: Galatians 5:1-5

BLOCKED IN

Therefore I will block her path with thornbushes; I will wall her in so that she cannot find her way.

— HOSEA 2:6

When I parallel park, I make sure to leave myself enough room to get out in case someone blocks me from behind. Sometimes I get back to my car and find that I didn't leave myself enough space. Other times the car behind me left me plenty of room, and I had no reason to worry.

Gomer had reason to worry. She felt blocked into a marriage. She was a former prostitute, and God told the prophet Hosea to marry her. Gomer married Hosea and was unfaithful to him numerous times. The Israelites were also unfaithful. The entire Old Testament shows us how unfaithful they were to God. Over and over again they rebelled, disobeyed, and did their own thing. And over and over again God took them back, disciplined them, provided for their needs, and fought against their enemies. The book of Hosea was written to show us God's redeeming love.

We can't get mad or upset when God blocks us in. Hosea couldn't get upset at Gomer because he knew God was using her to prove a point. God is still proving that point today. "Christ was sacrificed once to take away the sins of many people; and he will appear a second time, not to bear sin, but to bring salvation to those who are waiting for him" (Hebrews 9:28).

66 99 Amy, 21, said her goal is "to follow Jesus through life, with Matthew 24:14 and Matthew 28:18-20 as my guidance."

 Dear Unblocking Jesus,
Please give us space to confess our sins and be made right with you today; unblock our paths. Thank you, Lord, for caring enough to send your Son to die so that we can be set free. Amen.

Have you ever been blocked in? Please visit www.faithbookofjesus.com and click on "Community" to share.

To Read Further: Hosea 2:6-20

DON'T WORRY, BE HAPPY

Be happy, young man, while you are young, and let your heart give you joy in the days of your youth. Follow the ways of your heart and whatever your eyes see, but know that for all these things God will bring you to judgment.

— ECCLESIASTES 11:9

Are you happy? Do your present job, relationships, money, and health bring you all the happiness in the world? Whether you are young or old, we all dream of the perfect life, job, car, house, family, and health. But is that real happiness or just chasing after the wind?

If anyone had reason to be happy, it was King Solomon. God blessed him and gave him the spirit of wisdom plus all the riches the world had to offer. Solomon lived in mansions and ate the greatest foods. He was the richest man in the world and married hundreds of women.

At the end of his life, Solomon was a bit jaded. He said more than nine times in the book of Ecclesiastes that everything was "meaningless, a chasing after the wind" (1:14,17; 2:11,17,26; 4:4,6,16; 6:9). Maybe it's because he followed his heart and married hundreds of women. The world will tell you to be happy and follow your heart, but hear this: "Here is the conclusion of the matter: *Fear God and keep his commandments*, for this is the whole duty of man. For God will bring every deed into judgment, including every hidden thing, whether it is good or evil" (12:13-14, emphasis added).

❝❞ Tara, 25, said via Twitter, "Following your heart is wrong?"

 Dear Happy Jesus,
It's important to remember whom we are serving: ourselves or you. When our desires line up with your desires, we have joy and peace. When they don't, everything is meaningless. Show us today how to know the difference. Amen.

Are you serving yourself or Jesus? Please visit www.faithbookofjesus.com and click on "Community" to share.

To Read Further: Ecclesiastes 1:14,17; 2:11,17,26; 4:4,6,16; 6:9; 11:9; 12:13-14

DON'T LOSE HEART

Therefore, since through God's mercy we have this ministry, we do not lose heart.
— 2 CORINTHIANS 4:1

Moses is one person in the Bible who tried to accomplish what he knew God wanted him to do—but he tried it his way first and got himself in real trouble.

Moses tried to settle an argument between an Israelite and an Egyptian slave driver. He ended up killing the Egyptian. He didn't think anyone would find out. He probably thought he was being a hero at the time, but God had bigger plans. When people discovered what Moses had done, he fled for his life and spent forty years being prepped in the desert for his true calling.

Spending time in the desert is not glamorous. It's tediously long. How many of us are in a season of waiting? Working toward a degree? Married with young children? Single and waiting? After a while we grow restless. It becomes dull and routine. Some of us resign and make ourselves comfortable.

"Therefore, since through God's mercy we have this ministry, we do not lose heart. Rather, we have renounced secret and shameful ways; we do not use deception, nor do we distort the word of God. On the contrary, by setting forth the truth plainly we commend ourselves to every man's conscience in the sight of God" (2 Corinthians 4:1-2).

❝❞ Shawn, 26, said, "What stresses me out is my own inability to be assertive. I am *afraid* of upsetting anyone, and that causes me to be very, very timid . . . to a point that it's sometimes even damaging to me. I don't know how to stand up for myself."

 *Dear Big-Heart Jesus,*
Just because we are waiting doesn't mean that we can't be assertive and figure out what your will is for our lives. Give us a heart today that doesn't lose faith or hope in your Word. Amen.

Are you still waiting? Please visit www.faithbookofjesus.com and click on "Community" to share.

To Read Further: 2 Corinthians 4:1-3,13-18

ON GUARD!

You must be on your guard.
— MARK 13:9

When you are in a spiritual battle, there are three scenarios to remember in order to keep your guard up. The first is that life will sometimes catch you by surprise. The Enemy loves to attack without warning. For instance, just yesterday my roommate told me that she is moving out, and I have two weeks to find a new roommate (and $1,300 to cover the deposit). I can't even tell you how many curse words went through my head. Or there was the time when my mom said something so hurtful that caught me off guard, and I told her I'd rather be homeless than live with her again. Ouch!

The second scenario is because of the poor choices we make. I'm not going to read anyone's journal or go through your dirty laundry. I'll leave this one to your imagination. Mrs. Charles E. Cowman once said, "Someone who sheds great tears over a simple romance will not be of much help in a real crisis, for true sorrow will be too deep for him."[14]

The last scenario is learning how to guard your heart from the "what ifs" in life. We don't know what tomorrow will hold, and because of that, we respond in one of two ways: fear or trust. Fear says, "What I feared has come upon me; what I dreaded has happened to me" (Job 3:25). Trust says, "Everyone who calls on the name of the Lord will be saved" (Acts 2:21).

 Shannon, 31, said, "I am stressed when I cannot meet my bills—and have to humble myself and ask my parents for help."

 Dear Always-on-Guard Jesus,
We need your strength, help, and protection today. Shield us from surprise attacks, poor choices, and "what ifs" that have no end. Thank you for always being on guard and that we can trust you. Amen.

 Which scenario do you most relate to? Please visit www.faithbookofjesus.com and click on "Community" to share.

To Read Further: Mark 13:7-11

A HARSH WARNING

The LORD saw how great man's wickedness on the earth had become, and that every inclination of the thoughts of his heart was only evil all the time.

— GENESIS 6:5

What's changed since this verse? Not much!

Some people say that a man thinks about sex every seven seconds. But studies show that it's more likely that a man fantasizes about sex at least once a day.[15] As Christians, we struggle with sin, but if our actions and our character are defined by "every kind of wickedness, sin, greed, hate, envy, murder, quarreling, deception, malicious behavior, and gossip" (Romans 1:29, NLT), consider yourself warned.

The Bible says if we were to disassociate from people who do these things, we'd have to leave this world (see 1 Corinthians 5:9-10). Isn't that a crazy thought? Instead, it offers a warning for those who have faith in Jesus. If your friend claims to be a Christian and "is sexually immoral or greedy, an idolater or a slanderer, a drunkard or a swindler . . . with such a man do not even eat" (1 Corinthians 5:11). That's pretty harsh.

Think of all the people who refuse to be Christians or to set foot in church again because of the hurt and hypocrisy they have seen and felt. Jesus is pretty serious here. He does not put up with double standards. Jesus hates hypocrites.

Living the Christian life is not always easy. Obedience is hard, but it's not as harsh as what happens when we fall away. If your lifestyle does not match up today, consider yourself warned.

66 99 Burt, 24, said he'd like to know "how to stop acting like a teenager and not wait until he is thirty to grow into a mature Christian adult."

Dear Fair-Warning Jesus,
If you didn't care about us, you wouldn't discipline us. You would let us do whatever we want, whenever we want. Thanks for giving us harsh warnings because you care for us. Amen.

How does it feel to be warned? Please visit www.faithbookofjesus.com and click on "Community" to share.

To Read Further: 1 Corinthians 5:6-13

MY TESTIMONY

A matter must be established by the testimony of two or three witnesses.
— DEUTERONOMY 19:15

One witness is not enough to convict someone. Today's verse says that a matter must be established by at least two people. That's part of the reason I quote a twentysomething in every devotional. I don't want you to take just my word for it but the words of more than three hundred people who have also been there.

What drives me to share my testimony with you and use others to back it up? Passion! Since I was young, my parents taught me about Jesus. I remember reading the Bible at age four. At age five, I put my faith in Jesus. When I was seven, my parents moved us from Lincoln, Nebraska, to Oceanside, California, because they became full-time missionaries. I hated moving because I missed my best friend Laura, who lived two houses down and was born two days before me.

My parents sent me to a private Christian school. I was the awkward ex-home-schooled kid. After three years, my mom let me be homeschooled again, and that's when everything went wrong.

In junior high anxiety almost killed me — twice. Every day I'd read, "For God did not give [Renee] a spirit of timidity, but a spirit of power, of love and of self-discipline" (2 Timothy 1:7). Then I got eczema in high school that took the skin off my face, feet, and later my hands. The verse I prayed over and over was, "And the God of all grace, who called you to his eternal glory in Christ, after you have *suffered a little while,* will himself restore you and make you strong, firm and steadfast" (1 Peter 5:10, emphasis added).

66 99 Renee, 27, said, "I learned how to trust Jesus daily because of my suffering. Now I spend my life spurring others forward who feel alone and hopeless."

Dear Living-Testimony Jesus,
Thank you for forgiving our sins and transforming our lives. We ask you to help us consider how we may spur one another on toward love and good deeds. Amen.

What's your testimony? Please visit www.faithbookofjesus.com and click on "Community" to share.

To Read Further: Hebrews 10:24-36

THE WELL

With joy you will draw water from the wells of salvation.
— ISAIAH 12:3

A well holds water. Water is the source for all living things. We can draw water from a physical well or from the spiritual well that is Jesus (see Psalm 36:9). Jesus is the source of everything we need.

Second Peter 1:3 says, "His divine power has given us everything we need for life and godliness through our knowledge of him who called us by his own glory and goodness." What are you in need of in this life? A new roommate, a better paying job, or maybe you just want to know where the heck your life is going.

Just knowing that I can come to Jesus brings me joy. There is never an experience too deep that it can exceed the wells of salvation. No matter where I'm at, I can always count on Jesus to save me. He fills me up again with his love, new mercies, joy, strength, grace, and loving-kindness.

Watch Jesus turn your desert into an oasis of water. "See, I am doing a new thing! Now it springs up; do you not perceive it? I am making a way in the desert and streams in the wasteland" (Isaiah 43:19).

Come, drink from the wells of salvation today.

66 99 Kari, 24, said, "I'm not a deep person, but I do find joy in spending time with friends, going to church, and reading my Bible when I can."

 Dear Jesus, the Well,
I'd like to order a cup of fresh living water with a side of Jesus, please. Thank you that we can come joyfully before you and drink from the well of salvation. Fill our cup today. Amen.

Are you thirsty for living water? Please visit www.faithbookofjesus.com and click on "Community" to share.

To Read Further: Isaiah 12:2-6

A NEW HEART

I will give them an undivided heart and put a new spirit in them; I will remove from them their heart of stone and give them a heart of flesh.
— EZEKIEL 11:19

With the number of times my heart has been broken, I'm surprised it's still beating. What amazes me is how strong and resilient the heart is. The average adult heart beats about sixty to seventy beats per minute.[16] The heart should get paid overtime, right? And that's just the physical part.

Our hearts also feel and long to be loved. This is the emotional part of the heart. Have you ever seen a child drawing a picture of a heart? He or she doesn't actually draw a human heart but a pretty, red-shaped heart-looking thing.

The last part of the heart is the spirit. Jesus created our hearts with a space only he can fill. We sometimes try to fill this part of our heart with everything but him. Things like past hurts and relationships can take precedence. This is perfectly normal; after all, we are human, but Jesus is jealous and wants our whole heart (see Exodus 20:5).

Today's heart checkup involved a look at our physical, emotional, and spiritual heart. Which part of your heart needs the most attention?

"I [Jesus] will give you a new heart and put a new spirit in you; I will remove from you your heart of stone and give you a heart of flesh" (Ezekiel 36:26).

66 99 Steve, 24, said, "You can never be heartbroken if your heart is in the right place. If it's broken, that means you're not trusting your heart to Jesus."

Dear Heart-Dweller Jesus,
Please give a new heart to anyone in need. And bless those learning to live with a new heart today. Amen.

Do you need a new heart? Please visit www.faithbookofjesus.com and click on "Community" to share.

To Read Further: Ezekiel 36:25-29

EVIDENCE OF BLESSING

I loathe my very life; therefore I will give free rein to my complaint and speak out in the bitterness of my soul. I will say to God: Do not condemn me, but tell me what charges you have against me.

— JOB 10:1-2

Job is angry. No, he's pissed. He's not hiding it anymore. In fact, if he were standing in front of you and me today, he might drop a curse word or two. The poor man was clearly suffering. Sometimes we feel like that, too.

In the New Testament we're told to rejoice in suffering, and in the Old Testament we see suffering for what it is—tough. Our body's natural reaction is to fix whatever is wrong and to not experience pain. Pain hurts. It's uncomfortable, and sometimes it's too much for us to bear.

The hardest part of our pain is not getting angry at God. From the very beginning, Job's wife urged him to curse God and die (see Job 2:9). He never did. Job had too much class. In the midst of losing his children, material possessions, health, and sanity, he somehow kept it together.

This verse is one of my favorites in all of Scripture because it shows the appropriate response to our trials: vent to Jesus. He already knows anyway. Tell him. Complain to Jesus. Charles H. Spurgeon said, "Could this not be the reason God is dealing with you? Being left alone by Satan is not evidence of being blessed."[17]

Like Job, your trials could be the direct result of being in Jesus' will and the evidence of his blessing.

66 99 James, 32, said, "I would like to know more about spiritual warfare."

Dear Jesus Who Blesses,
Don't let Satan mess with us. When we feel we can't continue, remind us that there is a blessing waiting for us at the end of our trials. Amen.

Are you being blessed? Please visit www.faithbookofjesus.com and click on "Community" to share.

To Read Further: Job 1:6-12

EVERY LITTLE THOUGHT

We demolish arguments and every pretension that sets itself up against the knowledge of God, and we take captive every thought to make it obedient to Christ.
— 2 CORINTHIANS 10:5

Anything thought that stands in the way of Jesus — demolish it! Every lie. Every fear. Every sneaky, twisted sense of truth the Enemy uses against you. "You're not pretty enough." "You'll never get married." "You'll never be loved." Take every bad thought captive and make it obedient to Christ.

The concept is neat, but the practice is harsh. How do you take every thought captive? As someone who has struggled with anxiety most of my life, the process of taking every thought captive can take all day.

Here is a simple prayer that worked for me; it may help you uncover the lie and speak the truth over your thoughts.

Dear Jesus, I am sorry for believing that I am _____ [insert lie]. Please help me to realize the truth that I am _____ [insert truth]. In the name of Jesus and your shed blood on the cross, take my thought(s) captive to the obedience of Christ. Banish the power that the Enemy has had over me and do not let him infiltrate my thoughts any further. You are a big God, and I thank you for caring about what is happening to me today. Help me to go forth in peace, Jesus, for you have already set me free.

66 99 Alex, 30, said, "Stop, drop, and roll your thoughts on to Jesus."

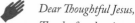 *Dear Thoughtful Jesus,*
Thanks for showing me an example in Scripture of what to do when negative thoughts come across my mind. Help me to get rid of them in your name. Amen.

What other things help you take your thoughts captive? Please visit www.faithbookofjesus.com and click on "Community" to share.

To Read Further: 2 Corinthians 10:4-6

A FOOTHOLD

"In your anger do not sin": Do not let the sun go down while you are still angry, and do not give the devil a foothold.

— EPHESIANS 4:26-27

When I get angry, I tend to curse. I also hold grudges. I don't want to let things go because I'm so angry at whomever has wronged me. I remember when a co-worker asked me out for drinks and proceeded to take advantage of me. When I said "no," he didn't stop. I asked him again, and he still didn't stop. Finally, the fourth time, after I was convinced he was going to force himself on me, I got him out of my car.

I drove home shaking and crying. I was so angry at this guy for thinking he could have his way with me. I was also angry with myself for putting myself in a situation where that could ever happen.

Like Jack Bauer from the TV series *24*, I have twenty-four hours to settle my anger. Anger is such a strong emotion that it's almost impossible not to self-destruct. Revenge consumes me. Once I let anger into my life, I allow the Enemy to have his grasp on me. My feet are now on shaky ground.

The best way to overcome anger is to deal with the situation before going to bed. If something happens close to bedtime, deal with it immediately . . . and then go to bed.

66 99 Meghan, 24, said relationships stress her out "when people don't communicate with me, and I feel like I am left in the dark and wondering why I am feeling rejected by them."

Dear Footrest Jesus,
If life were a couch, you would be the footrest. Help us to rest on you instead of the lies the Enemy makes us believe, such as the lie that we can't give up the right to be angry. Amen.

How do you handle anger? Please visit www.faithbookofjesus.com and click on "Community" to share.

To Read Further: Ephesians 4:25-31

FIRST PERSON

In the morning, O LORD, you hear my voice; in the morning I lay my requests before you and wait in expectation.
— PSALM 5:3

Have you ever taken one of those surveys on MySpace or Facebook that asks you a ton of questions? One of the questions usually is, "Who was the first person you talked to today?" or "Who was the last person you talked to today?"

The first person we talk to every day should always be Jesus!

In the morning, we offer him our prayers with thanksgiving and present every request to him. "And the peace of God, which transcends all understanding, will guard your hearts and your minds in Christ Jesus" (Philippians 4:7).

Here's another silly question: Have you ever noticed that when you give Jesus the first part of your day, everything else runs smoothly? It's kind of like tithing, too. When I write my first check to church, my funds last me until the next pay period. When I don't tithe, the money doesn't last. Go figure.

What about you? Do you prefer giving Jesus your requests in the morning or in the evening? The most important thing is that you're consistent and that you talk to him each day.

 Hillary, 22, said, "I fear not having enough time in a day."

 Dear First-Person Jesus,
You are pleased when we talk to you first. Thanks for giving us the floor in the morning to bring all our questions, desires, and requests to you. Amen.

 Who was the first person you talked to today? Please visit www.faithbookofjesus.com and click on "Community" to share.

To Read Further: Psalm 5:1-3

YOUR COMFORT

Praise be to the God and Father of our Lord Jesus Christ, the Father of compassion and the God of all comfort, who comforts us in all our troubles, so that we can comfort those in any trouble with the comfort we ourselves have received from God.

— 2 CORINTHIANS 1:3-4

Are you in mourning? The God of all comfort, whose name is Jesus, wants to comfort you. Are you sad? Let him wrap his big arms of love around you.

I remember when I first read the above passage. I was probably sixteen or seventeen. I was at home recovering from eczema, which covered my face and my feet. I thought that no guy would ever love me. My skin was hideous, and the weight I gained from the prednisone made me huge. I gained more than one hundred pounds in ten months. Talk about humiliation. I was living it!

Jesus comforts us in our troubles so we can comfort others who are also suffering. Why else would I be writing this book? Jesus healed me, and I want you to experience the same comfort he gave me every day (day after day after day).

If your best friend were sick, would you care? Of course! You'd probably take over chicken noodle soup and make sure he or she is drinking plenty of fluids. In order to receive the greatest amount of comfort from Jesus, you should be in his Word daily. When you're feeling better, then you can encourage your friends who need comfort, and you'll know what verses to share with them, too.

66 99 Hillary, 22, said, "How do a husband and wife comfort each other? By praying and reading the Word together."

Dear Jesus of All Comfort,
Some of us may be experiencing difficult trials. Please comfort each and every person with the same comfort I have received from you in difficult times. Amen.

Do you need comfort? Please visit www.faithbookofjesus.com and click on "Community" to share.

To Read Further: 2 Corinthians 1:3-7

POP GOES THE PROMISE

Praise be to the God and Father of our Lord Jesus Christ, who has blessed us in the heavenly realms with every spiritual blessing in Christ.
— EPHESIANS 1:3

The Bible's promises are like *Billboard*'s Top 40 pop songs. Every time you read a Scripture, the Holy Spirit inspires you and something "pops" out at you. Jesus has blessed us with every spiritual blessing, and we can take that as a promise.

Throughout Scripture there are a few promises that really "pop." The first is a promise of a Savior. "But I am the Lord your God, who brought you out of Egypt. You shall acknowledge no God but me, no Savior except me" (Hosea 13:4). Paul said, "I am not ashamed of the gospel, because it is the power of God for the salvation of everyone who believes: first for the Jew, then for the Gentile" (Romans 1:16).

Next our Savior promises us forgiveness of sins. "This is my blood of the covenant, which is poured out for many for the forgiveness of sins" (Matthew 26:28). We can come boldly before our Savior Jesus and receive forgiveness. These two promises should be enough, but there's more. . . .

Jesus also promises us eternity. "In my Father's house are many rooms; if it were not so, I would have told you. I am going there to prepare a place for you. And if I go and prepare a place for you, I will come back and take you to be with me that you also may be where I am" (John 14:2-3).

No matter how hard life may get with job loss, broken relationships, and loss of self, we can trust Jesus and his promises each and every day.

❝❞ Athena, 34, said, "I want to live the life God gave me unto him, seeking his face and [pop!] reflecting his love against the darkness."

 Dear Pop Jesus,
What an incredible promise: blessing us with every spiritual blessing we need. Thank you for being our Savior, forgiving our sins, and letting us spend eternity with you. Amen.

What promises pop out at you? Please visit www.faithbookofjesus.com and click on "Community" to share.

To Read Further: Ephesians 1:9-14

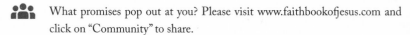

WAKE UP!

The Sovereign LORD has given me an instructed tongue, to know the word that sustains the weary. He wakens me morning by morning, wakens my ear to listen like one being taught.

— ISAIAH 50:4

Morning by morning I've spent time in the Word, waiting for Jesus to speak to me. Here are a few of my journal entries that I want to share with you.

September 23, 2002: Lord, let this be the day you change me forever. "The LORD will guide you always; he will satisfy your needs in a sun-scorched land and will strengthen your frame. You will be like a well-watered garden, like a spring whose waters never fail" (Isaiah 58:11).

September 27, 2002: Ah! My devotionals! Lord, the cool thing about you is when all other religions pray, you're the only one who actually speaks back. "I have told you these things, so that in me you may have peace. In this world you will have trouble. But take heart! I have overcome the world" (John 16:33).

September 19, 2004: God is not standoffish; he can get real with us. God is closer to us than ever before, ready to intervene in every situation, and now we rely on him in every unique situation we encounter.

Year after year, Jesus has been faithful to me. Every morning, I wake up and can count on him for new mercies and grace to get me through the day. I wonder what your journal says.

66 99 Christy, 23, said, "I believe that my purpose in life is to love others like Jesus and to give back where I can. I have been blessed with a lot in my life and want to give back what I can, where I can."

Dear Wake-Up-Call Jesus,
Every morning let your new mercies spur us on to great things. Inspire us daily as we draw near to you. Amen.

Do you need a wake-up call? Please visit www.faithbookofjesus.com and click on "Community" to share.

To Read Further: Isaiah 50:4-5,7-8

L - O - V - E

Love is patient, love is kind. It does not envy, it does not boast, it is not proud. It is not rude, it is not self-seeking, it is not easily angered, it keeps no record of wrongs.
— 1 CORINTHIANS 13:4-5

When you're in love, it shows. In fact, if you've been to a wedding recently, you probably heard 1 Corinthians 13 read aloud. This passage is popular because it talks about love.

Here is a fun way to remember what *l-o-v-e* is:

Look to Jesus. Today, look to Jesus. Let him be the first and last person you talk to. "But seek first his kingdom and his righteousness, and all these things will be given to you as well" (Matthew 6:33). Imagine how much better our relationships would be if we could grasp the love Jesus has for us.

Only you. The best kind of relationship is between two people. A husband and wife are popularly displayed as the ultimate love relationship. But for those of us who are single, we wouldn't have made it without the love and support of our best friends over the years.

Victory over your past. One of the best compliments I've ever received was from an ex-boyfriend who said he loved me just the way I am. Real love keeps no record of wrongs.

Expectation of the future. I love helping others reach their full potential. Being loved by someone makes me want to be a better person, too.

66 99 Suzanne, 24, said, "I share many of the typical stresses with most people my age in these categories: When will I meet that special someone? Will I ever meet him? Where the heck is he?"

Dear XOXO Jesus,
We love you. Lavish us with love today so we can be patient and kind and loving toward others in need. Show us that your love is all we need. Amen.

Are you in love? Please visit www.faithbookofjesus.com and click on "Community" to share.

To Read Further: 1 Corinthians 13:4-8,13

TORN TO PIECES

*Come, let us return to the L*ORD*. He has torn us to pieces but he will heal us; he has injured us but he will bind up our wounds.*

— HOSEA 6:1

I mention my eczema a lot. It was the most painful six years of my life. Before that experience I had difficulty reading through the Bible every day. My faith was okay, until I felt torn to pieces. Sitting in the hospital with no skin on my feet and on my face, I was in a state of despair. My mom shared with me from Hosea 6:1. I knew I couldn't live without knowing I had the strength to make it through.

The words from Hosea brought me hope and meaning. God would not only bandage my wounds but heal me as well. Henry David Thoreau said, "Do not despair of your life. You have force enough to overcome your obstacles."[18]

What about the broken pieces? After three days in the hospital, I made a vow. I decided to read through the Bible each day for one year so I wouldn't miss each time Jesus wanted to mend my wounds. Jesus wants to heal your wounds, too. Will you allow him to do just that?

 Linnea, 24, said she overcomes difficult life situations by praying it through "because I believe someone [God] is listening. And if he's listening, it means he cares."

 Dear Jesus Who Heals,
Be gracious to us. We long for you. Be our strength every morning, our salvation in times of distress. Amen.

 How has God taken your life and made it into something whole? Please visit www.faithbookofjesus.com and click on "Community" to share.

To Read Further: Hosea 6:1-3

TIME'S UP

The ax is already at the root of the trees, and every tree that does not produce good fruit will be cut down and thrown into the fire.
— MATTHEW 3:10

What if today was the last day you had to live? What would be said of your life? What would Jesus say when you stand before him?

When John the Baptist was preparing the way for Jesus to come and be baptized, he confronted the Pharisees and the Sadducees. John said, "You brood of vipers! . . . Produce fruit in keeping with repentance" (Luke 3:7-8).

What exactly does that mean? A person who is truly sorry will show it by his or her lifestyle and actions. The super-Christians showed up to display their knowledge and wealth but not to actually help people change.

I want to see lives changed. I want to lead you to the point where you can fall on your face and acknowledge Jesus Christ and worship him as your Savior (see 1 Corinthians 14:24-25).

We never know when our time will be up. Today, for instance, could be your last day. Rachel Joy Scott, the first victim of the Columbine High School massacre, didn't know her time was up.[19] She was the first to die at gunpoint because she prayed and acknowledged her belief in Jesus. She had written in her journal just days before, "This will be my last year, Lord. I have gotten what I can. Thank you."[20]

Now it's your turn. Don't wait until it's too late. Time's up.

❝❞ Rachel, 17, "I have this theory that if one person can go out of their way to show compassion, then it will start a chain reaction of the same."

 *Dear Jesus Who Calls Time,*
We never know when our time is up. Help us to come to a better understanding of how we should spend the time we have on this earth. Thank you for hearing our prayers. Amen.

👥 How will you spend the time you've been given? Please visit www .faithbookofjesus.com and click on "Community" to share. You can also visit Rachel's website (www.rachelschallenge.org) to learn more about her life. Don't wait until your time is up or it's too late to give your life to Jesus.

✝ To Read Further: Matthew 3:8-12

CASE OF THE MONDAYS

*By the seventh day God had finished the work he had been doing; so on the seventh day he
rested from all his work.*

— GENESIS 2:2

I love the movie *Office Space*. Every Monday, my co-workers and I say, "I'm having a
case of the Mondays!" I think it's ingrained in every one of us that our bodies need
rest. Did you know that from the very beginning Jesus rested? It's funny how I glossed
over that passage of Scripture.

Genesis 2:2 says the first thing God did after creation was rest. Jesus rested. How
cool would it be to end a workweek by resting? There would be no more cases of the
Mondays. The world would be an entirely different place.

Next time you're at the office and feeling like you'd rather be any place but work,
try to remember Genesis 2:2. Jesus wants to rest with you—not just on the weekends,
but at the start of the week, too. There are things he wants to accomplish with you in
your workplace, people he wants you to help. How else will people see Jesus?

❝❞ Brandon, 21, said, "Many of our generation want to make a difference but
don't know how or where to start."

 Dear Mondays Jesus,
We get through each week with you. Go with us today into our workplaces, homes,
and everywhere in between. Help others to see the kind of life and love they can
have if they rest in you—and not just on the weekends. Amen.

👥 How do you deal with a case of the Mondays? Please visit www
.faithbookofjesus.com and click on "Community" to share.

🐟 To Read Further: Genesis 2:1-3

THE FIRST AND LAST

I am the Alpha and the Omega, the First and the Last, the Beginning and the End.
— REVELATION 22:13

When I was growing up, I couldn't wait to be a teenager so I could drive a car. When I turned sixteen, I couldn't wait to turn twenty-one so I could legally have a beer. When I turned twenty-five . . .

The twenties are the most exciting times of our lives. Most of us get to choose where we live, work, and play. We even get to choose whom we marry (that's a scary thought). I wonder if, at the end of our lives, we'll look back and wish we were in our twenties again. Personally, I wonder when work is going to end, so I can retire and enjoy my life. But with Social Security and the state of our economy, who knows if I'll even be able to enjoy my senior years.

From the moment we are created in our mother's womb (see Psalm 139) to the time we die, Jesus is right there with us. Isn't that a comforting thought? Nothing or no one on this earth can claim that kind of sovereignty.

No matter what kind of pressure you are currently facing, count on Jesus to walk you through it. Spend a few moments this morning and evening thanking Jesus for getting you through another day and for his faithfulness in your life.

❝❞ Rachel, 20, said she is stressed about "deadlines that pile up, people who do not cooperate, and focusing on myself."

Dear First and Last Jesus,
From the moment we wake up until the moment we rest our head, you are there. Thank you that you're not going anywhere because of the everlasting covenant you made with creation since the beginning of time. Amen.

Who is your first and last? Please visit www.faithbookofjesus.com and click on "Community" to share.

To Read Further: Revelation 22:12-13

SCATTERED

Now those who had been scattered by the persecution in connection with Stephen traveled as far as Phoenicia, Cyprus and Antioch, telling the message only to Jews.
— ACTS 11:19

I never noticed the word *scattered* until my pastor pointed it out in a sermon last year. I probably skimmed over this passage because it was about killing. Stephen was the first Christian martyr.

After Jesus had been crucified, his disciples locked themselves in a room for fear they were next (see John 20:26). It wasn't until Stephen's death that they were forced to scatter. And he wasn't even a hero. Stephen was picked to look after the old ladies. Full of the spirit of faith, Stephen distributed food.

You don't have to be great in the kingdom or possess great faith to serve others. How many of you have worked at McDonald's, Jack in the Box, or some other fast-food place? There's no shame in that! But imagine being killed because you were such a great burger flipper. Now that's weird.

Because of Stephen, the Word of God spread rapidly (see Acts 6:7). People started taking notice. What was this faith everyone was talking about? Jesus? Who was he? Wasn't he a Nazarene from the town of Bethlehem, who claimed to be God?

Jesus used a horrific death (Stephen was stoned) to scatter the disciples throughout the regions of Phoenicia, Cyprus, and Antioch. Jesus can use your pain and suffering to scatter your testimony of faith throughout the world. Did you know that it was at Antioch that believers of faith were first called Christians (see Acts 11:26)?

66 99 Stephen, 20, said his goal is "to glorify God in whatever I happen to be doing. I can say that easily and know that in my head, but it sometimes doesn't transfer to my heart."

Dear Jesus Who Scatters,
Gather us back from the scattered places. Help us to see that you never allow pain unless there is a reason and a purpose. Increase our faith today. Amen.

What is the reach of your testimony? Please visit www.faithbookofjesus.com and click on "Community" to share.

To Read Further: Acts 11:19-26

CHOOSE LIFE

Do not worship any other god, for the LORD, whose name is Jealous, is a jealous God.
— EXODUS 34:14

When Jesus made us a deal, it came with a choice. Choose Jesus and choose life (see Deuteronomy 30:19). That doesn't mean we're allowed to have an open relationship. Jesus is committed to us and doesn't like it when we aren't exclusive with him.

Married people wouldn't like it if their spouse cheated, yet online personals are filled with mistress-wanted ads. Jesus is a jealous God, so what does it look like when we cheat on him? Here are some examples from the Old Testament:

- Jesus is jealous of our affections. "You shall have no other gods before me" (Exodus 20:3).
- Jesus is jealous over our conversation. "You shall not misuse the name of the LORD your God" (Exodus 20:7).
- Jesus is jealous of our time. "Remember the Sabbath day by keeping it holy" (Exodus 20:8; see also Genesis 2:2).

Wherever you were when you decided to make a deal with Jesus, remember that he is a jealous God, "who is jealous about his relationship with you" (Exodus 34:14, NLT). He wants our time and affection.

66 99 Lee, 22, said he's worried about "not being able to pay off my school loans and thus not being able to get married to my girlfriend."

 Dear Jealous Jesus,
You don't make me choose you, but if I do, I get to spend eternity with you. Help me to learn how to be faithful with my affection, my time, and how I speak about you in my conversations. Help me to choose life. Amen.

How does it make you feel knowing God is a jealous God? Please visit www .faithbookofjesus.com and click on "Community" to share.

To Read Further: Deuteronomy 30:19-20

UNBELIEF IS A KILLER

"O unbelieving and perverse generation," Jesus replied, "how long shall I stay with you and put up with you?"
— LUKE 9:41

No one likes to look bad in front of his or her boss. In the verse above, the disciples were ratted out in front of Jesus and the crowds. The boy's father said, "I begged your disciples to drive [the evil spirit] out, but they could not" (Luke 9:40).

Talk about a bad day at the office. The disciples' unbelief almost caused a death. The father was desperate. The evil spirit seized his boy, causing him to scream and convulse until he foamed at the mouth. There was no relief in sight, and it was killing him.

Unbelief has been killing man since the very beginning.

In her book *Lord, Heal My Hurts*, Kay Arthur said, "The Bible tells us that from the very beginning of the Garden of Eden, man's problem was unbelief. Unbelief . . . caused man to sin. Sin separated man from God, and God is love."[21]

Jesus, in his love, came to save us from our unbelief. He knew how much we would despair in unbelief that he was willing to die a sinner's death on a cross. Man's original doubt from the garden was nailed to the cross with Jesus. It wasn't until after Jesus' death and resurrection that even his closest friends (the disciples) believed.

Do you believe that Jesus is among us?

66 99 Allison, 27, said her unbelief kills her in regard to "the unknown and putting yourself out there. I feel like I'm running out of time to get married and have a family, yet there are still no prospects."

 Dear Believing Jesus,
Please help us check ourselves and our unbelief. Is our faith real? If not, then we have failed the test and still haven't believed that you are among us. Help us overcome our disbelief. Amen.

What belief are you holding on to? Please visit www.faithbookofjesus.com and click on "Community" to share.

To Read Further: 2 Corinthians 13:5 (NLT)

A BEAUTIFUL CADENCE

And we know that in all things God works for the good of those who love him, who have been called according to his purpose.

— ROMANS 8:28

I am coming to a place where I find my confidence in Jesus. Learning how to trust him is like a beautiful cadence.

I am created for Jesus' delight. I must learn to depend not on myself but on his desires for me. That is why Jesus sometimes removes those things in my life that have become an idol. Over and over I see how Jesus is jealous for my attention and affection.

I am created for Jesus' purpose. If Jesus didn't care for my ultimate good, he wouldn't bring me back again and again. He leaves the ninety-nine other lost sheep to find little lost me (see Luke 15:4-6).

I am created for Jesus' glory. I know that my God is refining me like gold through the fires of affliction. He won't walk away until he sees his reflection in me. Who am I to say "stop"? There might still be hidden corners with bitterness, dust bunnies of anger, and dark crevices that harbor fear.

I am confident that, like a beautiful cadence, my Jesus is daily working toward my good. He shares secrets of his kingdom, and when I listen and align myself with his will, he blesses me.

66 99 Jenni, 26, said, "Address the intense desire to find a life partner . . . and what it looks like to submit your will to Jesus over and over again."

 Dear Cadence Jesus,
Help us every day to listen, learn, and apply the knowledge that you are always looking out for our good, so eventually it will become a beautiful cadence. Thanks for teaching me how to trust you with my future. Amen.

What is your cadence? Please visit www.faithbookofjesus.com and click on "Community" to share.

To Read Further: Matthew 18:10-13

HAPPILY SINGLE

No more will anyone call you Rejected, and your country will no more be called Ruined.
You'll be called Hephzibah (My Delight), and your land Beulah (Married).

— ISAIAH 62:4 (MSG)

At times, I feel so lost, unwanted, and unloved. I don't know how I can go so long without human touch. It's been six years since my last significant relationship. I wish the Bible had passages that addressed my wants and needs. First Corinthians 7:9 says if you can't wait to get married, do it, but what about today's verse?

You will no longer be rejected. Oh! Pick me, pick me! I want that verse to be mine. I'm always the one picked last. So, now it's my turn, right?

But I know it means more than that. This verse is talking about the Israelite nation and how Israel just couldn't seem to get it together. Its land was in ruins. The people were not the talk of the town. Delight had been erased from their vocabulary.

I turn to my friend, Kay Arthur, once again: "O, Beloved, have you ever thought that maybe the reason you have hurt [been rejected] so badly is because you sought from man what only God could give? Your delight has been in the arm of flesh rather than in the Lord Himself . . . and the flesh will always fail. God won't."[22]

A one-night stand won't satisfy a lifetime of need. Let God meet your needs today and turn your rejection into his delight.

66 99   Mike, 26, is "happily single. I get along with everyone (I think)."

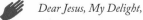 *Dear Jesus, My Delight,*
What a promise of hope we've been given. May we no longer be called rejected or ruined. No matter how deep the wounds of our past go, you make us beautiful again. Thank you for your covenant. May we never again doubt your love. Amen.

When was the last time you felt rejected? Please visit www.faithbookofjesus .com and click on "Community" to share.

To Read Further: Isaiah 62:1-5

WARNING SIGNS

The earth opened its mouth and swallowed them along with Korah, whose followers died when the fire devoured the 250 men. And they served as a warning sign.
— NUMBERS 26:10

The Bible's first warning sign cost 250 people their lives. Korah and his followers had challenged Moses. They refused to accept his leadership and, as a result, put God to the test. That should have been their first warning sign.

Because of this, the Lord's anger burned against Korah. The ground opened and swallowed these 250 men whole. This was the Bible's first mention of a warning sign. Maybe we should pay attention, too.

"Caution!" One of the first warning signs is a precaution. Perhaps you are taking on too much at work. Jesus wants to be there to meet your needs. Slow down. Bad behavior usually appears at this warning sign.

"Danger!" The second warning sign is an alert of oncoming danger. We are in harm's way when we fail to be cautious. Jesus has given us a counselor to show us how to listen. He is the Spirit within us. He shows us how to proceed when danger is ahead.

"Stop!" The Enemy's purpose is to stop us (see John 10:10). When we are faced with an obstacle that cannot be moved, we should ask Jesus for help and move on.

❝❞ Sheri, 25, said, "A major concern [warning] of mine is that I can hurt the people I love by how I treat them. How do I communicate when I'm tired and really don't feel like interacting with people?"

 *Dear Warning-Signs Jesus,*
Thank you for turns in this road of life. If everything were flat and boring, we'd never grow and experience the life you came to give us. When we come across a warning sign, show us how to proceed. Amen.

Which warning sign hits home with you today? Please visit www .faithbookofjesus.com and click on "Community" to share.

To Read Further: Numbers 16:1-15

NEVER GOING BACK

No one who puts his hand to the plow and looks back is fit for service in the kingdom of God.
— LUKE 9:62

I wrote this poem when I wanted to move forward in my life. I had no idea how or what I needed to do. All I knew was that I was twenty years old without a career, boyfriend, or sense of direction. I longed for the day when life would actually make sense.

"Ten years of a divine wound,"
The Lord said.
"It must be entire, complete
Not pierced with sharp metal,
But dull rock.

"It must hurt and wound
To break you.
So when the time comes for Me
To fulfill my prophetic promise to you,
You will cry out,
'I'm NEVER GONNA GO BACK!'

"In the stillness of My Presence you will
Feel the Harvest of Peace coming,
To restore and repair the loss.

"Come, Renee, return to Me.
I have broken you, now rejoice!"

Thankfully, my life makes a lot more sense now. The deep brokenness I experienced for so many years is gone. If it wasn't for Jesus and his presence meeting me where I'm at daily, I wouldn't have the kind of faith I have today.

66 99   Renee, 26, said, "It's so awesome to look back and see how far Jesus has brought me!"

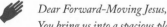   *Dear Forward-Moving Jesus,*
You bring us into a spacious place because you delight in us. Thank you that we don't
have to look back, go back, or fight back. Amen.

Do you need to move forward? Please visit www.faithbookofjesus.com and click on "Community" to share.

To Read Further: Luke 9:57-62

MY FATHER

Let us then approach the throne of grace with confidence, so that we may receive mercy and find grace to help us in our time of need.
— HEBREWS 4:16

Let me introduce you to my father. He gave me life. He taught me how to walk and read. He cares for my well-being and wants me to achieve things in life. He deserves my respect, and I want to honor him with my actions. These statements apply to both my earthly dad, Ron, and my heavenly Father, Jesus.

My dad didn't come from a Christian home. He found Christ in his late teens and decided to follow Jesus. My dad met my mom when he was twenty-two, and they married a few months before he turned twenty-three. Because my dad is not perfect, my view of Jesus is not perfect either.

God knew that imperfect people would need an example of what it means to be the perfect father. So he sent his Son, Jesus, to be born as a baby (see Luke 1:31). Jesus is someone we can sympathize with because he was fully man (human) and fully God. Yet when Jesus was tempted, he never sinned (see Luke 4:1; Hebrews 4:15).

Next time your earthly father does something to hurt you, remember our Father, Jesus, and approach him with confidence so you can receive the help you need.

❝❞ Jennifer, 35, said, "I want to be an agent of cheer. To raise my children. To please God. To be a great wife. To do the work set before me to the best of my ability."

Dear Jesus, My Father,
I'm so grateful that you came to this earth as a human so we could relate to you. Thanks for being the perfect Dad in our world and in the universe. Amen.

Does your view of your dad affect your view of Jesus? Please visit www .faithbookofjesus.com and click on "Community" to share.

To Read Further: Hebrews 4:14-16

THE EYE OF YOUR HEART

I pray also that the eyes of your heart may be enlightened in order that you may know the hope to which he has called you, the riches of his glorious inheritance in the saints.
— EPHESIANS 1:18

Every once in a while I catch a glimpse. A glimmer in time opens, and I see the future. Let's be honest: Most days are not like that. If you're like me, you're too busy with work, life, and social obligations to think about what your heart really wants.

If you were to look up "see clearly" in the dictionary, I believe it should say, "See Ephesians 1:18." Paul's letter to the Ephesians was an encouragement on the unity they could have in Jesus Christ.

If you were to ask a few hundred twentysomethings about the direction of their lives and how clearly they see the future, what do you think you'd find? From the hundreds I surveyed for this book, I can tell you that the answers were quite clear. We don't know what we want, and if we do, we're not sure how to get there.

That's why Paul said, "Keep asking that the God of our Lord Jesus Christ, the glorious Father, may give you the Spirit of wisdom and revelation, so that you may know him better. . . . Pray also that the eyes of your heart may be enlightened" (Ephesians 1:17-18).

66 99 Daniel, 26, said, "For singles, there can be a lot of feelings of loneliness and even jealousy when we see so many of our other twentysomethings in relationships."

Dear Jesus Who Sees Clearly,
You know the past, present, and future. May we be comforted by your unchanging nature today as some of us are still in the discovery process of figuring out who we are and what we want to become. Amen.

What does your heart really want? Please visit www.faithbookofjesus.com and click on "Community" to share.

To Read Further: Ephesians 1:15-23

EAGER DOES IT

Now finish the work, so that your eager willingness to do it may be matched by your completion of it, according to your means.
— 2 CORINTHIANS 8:11

Due to the state of the economy, I have never worked so hard in my life. The nature of sales has always been hard work, but throw in panic, budget cuts, and a stimulus package, and I'm scared. (Did I mention I sell to churches who have even less money?)

Eagerness is a great word to remember. I can never get too disappointed, or I won't make my sales goals. I also can't fear rejection, because it says in the Bible that Jesus will take care of my daily needs if I make God my primary concern (see Matthew 6:33).

The Bible never said we'd get rich staying home and sleeping in. To reiterate the point Paul was trying to make in 2 Corinthians 8:11, here are a few wise sayings to remind us that eager (not easy) does it:

"A little sleep, a little slumber, a little folding of the hands to rest — and poverty will come on you like a bandit and scarcity like an armed man" (Proverbs 6:10-11; 24:33-34).

"The sluggard craves and gets nothing, but the desires of the diligent are fully satisfied" (13:4).

"All hard work brings a profit, but mere talk leads only to poverty" (14:23).

❝❞ Danny, 21, said he's eager, but "people who want me to conform to what they *think* is a good walk with God" stress him out.

 Dear Eager Jesus,
Just as your work was to do the will of the One who sent you, we have our work cut out for us as well. Remind us who we're ultimately working for — you! In everything we do today, may we honor and glorify you. Amen.

Are you eager to please Jesus? Please visit www.faithbookofjesus.com and click on "Community" to share.

To Read Further: 2 Corinthians 8:10-15

THE PERFECT GIFT

So, my very dear friends, don't get thrown off course. Every desirable and beneficial gift comes out of heaven. The gifts are rivers of light cascading down from the Father of Light. There is nothing deceitful in God, nothing two-faced, nothing fickle. He brought us to life using the true Word, showing us off as the crown of all his creatures.

— JAMES 1:16-18 (MSG)

I would define the perfect gift with three E's: expensive, extravagant, and everything I've always wanted.

It's hard to imagine that Jesus would allow us to dream up the perfect gift without intending to fulfill it. He created us as perfect beings. His plan was to have perfect communion with us and with nature.

But after that stupid apple, everything we have tasted doesn't taste so perfect. You and I both know how to dream of the perfect-ten body, job/career, family/spouse, etc. I believe that if Jesus gave us the ability to dream about perfection, he intends to fulfill those dreams.

Gifts given by God are not fickle; they're "good and perfect" (see the NIV translation of today's verses). Mercy is really expensive. We can't buy it. Jesus doesn't give us mercy just once, but for a lifetime. His love is everything we could ever ask for, want, or imagine.

66 99 Peter, 23, said, "When you get one of God's gifts, you'll never be disappointed. You don't always know what you're going to get, or when, but it's something worth waiting for."

 *Dear Perfect-Gift Jesus,*
Let us taste and see your perfect gifts in our lives today. May we dance in the river of light, dream up an imaginable dream, and open up your storehouse of blessings before even leaving the house this morning. Amen.

What's your idea of the perfect gift? Please visit www.faithbookofjesus.com and click on "Community" to share.

To Read Further: James 1:16-18

NAME-DROPPING

But if I say, "I will not mention him or speak any more in his name," his word is in my heart like a fire, a fire shut up in my bones. I am weary of holding it in; indeed, I cannot.
— JEREMIAH 20:9

If you're passionate about someone, you're naturally going to share. I can't imagine my life as a celebrity because I can't keep my mouth shut about my relationships and who makes me happy. One of my biggest strengths is passion.

I have been blessed with new life. Jesus has healed me more than once. He has set me free in my health, my finances, and my relationships over and over. I think Jeremiah was blessed, too. He was called the weeping prophet. His passion for Jesus burned like fire deep inside his bones until he couldn't shut up.

If you are a follower of Jesus, you will mention his name!

If one of your friends were to ask you about your week over a beer or a cup of coffee, you'd probably name-drop about a new relationship at the office, a boy or girl you met online, or someone you really can't stand for whatever reason. When we mention Jesus' name, it should be a natural extension of the fire that's burning inside of us.

"You are to give him the name Jesus, because he will save his people from their sins" (Matthew 1:21).

66 99 Angel, 26, said, "There is always a yearning to learn more about God and our purpose in life. I only ask that that fire inside of me continues to burn."

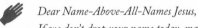 *Dear Name-Above-All-Names Jesus,*
If we don't drop your name today, may fire burn in our bones until we speak it out loud. Remind us to use it as often as we need to in our workplace, with our family, and in our prayers. Amen.

Does your passion for Jesus burn inside of you? Please visit www .faithbookofjesus.com and click on "Community" to share.

To Read Further: Jeremiah 20:7-9

FIREPROOF YOUR MARRIAGE

Each man should have his own wife, and each woman her own husband. The husband should fulfill his marital duty to his wife, and likewise the wife to her husband.
— 1 CORINTHIANS 7:2-3

The movie *Fireproof* premiered in theaters across the United States on September 26, 2008. Kirk Cameron stars as a firefighter who became the hero to everyone but his wife. Their marriage unfortunately was not fireproof.

In the movie Kirk Cameron's character reads a book called *The Love Dare* and tries for forty days to fix his marriage. But it isn't until his character becomes a follower of Jesus that he is able to save his marriage.

The Love Dare became an instant best seller. Thousands of couples saw the movie, went through the book, and saved their marriages. For about a year and a half around the release date of the movie, I received calls every day asking to book Kirk Cameron. It was such a pleasure knowing I helped influence marriages for the better when the staggering statistic in America says about 50 percent of marriages end in divorce.[23]

Want to fireproof your marriage? It's not too late. Whether or not you're already married, read what the Bible says about marriage in 1 Corinthians 7. No one is fireproof, and each person should take responsibility before entering into a marriage covenant. Ask Jesus to help make you a better spouse today or in the future.

66 99 Hilary, 22, asked, "How do we transition into building our faith as husband/wife?"

 Dear Fireproof Jesus,
As imperfect people, we humble ourselves before you today and ask that you show us how to change the statistic of marriage. Teach us how to be better wives and husbands to our spouses. In your name we pray. Amen.

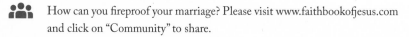 How can you fireproof your marriage? Please visit www.faithbookofjesus.com and click on "Community" to share.

To Read Further: 1 Corinthians 7

HOW TO MEASURE CONTENTMENT

The LORD is my shepherd, I shall not be in want.
— PSALM 23:1

I am a single twentysomething living in Southern California. We measure contentment by our job, our relationships, the size of our bank account, and how many times we dine out. Once a text message is sent, who knows what my group of friends will be doing next.

What is contentment anyway? In a world that promises "follow your heart" instant gratification no matter the cost, I know a lot of restless and empty people. I'm speaking to myself, too. There are many nights I sleep with my BlackBerry.

What is a healthy and well-balanced life? A relationship with Jesus in the twenty-first century takes finesse. Read Psalm 23 whenever you feel a lack of contentment.

GOD, my shepherd! I don't need a thing. You have bedded me down in lush meadows, you find me quiet pools to drink from. True to your word, you let me catch my breath and send me in the right direction.

Even when the way goes through Death Valley, I'm not afraid when you walk at my side. Your trusty shepherd's crook makes me feel secure.

You serve me a six-course dinner right in front of my enemies. You revive my drooping head; my cup brims with blessing.

Your beauty and love chase after me every day of my life. I'm back home in the house of GOD for the rest of my life. (MSG)

66 99 Delbarr, 25, said, "I want to reflect the *freedom* he's allowed me to know and walk in, whether that involves me working in ministry or in the workplace."

Dear Jesus, Our Contentment,
I know I'm not content. I need your help to make me lie down instead of chasing every dream and desire. I know once I give in and rest, I'll never be the same again.
Amen.

Are you content? Please visit www.faithbookofjesus.com and click on "Community" to share.

To Read Further: Psalm 23

THE TWO GREATEST QUESTIONS

I write these things to you who believe in the name of the Son of God so that you may know that you have eternal life.

— 1 JOHN 5:13

My mom loves to share her faith. She can talk to anyone about Jesus. Her boldness intimidates me at times because I'm not as good at sharing my faith with others, but it's also inspiring. In life we come across all kinds of people. Wouldn't it be nice to know how to share your faith? If your answer is "yes," then start with these two questions:

1. "Have you come to a place in your spiritual life where you know for certain that if you were to die today, you would go to heaven, or is that something you would say you're still working on?" The Bible says you can know for sure that you have eternal life! (See 1 John 5:13.)
2. "Wouldn't you like to know for sure that when you die, you will go to heaven?" Before you share how you can know, ask this: "Suppose you were to die today and stand before God and he were to say to you, 'Why should I let you into my heaven?' What would you say?"[24]

If you answered the first question with "I'm still working on it" and your answer to the second question is, "I've never done anything bad" or "It's up to God," then read tomorrow's devotional for the answer.

❝❞ Nathan, 26, asked, "What do you think is the best way to explain your faith to your non-Christian friends?"

Dear Jesus, the Son of God,
Show us to whom we should ask the two greatest questions. We never know who is spiritually seeking today. Thank you in advance for those friends you might bring into our circle of influence. Amen.

What are your answers to the two questions above? Please visit www.faithbookofjesus.com and click on "Community" to share. You can also go to www.eeinternational.org to put your faith into action.

To Read Further: 1 John 5:13-15

IT'S FREE

For the wages of sin is death, but the gift of God is eternal life in Christ Jesus our Lord.
— ROMANS 6:23

A lot of Christians believe you have to work your way into heaven. Heaven is a free gift. If it were possible for us to earn our way into heaven, God would not have sent his one and only Son to die on the cross for our sins.

So why can't man just accept this free gift of eternal life and quit striving to reach heaven by his own good deeds and works? Sometimes we feel the need to pay Jesus back for what he has done.

This is giving Jesus a knuckle sandwich. He doesn't want payment; he wants to give us a free gift: eternal life.

Jesus is the sinless Son of God, the only one who could pay the penalty for our sins. And he did that because he loves us so much.

So why can't personal effort, good works, or religious deeds earn you a place in heaven? Because they all represent *doing something* or *achieving something* in an attempt to pay back what can only be a gift from God.

Eternal life is a gift from God. It has nothing to do with what you do and everything to do with what Jesus has already done for you.

❝❞ Dianna, 24, said, "Allow the Word of God to be a foundation for your life and not just a 'set of rules' or something we 'talk about at church functions.' Let's take Jesus out of the box."

Dear Free Jesus,
It's silly to think how little we need to do to accept your free gift of eternal life. Help me be a witness to those around me and show them that earth is not our home; we have a better place to look forward to. Amen.

What is heaven? Please visit www.faithbookofjesus.com and click on "Community" to share.

To Read Further: Romans 6:15-23

NOT EARNED, NOT DESERVED

For it is by grace you have been saved, through faith—and this not from yourselves, it is the gift of God—not by works, so that no one can boast.

— EPHESIANS 2:8-9

Salvation is a free gift. We have the pleasure of spending eternity in heaven with Jesus if we accept this gift. However, what are some things we do to try to earn our way into heaven? Sometimes we think if we just go to church, Jesus will let us into heaven, right? Going to church doesn't make you a Christian any more than going to a barn will make you a cow.

Another false belief is that we can earn our way into heaven by being good and doing good to others. How many good acts is enough? Jesus set the standard that we cannot earn a place in heaven. What is a gift then?

For the sake of illustration, let's say it's your birthday. Your friend comes to your house and gives you a gift. You take off the bow, rip off the wrapping paper, and pull out a diamond bracelet. In your excitement you reach into your pocket and pull out a $100 bill and give it to your friend to pay for it. That would be insulting to your friend.

But let's say he accepts it. The diamond bracelet is no longer a gift. Any time you pay for something, it ceases to be a gift.

Because Jesus freely gives us eternal life, we cannot do anything to merit it.

66 99 Frank, 29, asked, "What does faith *really* mean, and how do you get there?"

 Dear Free-Gift Jesus,
How extravagant is your grace and how rich is your mercy to us today and every day. What a blessing to know we can accept this free gift of eternal life. After we accept, teach us how to put action to our faith. Amen.

How can you give feet to your faith? Please visit www.faithbookofjesus.com and click on "Community" to share.

To Read Further: Ephesians 2:1-10

I CAN'T SAVE MYSELF?

For whoever keeps the whole law and yet stumbles at just one point is guilty
of breaking all of it.
— JAMES 2:10

How do you explain your sin? We can all pick out at least one sin we've committed and say, "Yes, I've done that" or "Yes, I do that."

Have you ever hated someone? Then, by all admission, the Bible says you are a murderer (see James 2:11). Have you ever had lustful thoughts? Then you are an adulterer. Have you ever stolen something? You are a thief. What about lying? Everyone's a liar.

You might say, "I'm a good person and do good things." If you take a long, hard look back into your life, you'll find at least a few sins. For example, let's say on a Saturday morning you make scrambled eggs for yourself or your family. You break the eggs—one, two, three . . . oops, the fourth is rotten. Would you serve the scrambled eggs to your family with one rotten egg in it? Of course not.

Our lives are like scrambled eggs. We do good things, but there is also sin in our lives. We could never serve our lives up to Jesus because there is sin mixed in. At some point in our lives, we have sinned. We will never be able to save ourselves; we would have to be sinless to enter heaven. It is impossible for our good works to get us into heaven.

❝❞ Brian, 26, asked, "How can I be faithful with the Christian lifestyle while still being normal?"

 Dear Saving Jesus,
While we were still sinners, you died for us. Show us that we are guilty no matter if we sin a little or a lot. Cover us with your blood and wash us clean today. Amen.

👥 How does it feel to know that nothing you do can help you get into heaven? Please visit www.faithbookofjesus.com and click on "Community" to share.

✠ To Read Further: James 2:8-13

AM I A SINNER?

For everyone has sinned; we all fall short of God's glorious standard.
— ROMANS 3:23 (NLT)

This week I've been using examples from Evangelism Explosion on how to share your faith in an attempt to convince you that it's not works alone that can save us. Here is today's illustration: When you go into a store and buy a new appliance, a manual comes with it. The manual is the guidebook to explain how the appliance should run. It also tells you how to fix certain problems that might arise. Usually there is also a 1-800 number to call if you have any questions concerning your appliance.

Human beings come with a guidebook that explains how we should live our lives. It is the Bible, Jesus' holy Word. It explains that we are sinners.

What is *sin* anyway? Sin is anything that doesn't please Jesus and falls short of his standards. Sin is doing things we shouldn't do, such as stealing or getting angry. There are also sins of word and thought, such as cursing, lust, pride, and hatred.

Let's say I sin three times a day (this is a conservative number) by thinking an unkind thought, losing my temper, or failing to do right. In a year's time I would have sinned more than a thousand times. By the time twenty years had passed, I would have sinned 21,900 times.

I know this sounds pretty absurd, but what would happen to me if I walked into a traffic court with seventy-four thousand speeding tickets on my record? What would the judge do to me? He'd put me in jail. I am not only a sinner, but my sin is actually a serious issue before Jesus.

66 99 Alicia, 23, said, "I hate the feeling that I'm not measuring up to expectations of me."

Dear Jesus Who Did Not Sin,
You are a good God who does not tolerate sin. We confess our 21,900-plus sins to you. Cleanse us and forgive us today. Thank you for making us new. Amen.

Do you count your sins? Please visit www.faithbookofjesus.com and click on "Community" to share.

To Read Further: Romans 3:21-26

GOD IS JUST

Yet he does not leave the guilty unpunished.

— EXODUS 34:7

The same Bible that says that Jesus is merciful and loving and doesn't want to punish us says that God is just and must punish our sin. So which is right? Can Jesus, who loves us *and* is just, allow anyone into his presence?

To man, this is a problem, but to Jesus, it is not because he is God!

So what does it mean that God will punish sin? God provided a sacrifice, his Son Jesus Christ, to pay for our sins, so we will not be punished if we accept his forgiveness. If we do not accept his payment for our sins, then we need to fear his wrath and judgment someday.

The good news is that Jesus took our punishment. We need to accept this and stop thinking we can get into heaven any other way. Remember the last few devotionals? Salvation is a free gift. Eternity is something we cannot earn.

God solved this apparent problem of being loving and just in the most wonderful way: the person of Jesus Christ.

 Scott, 30, said, "Sometimes I feel like I am the only one who can handle taking care of everyone's problems. I have this 'savior' complex."

 Dear Just and Loving Jesus,
You are just toward our sin and loving toward us as people. Help us to hate the sin and not ourselves, the sinner. Change our hearts to accept the gift of God, who is Jesus Christ our Lord. Amen.

 Do you view Jesus as a just or loving God? Please visit www.faithbookofjesus .com and click on "Community" to share.

To Read Further: Exodus 34:5-7

AMERICAN IDOL

The Lord your God is with you, he is mighty to save. He will take great delight in you, he will quiet you with his love, he will rejoice over you with singing.

— ZEPHANIAH 3:17

I love today's verse. It reminds me that Jesus is the ultimate American Idol because he sings to us daily. I wonder what his singing voice sounds like. I'm sure he doesn't sound like William Hung, who is known for singing Ricky Martin's "She Bangs," or the British sensation Susan Boyle, who got discovered on *Britain's Got Talent* at age forty-seven.

Zephaniah isn't one of the most popular books in the Bible, so today's verse is often overlooked. If I asked if you knew anything about it or had read it before, I'm sure I wouldn't get much of a response. I'd probably get a better response if I asked you who got kicked off *American Idol* last week.

If the Bible is still as relevant today as it was two thousand years ago, why do we find more satisfaction in knowing who got kicked off *American Idol*? We watch television and talk about it the next day at work and with our friends on Facebook (I'm personally a huge *Burn Notice* and *Lost* fan); we should also talk about God's Word. Today's verse could spark a conversation like this: "In my quiet time last night I found out that Jesus sings over me because he loves me. Isn't that crazy? What was the last thing you read?"

Get to know the book of Zephaniah today. The more you read, the more you'll realize why the Bible is called God's love story and how much he truly delights in you and wants to be your friend. You can even read it on your iPhone or BlackBerry.

66 99 Megan, 24, said, "I would love to be a singer/songwriter. I play locally every now and then and have a few recorded tracks, but I would love to be able to share my heart with more people."

 *Dear Singing Jesus,*
What a delight and joy to hear your voice as you sing over me in the morning when I get ready for work and in the evening when I lay my head down to sleep. Thank you for taking delight in me. Amen.

What's the last verse you read in the Bible that stuck with you? Please visit www.faithbookofjesus.com and click on "Community" to share.

To Read Further: Zephaniah 1–3

I FOUND LIFE

The thief comes only to steal and kill and destroy; I have come that they may have life, and have it to the full.
— JOHN 10:10

I wrote the poem below more than five years ago. It was read on a nationally known radio show, *Revive Our Hearts* with Nancy Leigh DeMoss. I hope you find your life today.

I have an addiction that has taken over my life. It's turned my pure desires into fleshly, evil dark pleasures. I have this need to satisfy my wants and needs immediately—instant gratification. I have been overcome. I can't take breaks or go away on vacation.

Looking this addiction straight in the eye has brought me to my knees—to the cross. But, what does it mean to take up my cross?

I crucify my flesh and all its desires and lay down on my cross of guilt and shame.
I feel the nails being driven into my hands and the evil one driven out.
Not I, but Christ lives in me—now I have the choice to live each day for Jesus.

To say yes to Him and no to my addictions.
Through my death comes life and the power to choose.
A new life, with new and right desires.

My life's view is no longer twisted and perverted. It has been turned right-side up.
Today I have the power over my evil desires, over my addictions, over the things that overcome me and take me down.

I no longer desire power for the sake of power, a relationship for the sake of not being alone,
Nor the gym for the sake of being skinny, or money for the sake of being rich, alcohol for the purpose of losing touch with reality, music to drown out the silence, or food for the sake of comfort.

What I really want is what God wants for me: Life and life abundantly.

66 99 Frank, 29, said, "My life came alive for the first time when I put my faith in Christ."

 Dear Abundant-Life Jesus,
The Enemy is trying to steal our life. With all of our breath, help us to praise you today even in the midst of sorrow. Amen.

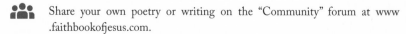 Share your own poetry or writing on the "Community" forum at www .faithbookofjesus.com.

 To Read Further: John 10:10-18

GOD IS MERCIFUL

Whoever does not love does not know God, because God is love.

— 1 JOHN 4:8

Another great way to share your faith with your friends is by showing mercy. Most people are tuned in to a god who is all-powerful. The good news is that Jesus exists; he is alive; and he has forgiven you of all your sins, past, present, and future, no matter what you've done! He is merciful and does not want to punish you.

God sent his Son, Jesus Christ, to take your punishment, the debt you owed to God for your sins. God knew that the only perfect sacrifice for our sins was his one and only Son, who was sinless and who would bear our sins in his own body. God knew we would sin and that we couldn't save ourselves; that's the reason he provided a substitute for us.

"This is love: not that we loved God, but that he loved us and sent his Son as an atoning sacrifice for our sins" (1 John 4:10). But can't we do something to pay for our sins?

Most young people think that if they do good to others and live a life that is good or exemplary, the good will outweigh the bad and God will accept them into heaven. In God's economy, it doesn't work this way. The good will never outweigh the bad. On one hand, God loves us and doesn't want to punish us, but on the other hand, he is also just—and what will he do to us then?

❝❞ Sako, 22, said, "My purpose in life is to bring glory to the One who created me."

 Dear Merciful Jesus,
Thank you for your mercy. Please don't let us take for granted how much you love us and are not eager to punish us. Today may we learn what it's like to be your sons and daughters. Amen.

👥 What is your definition of *mercy*? Please visit www.faithbookofjesus.com and click on "Community" to share.

✢ To Read Further: 1 John 4:8-10

SONS AND DAUGHTERS

For you did not receive a spirit that makes you a slave again to fear, but you received the Spirit of sonship. And by him we cry, "Abba, Father."

— ROMANS 8:15

Have you ever met a child who was never told the word "no"? Those kids are complete brats! They get their way in every situation and have horrible attitudes. Yes, they can be cute little angels from time to time, but every child comes out of the womb screaming. Parents need to discipline their children because we all must be taught how to live, love, and respect others.

Jesus disciplines us, his children. He is a not a mean and vengeful God. Yesterday we read that Jesus is merciful and is not eager to punish us. The reason we know love is because we have Jesus. Today's verse is a mirror reflection of that.

If we love Jesus, we'll come to him as a child would. Have you ever seen a little girl asking her daddy to help her? The father shows mercy by feeding, clothing, and providing the child with whatever she needs.

We have not received a spirit of fear that makes us shy away from God. We can come directly to him and yell, scream, or cry, "Abba, Father," which means "Daddy, Daddy!"

❝❞ Alexandra, 23, said, "Currently I am a graduate residence director. I plan on becoming a dean of students; I also want to be a mother."

Dear Abba Father Jesus,
You are the best Daddy in the world. May we come to you today with our problems, struggles, and concerns because of your great love for us. Amen.

What does receiving a Spirit of sonship mean to you? Please visit www.faithbookofjesus.com and click on "Community" to share.

To Read Further: Romans 8:11-15

MISS-INFORMED OPINION

Always be prepared to give an answer to everyone who asks you to give the reason for the hope that you have. But do this with gentleness and respect, keeping a clear conscience, so that those who speak maliciously against your good behavior in Christ may be ashamed of their slander.

— 1 PETER 3:15-16

In April 2009 at the Miss USA Pageant, Carrie Prejean, Miss California and runner-up for Miss USA, was asked a question by judge Perez Hilton: "Vermont recently became the fourth state to legalize same-sex marriage. Do you think every state should follow suit? Why or why not?"

Carrie responded by saying, "I think it's great that Americans can choose one or the other. We live in a land that you can choose same-sex marriage. . . . In my country and my family, I think that I believe that a marriage should be between a man and a woman. No offense to anyone . . ."[25] No offense? Her answer sparked a national controversy. She became the target of national media, including Perez Hilton, and ended up losing her crown. I believe (and so does Carrie) that she lost the competition because she spoke the truth of her convictions.

Now more than ever, twentysomethings are full of tolerance. The right opinion could land you the right job or even the right relationship. Jesus came to show us the way, the truth, and the life (see John 14:6). Next time you respond to your friends, co-workers, or Perez Hilton on Twitter (@perezhilton), don't be misinformed. The world will tell you one thing, but what Jesus says is always correct (see Ezekiel 2:7; Matthew 24:35).

66 99 Daniel, 29, said, "Perez Hilton called her a dumb b**** not for her belief but for her misinformed opinion."

 Dear Jesus Who Allows Us Opinions,
When we're asked a question about the hope we have, may we respond with gentleness and respect, keeping a clear conscience so that we will not be ashamed. No matter who is right or wrong, help us to remember that a gentle response turns away wrath. Amen.

How do you respond to difficult questions? Please visit www .faithbookofjesus.com and click on "Community" to share.

To Read Further: 1 Peter 3:14-16

TELLING JESUS OFF

The LORD said to Job: "Will the one who contends with the Almighty correct him? Let him who accuses God answer him!"

— JOB 40:1-2

Telling someone off is like giving someone the finger. It means you're mad and you want that person to know how you feel. In today's passage the Lord is responding to Job's monologue.

For those of you who don't know, Job was a righteous and God-fearing man with a large family. He was very wealthy. In the first chapter of Job, Jesus was bragging about his servant Job. Satan asked to mess with Job, because why would Job fear God for nothing?

In a twenty-four-hour period Job lost everything. (Take that, Jack Bauer!) His wife told him to curse Jesus and die, but Job refused (see 2:9). Then Job's friends told him off because they figured he must have done something to deserve his sufferings.

The story is quite fascinating. I love how the Bible doesn't hold back. It shows how we treat our friends. When the Lord steps in to correct Job's friends, put Job in his place, and remind Job of his faith, watch out! "Brace yourself like a man; I will question you, and you shall answer me. Would you discredit my justice? Would you condemn me to justify yourself?" (40:7-8).

It's okay to tell Jesus your needs. Be honest. He already knows anyway. I can remember the first time I told Jesus off. I felt awful and didn't know what else to do. Let Jesus know you're upset and angry with him, but be prepared when he responds.

66 99 Justin, 29, said, "Sometimes I just don't like people."

Dear Correctional Jesus,
We all have days when we feel the need to get angry and tell someone off. When we're in pain, help us to choose our words and friends wisely. May we come to you first and allow you to heal our hurts. Amen.

When was the last time you felt like telling someone off? Visit www .faithbookofjesus.com and click on "Community" to share.

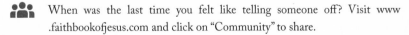  To Read Further: Job 40:1-8

OLD HABITS DIE HARD

As a dog returns to its vomit, so a fool repeats his folly.
— PROVERBS 26:11

I once made out with a guy who worked in my building. I was extremely attracted to him. I saw him every day on my breaks when I went for a walk. He was outside smoking. I'm not a big fan of smoking; in fact, I never thought I'd make out with a smoker. But he looked like McDreamy. Enough said.

Up until that point I had responded to temptation by running away, but I had never encountered the law of close proximity. His bad-boy charm eventually got to me. So I pushed him against the side of the elevator (like in a scene from a movie). Michael's jaw dropped to the ground. I had become the bad girl.

I had just made the worst decision of my life. Afterward, I'd find ways to meet him in the stairwell or the elevator. Never mind that I was bored at work. I hated my life and was looking for an escape. When I tried to stop, I couldn't.

I wrestled with myself for months until I finally gave up. I was twenty-three, and my life was going nowhere fast. The moment I finally stopped, he walked off the job. My temptation was never to be seen again. I think sometimes Jesus waits for us to walk away before he can clean up the mess.

Tired of old habits keeping you up at night? Going back to the same old place (like the vomit in today's verse) is easy, but once you surrender your pride to Jesus, he comes in and cleans you up from the inside out, giving you a way to stay strong and stand up under temptation (see 1 Corinthians 10:13).

❝❞ Ashley, 27, said, "My lack of self-discipline really stresses me out. I know what I need to do, but I just don't do it. I have an all-or-nothing personality, which I am asking Jesus for help to overcome."

Dear Return-to-Me Jesus,
Temptation is an appealing trap. Please help us see the lies we believe. Thank you for providing a way out of temptation. Help us to walk away when temptation is strong. Amen.

What habits are tripping you up? Please visit www.faithbookofjesus.com and click on "Community" to share.

 To Read Further: Proverbs 26:9-12

HEMMED IN

You hem me in—behind and before; you have laid your hand upon me. Such knowledge is too wonderful for me, too lofty for me to attain.
— PSALM 139:5-6

Can you tell the difference between a problem and Jesus' hand in your life? When we're going through a tough time, the answer is "no, not right away."

How do you put your hope and trust in Jesus when your life is in utter chaos? Do you choose to find rest in Jesus and let him work out the details, or do you try to fix it? It is in these times that the Enemy tries his hardest to exploit our weakness. He knows when we're most vulnerable. Satan tries to distract us from seeing God's hand, his fingerprints, or his sovereignty.

The truth is Jesus is hemming us in for his purposes. Maybe we have some more growing up to do, some maturing. Maybe it's for our own protection. Maybe it's because we need more faith. "Restore our fortunes, LORD, as streams renew the desert. Those who plant in tears will harvest with shouts of joy. They weep as they go to plant their seed, but they sing as they return with the harvest" (Psalm 126:4-6, NLT).

" " Matt, 27, said, "Sometimes I feel like people don't actually care, that they're in the relationship for selfish reasons instead of mutual benefit."

  Dear Hemmed-In Jesus,
Thank you that you hem us in before, behind, and on both sides. Help us to see the full measure of your protection in our lives today. Amen.

  Are you hemmed in? Please visit www.faithbookofjesus.com and click on "Community" to share.

  To Read Further: Psalm 139:5-12

FAITH IMPOSSIBLE

And without faith it is impossible to please God, because anyone who comes to him must believe that he exists and that he rewards those who earnestly seek him.

— HEBREWS 11:6

Some of you might remember today's verse from Sunday school. Paul, the writer of Hebrews, told us that it's impossible to please Jesus without faith.

If you wanted to speak with your best friend but never picked up the phone, what good would that do to improve your relationship? With Jesus the hard part is that we can't exactly see, touch, feel, or have a two-way conversation as we would with our best friend here on earth.

Some churches will tell you that you have to hear God's voice, speak in tongues, or prophesy to be saved. Not true. Paul tells us we should eagerly desire certain spiritual gifts, especially prophecy (see 1 Corinthians 14:1).

Start with faith. Want to get to know Jesus daily? Read your Bible and learn how to pray. Discover the important spiritual truths by putting your faith in action.

Test everything. Hold on to your faith (see 1 Thessalonians 5:21). Without developing your faith, it will not only be impossible to please God but also to serve others.

❝❞ David, 30, said, "I am an insurance agent. I enjoy it very much. But I struggle with faith. Some of it is me, some of it is others. Ultimately though, I feel this is where God called me, to help others make good financial decisions."

🤚 *Dear Faithful Jesus,*
I want to experience the rewards of a faith that pleases you. Teach me how to put my faith into action everywhere I go—even when I don't understand exactly where you're leading me. Amen.

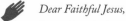 Want to learn how to put your faith into action? Go to www .putyourfaithinaction.org.

🐟 To Read Further: Hebrews 11:4-6

YOU + ME + ? = US

Then God said, "Let us make man in our image, in our likeness, and let them rule over the fish of the sea and the birds of the air, over the livestock, over all the earth, and over all the creatures that move along the ground."

— GENESIS 1:26

Nothing in the Bible is more puzzling than the Trinity. Since the Bible doesn't clearly spell out or say, "This is the Trinity," it can get confusing. However, starting in Genesis 1:26, the Bible strongly hints at a three-in-one God.

Mark Driscoll, pastor of Mars Hill Church in Seattle, said, "The Trinity is one God who externally exists in three distinct persons—Father, Son, and Spirit—who are each fully and equally God." Each member of the Trinity is equally God (the reason for the equation): Father + Jesus + Holy Spirit = God.

In his series on the Trinity, Mark Driscoll said there is only one God (see Deuteronomy 4:35; 32:39; Psalm 86:10; Isaiah 43:10; 45:5; 1 Timothy 1:17; 2:5). All other gods are demonic false gods (see Deuteronomy 32:17; John 17:3; 1 Corinthians 10:20). The Father is God (see John 6:27; 1 Corinthians 8:6). The Son is God (see John 1:1,14; 8:58; 20:28; Romans 9:5; Titus 2:13; 1 John 5:20). The Spirit is God (see Acts 5:3-4; 2 Corinthians 3:17-18).[26]

66 99 Phoebe, 27, said, "There was a long time where I hated not understanding this aspect of God. Since then I've come to terms with, and even rejoice in, the fact that there are some aspects of God that I cannot fully understand in this life."

Dear God + Jesus + Holy Spirit,
What an incredible gift we receive when we become followers of Jesus. We have full access to the Father, the Son (who is Jesus), and the Spirit who guides us and counsels us where we should go—all wrapped up in the present of God. Amen.

What do you know about the Trinity? Please visit www.faithbookofjesus.com and click on "Community" to share.

To Read Further: Deuteronomy 4:35; John 17:3; Romans 9:5

SO MUCH MORE

Amaziah asked the man of God, "But what about the hundred talents I paid for these Israelite troops?"
— 2 CHRONICLES 25:9

Israel's king, Amaziah, was twenty-five years old and about to go into battle. The Bible says he followed the Lord, but not wholeheartedly. When the man of God told him to let his soldiers go, Amaziah was faithful because he knew God was on his side.

I can relate. I try too hard to get what I want. What Jesus was really saying was, "Even if you go and fight courageously in battle, God will overthrow you before the enemy, for God has the power to help or to overthrow" (2 Chronicles 25:8).

Amaziah even paid a hundred talents of silver (let's say $100 in our day) to hire soldiers to fight on his behalf. But the man of God told Amaziah God didn't need his money and could do so much more.

I ask others for help all the time. In fact, I've paid well over $100 to different doctors and counselors to help me overcome health issues. When they all failed me, I realized God wanted to be the one to come through for me. As Amaziah learned, God doesn't need our money. Sure, it's great to seek help. Don't be stupid, right? But the Bible is filled with examples of the kind of faith that pleases him.

Next time you're tempted to splurge and go on a shopping spree or buy a new car, consider the Source. Jesus can give you so much more if you just ask him.

" " Phil, 31, said, "I don't know why God chooses to use us to accomplish his will. Why not send a battalion of angels and get the job done quickly?"

Dear Much-More Jesus,
I confess that I want so much more, but I'm afraid to give up what I feel my needs are. If you can help King what's-his-name thousands of years ago through a difficult situation, then you can definitely supply my needs today. Amen.

Do you want more? Please visit www.faithbookofjesus.com and click on "Community" to share.

To Read Further: 2 Chronicles 25:1-9

THE BLACK HOLE

What gain is there in my destruction, in my going down into the pit? Will the dust praise you? Will it proclaim your faithfulness?
— PSALM 30:9

When David was young, he was anointed by the prophet Samuel to become the next king over Israel. But he had to wait years to actually become the king.

The current king, Saul, couldn't accept his fate, and he made it his vendetta to kill David. As he was fleeing for his life, David wrote the book of Psalms. If David became king right away, we wouldn't have this book. Each psalm is a testimony to David's honesty and Jesus' faithfulness.

David trusted Jesus with his life. David trusted in the Lord: "God did not give David into [King Saul's] hands" (1 Samuel 23:14). David even had a few opportunities to take the throne away from King Saul. The first could have been the perfect kill—when Saul was using the bathroom (see 24:2-9). The second was when David found Saul sleeping (see 26:5). Both times David trusted Jesus and did not kill Saul. If only we could learn a lesson or two from King David.

Are you stuck in a black hole? Pour your heart out to Jesus as David did. Record your journey in a journal or blog. You might be able to encourage others down the road.

66 99 Veronica, 23, said, "I am not currently in a career. It's more of a black-hole, part-time job that sucks the fun right outta me. I would love to be done with school so that I can begin my career."

 *Dear Black-Hole Jesus,*
Life is tough when we are waiting for you to rescue us from our dead-end jobs and lives. You know the proper timing, and we need your strength and peace to trust your perfect timing today. Amen.

Are you in a black hole? Visit www.faithbookofjesus.com and click on "Community" to share.

To Read Further: Psalm 30

OWE NO ONE NOTHING

Let no debt remain outstanding, except the continuing debt to love one another, for he who loves his fellowman has fulfilled the law.

— ROMANS 13:8

What was your first thought this morning (besides "Thank God it's Friday!")? So often I find myself complaining because there are not enough hours in the day.

One of the phrases my mom tells me when I'm stressed is "I owe no man nothing." I have a fear of being alone, and I don't know how to say "no." I remember trying to balance school, work, and social obligations — and I had to go back on my happy pills because I couldn't deal with my life. If you're in a similar situation, read these verses for encouragement:

"The LORD is my light and my salvation — whom shall I fear? The LORD is the stronghold of my life — of whom shall I be afraid? When evil men advance against me to devour my flesh, when my enemies and my foes attack me, they will stumble and fall" (Psalm 27:1-2).

"So do not worry, saying, 'What shall we eat?' or 'What shall we drink?' or 'What shall we wear?' For the pagans run after all these things, and your heavenly Father knows that you need them. But seek first his kingdom and his righteousness, and all these things will be given to you as well" (Matthew 6:31-33).

66 99 Lee, 24, said, "My life all seems to happen at once — either I'm sitting around waiting for things to happen or I can't sit still because I am doing a million different things with a million different people."

Dear Owe-No-One Jesus,
The debt you paid so we could be free is priceless. I accept your free gift of salvation and thank you for it. Amen.

Do you have trouble telling others "no"? Please visit www.faithbookofjesus .com and click on "Community" to share.

To Read Further: Psalm 27:1-2; Matthew 6:31-33; Romans 13:8

MINISTRY OF RECONCILIATION

All this is from God, who reconciled us to himself through Christ and gave us the ministry of reconciliation.

— 2 CORINTHIANS 5:18

We are called by Jesus to minister the gospel. The gospel is the good news of Jesus Christ. Second Corinthians 5:17-20 is a key passage that explains what most of us will spend the rest of our lives doing.

1. **We are a new creation** (verse 17). If we follow Jesus Christ as our Lord and Savior, he makes us into a new creation. We are born again in him.
2. **We are reconciled** (verses 18-19). Through his death, burial, and resurrection, we are saved and reconciled. Jesus Christ's reconciliation means our sins are forgiven. The debt of our sins has been settled. If you remember only one thing, tell others their sins are not counted against them.
3. **We have a ministry** (verse 18). Ever wondered what your purpose in life is? Don't fool yourself! You are a minister of the good news of Jesus Christ whether you are on paid staff at a church or working at Wal-Mart.
4. **We are ambassadors** (verse 20). We have the pleasure of "imploring" or urging others earnestly on Jesus' behalf to be reconciled to him just as we are.

66 99 Stephen, 30, said, "Am I doing the best I possibly can to improve others' relationships with God? How better can I care for them? Be more selfless by giving 51 percent and taking 'just' 49 percent every day."

Dear Reconciled Jesus,
Thank you for the incredible ministry of sharing the gospel of Jesus Christ with others. May we not take it lightly but boldly proclaim your name wherever you lead us today. Amen.

Are you reconciled? Please visit www.faithbookofjesus.com and click on "Community" to share.

To Read Further: 2 Corinthians 5:17-20

THE CONFIDENCE MAN

You must not eat fruit from the tree that is in the middle of the garden, and you must not touch it, or you will die.

— GENESIS 3:3

Over the next few days we'll study hindrances that keep us from becoming the healthy individuals God wants us to be.

Today we'll learn about false confidence: where it came from, what it looks like, and how to believe the truth about who we really are—free in Jesus.

To understand how confidence in ourselves can be a hindrance, we must first look at what happened long ago in a little garden known as Eden. The serpent tricked Eve into believing that God couldn't be trusted. His lie went like this: "Did God really say, 'You must not eat from any tree in the garden'?" (Genesis 3:1).

We're not exactly faced with a forbidden tree today, but if we're honest with ourselves, our healthy ambition can turn into pride. We put our needs before others. We take the bite out of the apple as Eve did. Sometimes we even pass it along.

Let's pay close attention to the kind of confidence we have today. Does it glorify God or us?

66 99 Eric, 33, said, "My purpose is to reach out to divorced men and help them get their lives back and become strong Christian men."

Dear Confidence-Giving Jesus,
Thank you for showing us this hindrance through the example of Eve in the Garden of Eden. Help us see when we're placing too much importance on ourselves instead of on the needs of others. Help us place our confidence in you instead so we can walk in your freedom. Amen.

Does your confidence glorify God? Please visit www.faithbookofjesus.com and click on "Community" to share.

To Read Further: Genesis 3:1-7

YOU'VE GOT SOME EXPLAININ' TO DO

Blessed is he whose transgressions are forgiven, whose sins are covered. Blessed is the man whose sin the LORD does not count against him and in whose spirit is no deceit.
— PSALM 32:1-2

Sometimes we hold things in. I know I'm guilty of that. It starts out as something small, like believing a lie, but if we don't address it right away, the anger, bitterness, strife, slander, gossip, hate—you get the point—strangles us and forces us to surrender.

This is unconfessed sin. An example of unconfessed sin in the Bible is found in Psalm 32:3-5. David shared what sin tastes like when left inside our bodies:

> When I kept silent, my bones wasted away through my groaning all day long. For day and night your hand was heavy upon me; my strength was sapped as in the heat of summer. Then I acknowledged my sin to you and did not cover up my iniquity. I said, "I will confess my transgressions to the LORD"—and you forgave the guilt of my sin.

See what happens when we open our mouths and confess what's going on inside, even if it's messy and could spill all over the place? At least it's better than being choked up in silence.

Let's choose to confess our sins before Jesus and be set free.

66 99 Laurie, 25, said, "I freak when people are not listening to me. Lack of communication."

Dear Sinless Jesus,
Thank you for showing us what unconfessed sin looks like. Don't let us hold on to the bad stuff, but instead help us to confess our grievances and move on. Thank you for your grace and mercy, which have no limit. Thank you for putting up with us even when we don't deserve it. Amen.

Are you holding something in that you need to let go? Please visit www.faithbookofjesus.com and click on "Community" to share.

To Read Further: Psalm 32:1-8

WHAT'S NEXT, PAPA?

This resurrection life you received from God is not a timid, grave-tending life. It's adventurously expectant, greeting God with a childlike "What's next, Papa?"
— ROMANS 8:15 (MSG)

I love hugs. I can't go a day without the embrace of a loved one. Imagine the feeling that you are loved, secure, and accepted. All my worries seem to fade away when I'm in the arms of a friend.

We are called to be like a child in the arms of our Papa. How can we fear when we trust our Papa Jesus? How can we be upset? How can we worry when the cares of the day will fade away and a new day will take its place? Every day we encounter trials just by waking up and turning on the news, walking out the door, and facing the troubles of life.

In the same way that a child trusts his or her parents, we can trust Jesus. A newborn baby doesn't have the ability to say to his dad, "Make sure you feed me every two hours for the next year because I don't know how to feed myself." No. The parents already know this.

Jesus knows our weaknesses. If we want to be healthy people, we must not give way to fear. Instead we can embrace our Father and simply trust him as a child and say, "What's next, Papa?"

❝❞ Cassandra, 30, said, "I wish when I was twenty someone had taught me about being unequally yoked, picking a husband, and preparing to be a mom. I bought into culture's lie that I can have it all. I can't, and now I regret that I have to work while my two-year-old is in day care."

 Dear Papa Jesus,
When we are in pain or scared, show your love to us. Tenderly come to us and replace our fears with the security of your touch. Help us cry out to you when we are in need and know that you are only a hug away. Thank you, Papa. Amen.

Do you trust Papa Jesus? Please visit www.faithbookofjesus.com and click on "Community" to share.

To Read Further: Ephesians 6:1-4

PICTURE PROMISES

For the vision is yet for an appointed time; but at the end it will speak, and it will not lie.
Though it tarries, wait for it; because it will surely come, it will not tarry.
— HABAKKUK 2:3 (NKJV)

What if Jesus were to snap a picture of you right now and hand it to you? You look at the picture and say to him, "Wait, who is that?" Of course, that would never happen. Why? Pictures never lie. What Jesus promises, he will fulfill. Think of his promises as picture promises.

Commit to memory three picture promises you'd like to see Jesus fulfill in your life. "This vision is for a future time. It describes the end, and it will be fulfilled. If it seems slow in coming, wait patiently, for it will surely take place. It will not be delayed" (Habakkuk 2:3, NLT). Want to know my three things?

1. Publish a daily devotional—This was my written prayer request since 2004, and it was fulfilled March 8, 2010, with the release of this book.
2. My health to improve—This was my written prayer request since 1997, and it was fulfilled in 2007 when I graduated from Biola University, got a full-time job (my dream job), and was able to finally move on.
3. My future husband—This has been a written prayer request since I was fifteen. I'm still waiting on this one. . . .

66 99   Carrie, 25, said, "I'd like to start my own company to serve and pour into other people's dreams, to encourage and mobilize them to go after what they were made to do."

Dear Picture-Promise Jesus,
While we wait for life to develop into portraits of promise, help us to remember that we can trust you. When we grow impatient, remind us that you do not lie and that the best things in life are worth waiting for—and are still to come! Amen.

What are your three picture promises? Please visit www.faithbookofjesus.com and click on "Community" to share.

To Read Further: Habakkuk 2:2-3

HELP, I'M SLIPPING!

When I said, "My foot is slipping," your love, O LORD, supported me.
— PSALM 94:18

This week we looked at hindrances that keep us from becoming healthy people. If left unchecked, each hindrance (confidence, unconfessed sin, fear, and impatience) can lead to unbelief. Why? Weeks can go by while we're waiting for the answer we needed yesterday. We know that Jesus has promised us victory over the Enemy, but sometimes our trials are just too big. They cover us in despair until we give up and lose faith.

David was a man of great sorrow. He waited a long time to be the king of Israel. Unbelief could have cost him his life, but each time he felt his foot slipping, he cried out to Jesus.

What are you waiting for? Could it be a promotion at work? Maybe you're waiting for test results to come back. What about changing that major of yours three times? Maybe you're hoping that graduation will happen before you turn the big 3-0.

Today is the day to bring your slipups and worries to the foot of the cross and leave them there, exclaiming, "My foot is slipping!"

❝❞ Casey, 19, said, "I'm afraid for my family to lose what they have because I can't always help financially."

 Dear Supportive Jesus,
You see all of our anger, guilt, loss, grief, betrayal, despair, and pain. Restore our faith and help us to believe that you can make us into healthy people. Support us as we slip away from the things that lead us away from you. Amen.

Are you slipping? Please visit www.faithbookofjesus.com and click on "Community" to share.

To Read Further: Psalm 94:11-23

THE SUPERHERO

Stand firm then, with the belt of truth buckled around your waist, with the breastplate of righteousness in place.
— EPHESIANS 6:14

What happens when a superhero dons his supersuit? He's changed from an ordinary man with weaknesses into a man who performs the extraordinary. That's kind of like us when we put on the belt of truth and the breastplate of righteousness.

So what happens when you don't buckle your belt? Your pants may fall down! Did you know that Jesus said "I tell you the truth" more than seventy-eight times in the New Testament? You can't hang your sword of the Spirit unless your belt is buckled firmly in place.

How about a breastplate? What does that do? It protects your heart! "Above all else, guard your heart, for it is the wellspring of life" (Proverbs 4:23). We could all use some pointers on how to protect our hearts from the many relationships we encounter.

If we want to be healthy superheroes, we must learn how to protect our identity in Christ. I'm ready to wear the armor. Are you?

66 99 Yasmine, 20, said, "I am currently studying digital media/Internet web development. I have an internship with a design company, but my superhero job would ideally be to create media/web work for nonprofit organizations."

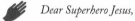 *Dear Superhero Jesus,*
What a precious gift you have given us: the ability to protect ourselves. Show us what it means to apply truth and righteousness in our everyday lives. Transform us from ordinary men and women into extraordinary superheroes armed and ready for battle. Amen.

Ready to be a superhero? Please visit http://en.wikipedia.org/wiki/Armor _of_God to learn more.

To Read Further: Ephesians 6:10-18

YOUR FEET

And with your feet fitted with the readiness that comes from the gospel of peace. In addition to all this, take up the shield of faith, with which you can extinguish all the flaming arrows of the evil one.

— EPHESIANS 6:15-16

I recently visited Disneyland with my best friend Monique. She flew in from Texas to spend her vacation with me. We knew it was going to be the last time we would share together for a while because she's moving to Uganda for three years.

We walked around all day enjoying rides, interesting people, and great food. Monique and I even wore tiaras all day so we could feel like Disney princesses. We were having a blast until our feet started hurting in the evening. But, that's what happens when you walk all day—your feet get tired and weary (see Isaiah 40:31).

I wonder what would've happened if we had brought shields along with us to Disneyland. People might have thought we were crazy for trying to dress the part of a hero. Or we might have been kicked out. It makes me wonder: Maybe the shield of faith isn't about Captain America showing off his supercool shield.

Maybe it's about serving others with hurting feet whether you're in Anaheim, California, or Uganda, Africa. Hmm . . . What do you think?

66 99   Jacob, 34, said, "My friends who are twentysomething and single can only think about themselves and what works best for them, regardless of how it affects others. I think we're prone to this sort of behavior because of our sin nature, and when we don't put ourselves in their shoes, it ruins our testimony and stands in the way of true friendship."

Dear Serving-Feet-Everywhere Jesus,
Not all superheroes need to be flashy like in the comic books. Heroes can appear in all different forms. Some are college students, mothers, or office workers. Help us to see the value of real faith by serving others in need today. Amen.

Do your feet hurt? Please visit www.faithbookofjesus.com and click on "Community" to share.

To Read Further: Ephesians 6:10-18

GO OFFENSE

Take the helmet of salvation and the sword of the Spirit, which is the word of God.
— EPHESIANS 6:17

Sometimes after work I jump on my bike and ride for eight miles. I wear a bike helmet to protect my head in case I fall. Protecting what's inside my head is what really matters.

Have you ever noticed that every action comes from a thought that begins in your mind? For instance, take the movie *Star Wars*. Anakin doesn't turn into Darth Vader and become Mr. Darkside overnight. No, it's careless mistakes over time that cost him his future.

Which leads me to our last piece of armor, the sword — or should I say lightsaber? Do you want to use your sword for harm or good? If, like Anakin, we choose evil, we will end up hurting ourselves and others in the process. But if we choose to use our swords for good, then we'll go further than we ever imagined.

The sword is the only offensive tool in the armor of God. Every piece of the armor has been designed to defend and protect. Even Obi-Wan understands the importance of the lightsaber. It can cut through any material and deflect bullets and lasers. If you're facing a situation at work or home and you need more peace, faith, or truth, pick up your sword, which is the Word of God, and go on the offensive.

66 99 Donnie, 26, said, "God had to trick me into prayer, but once I gave in, he changed my whole life by giving me a tool that would help [me go on the offensive]."

 Dear Obi-Jesus,
Who are you that you allow us to know the mind of Christ? And beyond that, you let us carry around the Word of God and apply it to our lives. I pray there would be a movement of swords that brings health and healing to advance your kingdom today. Amen.

Do you know what it means to go on the offensive? Please visit www.faithbookofjesus.com and click on "Community" to share.

To Read Further: Hebrews 4:12-13

FIVE LOVE LANGUAGES

God created man [and woman] in his own image. . . . [And] on the seventh day he rested from all his work.
— GENESIS 1:27; 2:2

I find it fascinating that God spent time resting in the Garden of Eden with man and woman.

Maybe it was because Jesus knew that investing quality time in relationship with his created beings was the single most important act he could do. So they rested together.

Over the next few days we're going to study five different ways you can find and rest in Jesus' love. I'm taking the concept of the book *The Five Love Languages* by Gary Chapman and turning it into God's guidebook on what Scripture has to say about accepting Jesus' love for us.

I don't know about you, but when I come home from work, it's nice to see a smiling face. Working hard has its rewards, but even Jesus said, "It is not good for the man to be alone" (Genesis 2:18).

Just as I need money to support myself and pay the bills, I need time with Jesus, family, and friends to feel their love and support.

Try loving on someone today by giving them your time.

❝❞ Phil, 30, said, "I don't want to spend time with my relationships in the wrong priority order (i.e., family getting bumped for people with little significance in the overall scope of life)."

Dear Quality-Time Jesus,
Thank you for making time your top priority. What an incredible blessing it is to rest with the Creator of the universe. Amen.

 What's your love language? Go to www.fivelovelanguages.com/30sec.html to find out.

To Read Further: Genesis 1:27–2:3

TELL EVERYONE

Publish his glorious deeds among the nations. Tell everyone about
the amazing things he does.
— PSALM 96:3 (NLT)

When it comes to using words to express our love toward God and each other, I'm a little biased. I'm a writer. I love using words to encourage others.

What about you? How do you tell someone you love him or her? Do you say it out loud, or do you write it down?

In Psalm 96:3, David can't wait to tell others about the amazing things God has done. If I had to recount all the amazing things the Lord has done for me, the list wouldn't stop for days.

It's important to remember that our family and friends can't read our mind. They don't know why we love them. That's why we tell them. In the book of Joshua, the Israelites were told not to let the words of the Law depart from their mouths. They were told to meditate on it day and night (see Joshua 1:8).

Thankfully we have more than the Law to read today. We have the Old and New Testaments, which are God's love letters written to teach, rebuke, correct, and train us in righteousness (see 2 Timothy 3:16).

" " Caleb, 24, said, "I don't really get stressed out by relationships . . . maybe occasionally bummed out by unmet expectations."

 Dear Tell-Everyone Jesus,
Thank you that you are not shy in expressing your love toward us. Help us to express to our family and friends how much we love, value, and appreciate them in our lives. Amen.

How do you express your love? Please visit www.faithbookofjesus.com and click on "Community" to share.

To Read Further: Psalm 96

DON'T GO TO CHURCH

For we are God's workmanship, created in Christ Jesus to do good works, which God
prepared in advance for us to do.
— EPHESIANS 2:10

Don't Go to Church. That's the slogan of the Faith in Action campaign put together by Outreach, Inc. What an incredible tool for Christians to be the church and make a difference.

Imagine if every church in the United States and the world shut its doors for one weekend to meet the needs of the community. The response would be overwhelming.

When we choose to put the needs of others above ourselves, we serve the greater good. "Church" gets old and buildings collapse. The only things that last are the relationships formed. Your service makes an impact.

Every year North Coast Church in Vista, California (the church I attend), closes weekend services to serve the community. More than seven thousand people went into the community, schools, homes, and parks last year. It was amazing to see what was accomplished.

The last thing Jesus wants is for us to get comfortable in church. Try skipping church this Sunday and instead serve someone in need.

66 99 Ben, 33, said, "Service! . . . Twentysomethings who are connected and involved in ministry stay connected to a church and deepen their faith. If we can find ways to plug twentysomethings into service and also have some 'gatherings' where they receive, then we'll not only be able to help them *stay* involved but also help them foster their own spiritual maturity."

Dear Nonchurchy Jesus,
I confess that I'm not a natural at serving. I'm selfish and usually put my needs before others. Will you please forgive me? Help me to be humble and consider others better than myself, not only looking to my own interests but also to the interests of others. Amen.

If you'd like to sign up for a service project or volunteer your church for a Faith in Action campaign, visit www.putyourfaithinaction.org.

To Read Further: Luke 9:62

HEALING TOUCH

Then the woman, seeing that she could not go unnoticed, came trembling and fell at his feet. In the presence of all the people, she told why she had touched him and how she had been instantly healed.

— LUKE 8:47

The last thing this woman wanted was to be noticed. Why? Because she had an incurable disease, and it was not the kind any woman talks about.

Mark 5:26 says that "she had suffered a great deal under the care of many doctors and had spent all she had, yet instead of getting better she grew worse."

I believe this verse was placed in the Bible to declare healing over those who have been abused at the hands of doctors, husbands, children, pastors, roommates, and even those who will kill to stop the spread of Christianity.

The power of touch is just that—powerful. There are many ways we can touch one life. "If the foot says, 'I am not a part of the body because I am not a hand,' that does not make it any less a part of the body. And if the ear says, 'I am not part of the body because I am not an eye,' would that make it any less a part of the body? . . . If one part suffers, all the parts suffer with it, and if one part is honored, all the parts are glad" (1 Corinthians 12:15-16,26, NLT).

Reach out to Jesus and receive your healing touch today.

66 99 Jennifer, 27, said, "I want to be a sign-language interpreter. I love to sign and want to use that in some way for God."

Dear Healing-Touch Jesus,
I come boldly asking for a healing touch for those who have been abused by the hands of others. I fall on my knees and ask you to bring instant healing in the name of Jesus. Amen.

Do you need a healing touch? Please visit www.faithbookofjesus.com and click on "Community" to share.

To Read Further: Luke 8:40-47

GOOD GIFT, BAD GIFT

Shall we accept good from God, and not trouble?
— JOB 2:10

I just finished watching a great movie called *Facing the Giants*. It's about football and the underdogs. Coach Taylor told his team that no matter if they won or lost, they would give praise to God.

It reminds me of Job 2:10. How many times in your life have you felt the sting of defeat but still got on your knees and cried out to the Lord, saying, "Yet I will praise you!"?

This is a gift.

To praise the Lord in the midst of our struggles is true joy. The power of sin is broken, and we are free. We are no longer held under the power of the Enemy's grasp. In that moment we are lifted higher into Jesus' presence.

God knew what he was doing when he sent his Son to be born as a baby on this earth. He knew what he was doing when Jesus didn't immediately take the throne but instead spent time with people touching and healing them. His power was not taken away when he was crucified on the cross.

Jesus is risen—that's why we celebrate. No matter what we face here on earth, it's nothing compared to the future glory that awaits us. Today, choose to stand in awe, whatever the circumstances.

66 99 Phillip, 22, said it would be bad "not being able to find work."

 Dear Gift-Giving Jesus,
Where would we be without the trials and sufferings that make us better people?
Help us to see the good gifts even when the giants get too big and we can only see the bad. Amen.

 How do you accept the bad from Jesus? Please visit www.faithbookofjesus .com and click on "Community" to share.

To Read Further: Job 2:9-10

WHAT'S YOUR THING?

Now a man came up to Jesus and asked, "Teacher, what good thing must I do to get eternal life?"
— MATTHEW 19:16

Jesus was the perfect Teacher. He had students and followers who yearned for his knowledge. People came from surrounding cities to hear him speak. There was something different about this man they called Teacher.

Matthew 19 says that a man came up to Jesus and asked him what he needed to do to get into heaven. Because Jesus knew his heart, he used the opportunity to teach his students along with this rich young man. He said, "If you want to be perfect, go, sell your possessions and give to the poor, and you will have treasure in heaven. Then come, follow me" (Matthew 19:21).

Could there be a reason Jesus asked this man to do the one thing he could not do? In the same way Jesus knows our hearts and what we are truly capable of. I wonder what your thing is? Mine is pride.

It's hard to let go of what I want and what I think I need. I recently realized it goes even deeper to my childhood (that's what therapists are for). When I don't feel loved, I start acting out and become proud. Just turn on an episode of *The Real World* and you'll know what I'm talking about.

Next time we find ourselves face-to-face with Jesus in a teaching moment, let's ask him to help us let go so we can follow him today.

66 99   Sarah, 24, said, "I homeschool four of my cousins I am helping to raise. More than anything I just want Jesus glorified. It's not what I was expecting, but it's rewarding."

Dear Perfect-Teacher Jesus,
Please give us a teachable spirit so we can learn what things we're holding back. Thank you for seeing our hearts and knowing what we need. You're the perfect Teacher. Amen.

What's your one thing? Please visit www.faithbookofjesus.com and click on "Community" to share.

To Read Further: Matthew 19:16-21

STUDY HALL

Do not conform any longer to the pattern of this world, but be transformed by the renewing of your mind. Then you will be able to test and approve what God's will is — his good, pleasing and perfect will.

— ROMANS 12:2

We've established that God is our Teacher. Today let's take our books and head to study hall so we can evaluate and act accordingly when testing time comes.

Here are three ways to respond to a teaching moment:

1. **Are we being disobedient?** Are we overstepping biblical principles that God has placed in our lives to protect us?
2. **Is God preparing us?** I recently read the book *Secrets of the Vine* by Bruce Wilkinson, and he mentioned three different teaching moments, one being about pruning. Sometimes God is preparing us for the future, and he does so by cutting off the parts that might hinder any future glory (see John 15:1-5).
3. **Is there a lesson to be learned?** Maybe God is trying to get your attention to help you understand that he has something better. This is your chance to listen up and pay attention in class.

Teaching moments are difficult no matter which type you're dealing with. Disobedience sucks. Giving up our pride to follow Jesus is never easy. The pruning process can sometimes be painful, but it's also rewarding. As students, we can take full advantage of Jesus and learn from his Word daily. When testing time comes (and it will), we'll know what to do and how to pass that stupid test. Amen?

66 99 Hannah, 18, said, "I am a student. After undergraduate school (for theology and catechetic), I would like to study at Gallaudet University for graduate school and then work with the Catholic Church and the deaf."

Dear Studious Jesus,
As we spend time with you in study hall, help us to test and approve what your will really is. Thank you for showing us just a couple of options of how to do that today. Amen.

Which lessons are you learning today? Please visit www.faithbookofjesus.com and click on "Community" to share.

To Read Further: Romans 12:1-3

POP QUIZ

Don't worry about anything; instead, pray about everything. Tell God what you need, and thank him for all he has done.
— PHILIPPIANS 4:6 (NLT)

If the words "pop quiz" cause your blood pressure to rise, might I suggest you write down the correct answers to the multiple-choice questions listed below. The Bible verse or *right answer* will help you be prepared next time you come across a trial. Got your pen ready?

Question #1 — What should you do when you feel like asking God, "Where the heck are you?"

    a. Tell God how you really feel; it's not like he cares anyway.

    b. Ask all your friends how you should handle the situation, and then ask God.

    c. *Read Romans 10:11, "Anyone who trusts in [the Lord] will never be put to shame."*

Question #2 — Surprise! How should you react when a trial happens and causes you to stress and worry?

    a. Freak out and dial 9-1-1.

    b. Tell everyone you see that day that you are really stressed out.

    c. *Read Isaiah 30:15, "In repentance and rest is your salvation, in quietness and trust is your strength."*

Question #3 — What should you do when someone has unexpectedly wronged you?

    a. Take revenge. Nobody likes a pushover.

    b. Call your mom.

    c. *Read Isaiah 57:15, which says that God will "restore the crushed spirit of the humble and revive the courage of those with repentant hearts"* (NLT).

I hope this quiz (as silly as it may seem) helps prepare you for life's little surprises.

66 99 Chad, 25, said, "I see people not succeeding and not living up to their fullest, and I hate not being able to do anything about it."

 Dear Pop-Quiz Jesus,
Thank you that nothing catches you by surprise. Help us to stay calm and pray through each insta-trial we come across, even if it's for others and not ourselves. Amen.

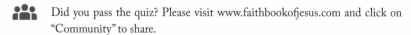 Did you pass the quiz? Please visit www.faithbookofjesus.com and click on "Community" to share.

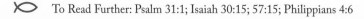 To Read Further: Psalm 31:1; Isaiah 30:15; 57:15; Philippians 4:6

TRUE COLORS

You know that under pressure, your faith-life is forced into the open and shows its true colors. So don't try to get out of anything prematurely. Let it do its work so you become mature and well-developed, not deficient in any way.

— JAMES 1:3-4 (MSG)

No matter how big or small the test, it always reveals my true colors. Do I freak out and stress about every little detail, or do I learn how to trust Jesus and stay calm? L. B. Cowman said, "The prison became a palace [for Paul], with its corridors resounding with shouts of triumphant praise and joy."[27]

How in the world do I do that? There have been a few instances in my life when I have not had skin on my hands, feet, and face due to eczema. My true colors were flying all over the place. I had to be homeschooled again. Red. I didn't get to go to prom. Orange. I didn't have my first kiss until I was nineteen. Yellow. I think you get the point.

The great thing about Jesus is he doesn't allow trials for no reason. He knows the pressure will force our faith to grow. He's not afraid of our colors—and wants to help us show our true colors. Jesus uses our own personal prisons (work, home, school, our bank account, fill in the blank) to move us from prisoner to palace guard—like Paul—if we'll let him. Let's remember that the next time we find ourselves in a teaching moment.

❝❞   Sara, 24, said, "Don't just deal with the surface struggles and trials and frustrations; get to the heart of the issue."

   Dear True-Colors Jesus,
You see our true colors even before we show them. Show us the heart of the issue—our maturity. If we need wisdom, may we ask so we are well-developed and not deficient in any way. Amen.

👥   What's your true color? For a fun color test, go to www.viewzone.com/luscher .html.

✦   To Read Further: James 1:2-5

GRADUATION TIME

It is finished!
— REVELATION 21:6 (NLT)

Everyone loves a big finale. The end of something is the promise of a new beginning. It's always a great relief to know we have mastered our teaching moment. We can move on to bigger and better things.

I'll never forget the day I read those three words: "It is finished!" It was December 28, 1998, and I had just been through the toughest year of my life.

I was only fifteen and was supposed to be starting my sophomore year in high school. As far as I was concerned, my life was over. When I read that verse, I took it as God literally telling me, "It *was* finished!" No more suffering.

Maybe you need to hear those three little words. Today, don't be afraid. It says three times in Scripture that if we share in the sufferings of Jesus, we will also share in his glory (see Romans 8:17; 2 Corinthians 1:7; 1 Peter 5:1).

Imagine the future glory that awaits us in heaven (the final graduation day). "Blessed is the man who perseveres under trial, because when he has stood the test, he will receive the crown of life that God has promised to those who love him" (James 1:12).

❝❞ Angel, 32, said, "I am in college at thirty-two, and I am not sure what I will do after."

Dear It-Is-Finished Jesus,
I can't wait to reach final graduation. In the meantime, help us to celebrate life's smaller graduation days from finishing school, finding a mate, and discovering our purpose. Amen.

When is your next graduation? Please visit www.faithbookofjesus.com and click on "Community" to share.

To Read Further: Revelation 21:5-7

WHAT DRIVES YOU?

If you carefully observe all these commands I am giving you to follow—to love the LORD your God, to walk in all his ways and to hold fast to him—then the LORD will drive out all these nations before you.

— DEUTERONOMY 11:22-23

What drives your life? Is it food, money, your job, or maybe relationships? Today's devotional focuses on what fuels your worship. Your worship shows others what really drives your life.

I like to use a Ferrari to represent how we worship because of what it can do. A Ferrari can drive very, very fast (and it's also easy to worship). The fancier the car, the faster and farther it can go. For us, the more sensitive we are to spiritual matters, the further we can go in our walk with God. Understanding his leading doesn't need to be long and tedious but fast and furious.

And if that weren't enough, as we begin to fuel our lives by worshipping Jesus and getting to know him, we'll go very far (see Deuteronomy 11:22-23).

For years I was driving in first gear, hoping to someday get the chance to do something meaningful. I wrote in my journal every day pouring out my heart to Jesus. I never thought it would turn into a book that could encourage hundreds of thousands of people.

What about you? Let worship be a driving force in your life today. The more time you spend worshipping Jesus, the more he can show you how to drive fast and go far with him.

66 99 Emily, 18, said, "I would like to know more about reading the Bible. Sometimes, it can be intimidating to do all on your own. When you feel that God is presenting more than one path for you to follow, how do you choose?"

Dear Red-Ferrari Jesus,
Help us to consider what is fueling our lives. Are we worshipping you first, or are we driving our Ferrari as far and as fast as we can away from you? Amen.

What drives your life? Please visit www.faithbookofjesus.com and click on "Community" to share.

To Read Further: Deuteronomy 11:22-32

AT YOUR COMMAND

And Peter answered Him and said, "Lord, if it is You, command me to come to You on the water."

— MATTHEW 14:28 (NKJV)

Sometimes we please people because we don't want to rock the boat. Letting others down can be excruciating, especially if their influence means something. It's easier to say "yes" and go with the flow than break the tide of people's expectations of you. Have you noticed it's sometimes easier to make new friends? They don't judge you based on the old you!

When Peter saw Jesus walking on water, he didn't care about anyone else; he just wanted to please Jesus. Peter asked Jesus to command him to get out of the boat. Jesus answered and commanded him to come. And when Peter had come down out of the boat, he walked on the water toward Jesus (see Matthew 14:29).

I'm sure Peter wanted to boast about his walking-on-water experience. Peter was the bold one, always getting ahead of himself. I can relate to Peter. I often find myself getting impatient and desiring more out of life. Yes, please.

Are we driving our boats around in the harbor waiting for a chance to do something dangerous and exciting like Peter? It's easier for Jesus to steer a willing vessel than an anchored one. If we truly desire to please Jesus and get a little dirty, then let's ask him to command us, too. We might find ourselves walking on the water next to Jesus.

❝❞ Jennie, 27, said, "The guys call me 'Smiley' at work, and I've been told I'm good for morale. I may never save the world, but if I can lift someone's spirits for a moment, that just may be good enough."

✋ *Dear At-Your-Command Jesus,*
I confess that I have been afraid to come and join you on the water. I let my many responsibilities at the office, at home, and in life stop me from driving my boat into the open sea. Please help me to trust you completely each and every day. Amen.

👥 Do you trust Jesus enough to follow him out of the boat? Please visit www .faithbookofjesus.com and click on "Community" to share.

✝ To Read Further: Matthew 14:22-29

RIDIN' DIRTY

Seek first his kingdom and his righteousness, and all these things will be given to you as well.

— MATTHEW 6:33

Oftentimes, our time and money control what we eat, how much we spend, when we're going to get married and have a family, and when we'll retire. As I mentioned a few weeks back, the easiest way to see what's controlling you is to take a look at your calendar and your bank account.

How much room for change does your clean and perfect life leave? And the mystery of the Holy Spirit?

It's easy to get stuck in responsibility and never venture outside to the realm of possibilities. Jesus has no problem allowing unfortunate circumstances in our life to get us dirty if it brings our attention back to him.

Today if you feel rushed in life, work, school, and relationships, why not slow down and take a ride with God? Don't wait for Jesus to find you when you're in trouble. A spiritual life isn't always a dirty life. It can be fun, challenging, and exhilarating.

Think of it like this: Your spiritual life is like riding in the sidecar of a motorcycle. Staying closely connected with Jesus daily and putting him first will help you. The next time you experience a speed bump, roadblock, flat fire, or engine failure, you won't get caught ridin' dirty.

66 99 Lee, 26, said, "We need to practice changing our mind-set of judging someone (especially ourselves) by the clothes, car, or career they have."

Dear Copilot Jesus,
I struggle for control of my life daily—where I eat, live, work, and worship. Help me to seek you first and have fun ridin' shotgun whether I'm in a sidecar or a smokin' hot car. Amen.

How are you ridin' dirty? Please visit www.faithbookofjesus.com and click on "Community" to share.

To Read Further: Matthew 6:28-34

DRIVING MISS TAMAR

About three months later Judah was told, "Your daughter-in-law Tamar is guilty of prostitution, and as a result she is now pregnant." Judah said, "Bring her out and have her burned to death!"

— GENESIS 38:24

One of the most bizarre stories in the Bible is about Tamar. Really, you should read the whole thing sometime.

Judah (an Israelite) found a wife—Tamar (also an Israelite)—for his son Er. Because of Er's wickedness, Jesus executed him. Talk about the original gangsta! He meant business. Next, Judah gave Tamar to his son Onan. Now here's where the bizarre part of the story plays out. It was customary during that time for a widow to marry the next brother in line. That was Onan. His responsibility was to get her pregnant to carry on his dead brother's lineage.

But Onan, also a wicked man, thought he was crafty, and every time he had sex with Tamar, he spilled his semen on the ground (see Genesis 38:9). He died. Surprise, surprise! The youngest son, Shelah, was too young to marry Tamar, so Judah sent her home to live at her father's house (see verse 11).

Tamar lived the life of a widow for a long time. Many years later, Tamar heard that Judah was in town shearing his sheep, so she dressed up as a prostitute, slept with him, got pregnant, and continued the family line. Even more bizarre, right?

Like the reality shows of our time, Tamar's fifteen minutes of fame in the Bible actually landed her in the lineage of Jesus (see Ruth 4:12). We'll never know why God chose to put this story in the Bible, but doesn't that comfort you about *your* family? You may think your family is pretty screwed up, but don't stop praying. You never know where they might end up someday.

66 99 Esther, 28, said, "My favorite Bible verse is Proverbs 3:27, which says, 'Do not withhold good from those who deserve it [no matter how bizarre they really are], when it is in your power to act.'"

Dear Bizarre-Working Jesus,
Please provide for us even when those in power withhold the good we deserve. Show us how to keep driving so we can be the ones to make an impact today. Amen.

Are you waiting for something? Please visit www.faithbookofjesus.com and click on "Community" to share.

To Read Further: Genesis 38

SUNDAY DRIVING

Surely goodness and lovingkindness will follow me all the days of my life.
— PSALM 23:6 (NASB)

After facing tough times, how easy is it to settle and get comfortable? Rest could be for survival purposes. Or we could just be tired and need a place of safety. That's where a Sunday drive could help. Sometimes we need to get away and take a drive.

Jonah needed to get away. Instead of taking a drive, he ran away from God. Most of us know him as the man who got swallowed by a whale. But what you may not know is the reason *why* he ended up there in the first place.

Jonah was having a hard time obeying God. God wanted him to travel to the city of Nineveh to share God's love with the people. But, Jonah thought he could run away and get out of this particular assignment. After being spit up by the whale, Jonah grudgingly went to Nineveh. Afterward, he sat down underneath a bush to sulk. Let's just say there was no Sunday drive that day.

The Bible says, "Jonah was greatly displeased and became angry" (Jonah 4:1). He knew how wicked the people of Nineveh were, and he resented the fact that God wanted to use him to save the city. Jonah's anger caused him to see only his selfish pride instead of caring for the needs of others.

There may be special circumstances in your life that God has asked you to fulfill, and you may not be too excited about that. Jump into your car and take a drive with God. Hash it out. Don't let your anger gain control of you and cause you to sin (see Psalm 4:4). Today's drive could not only save your life but the lives of other people as well.

66 99 Jessica, 23, said, "I'm an accounting clerk at a Chevrolet dealership. I also took over the cashier/reception duties because that chick quit. I wish I had a job where I could be proud of my work product and feel like I was making a difference."

 Dear Sunday-Drive Jesus,
Help us to be obedient and go where you want us to go so that goodness and loving-kindness can follow us all the days of our lives. Amen.

Do you need a Sunday drive? Please visit www.faithbookofjesus.com and click on "Community" to share.

To Read Further: Jonah 1:1-6

WE'RE SELFISH

Do nothing out of selfish ambition or vain conceit, but in humility consider others better than yourselves.

— PHILIPPIANS 2:3

Everyone is selfish. Being confident in who you are is not a bad thing. In fact, most of us would probably say that we are *good* people. But we shouldn't judge ourselves based on how "good" or "selfish" we are. The real test of selfishness ends with ourselves and begins with focusing on others.

It is not a natural response to put others first. Instead of thinking of selflessness as a grand gesture, think of it this way: When work and school overwhelm and overload you, take a few minutes to make a phone call to a hurting friend. Stop by your parents' house to give them a hug or tell them you love them. Maybe a younger sibling who looks up to you could benefit from playing a game or two.

My roommates tell me I'm being selfish when I come home and go straight to my room. It's not that I don't want to see them; I just know how much work I need to finish.

Focusing on others for a few minutes a day will enhance our quality of life. I'm guessing it's in the Bible for a reason. The least we can do is obey!

66 99 Adam, 29, said, "I am stressed out by the lack of sleep I get because I get up early to run or walk the dogs and stay up late (occasionally all night) to finish homework. By the time the weekend comes, I don't want to do anything or see anyone."

Dear Selfless Jesus,
Help us choose not to be selfish, but instead be ready and willing to help others. Thank you for giving us the ability to look not only at our interests but the interests of others. Amen.

Are you selfish? Please visit www.faithbookofjesus.com and click on "Community" to share.

To Read Further: Philippians 2:1-4

YOUR GIFTS

Each one should use whatever gift he has received to serve others, faithfully administering God's grace in its various forms.
— 1 PETER 4:10

Everyone has gifts. It says so in the Bible. We all have something to give.

We—every one of us—are called to faithfully use whatever gifts we may have to administer God's grace. If you're curious what the Bible says about these gifts, consider an in-depth reading of Romans 12 and 1 Corinthians 12.

One of my favorite Bible verses that keeps me in check whenever I'm being selfish with my time, money, and gifts is Matthew 20:28: "For even the Son of Man came not to be served but to serve others and to give his life as a ransom for many" (NLT).

Jesus' life is a great example. He was a man who gave out of his giftedness. Wherever he went, he was called Good Teacher. He had compassion on others and healed the sick. He even gave people bread to eat so that they wouldn't go away hungry.

You may have the gift of serving others. It could be offering someone a drink of water on a hot day or opening up your home to someone who is unemployed and letting them crash on your couch for a few weeks. Whatever it is, we should feel blessed to use our gifts to serve the needs of others. We all have something to give. How will you serve others today? "Now you have every spiritual gift you need as you eagerly wait for the return of our Lord Jesus Christ" (1 Corinthians 1:7, NLT).

66 99 Laine, 27, said, "We're such a rich country, and yet we fritter away what Jesus has given us. Just imagine if we all worked as the hands and feet of Christ instead of working to pay our car payments. I have multiple friends who have multiple jobs to make ends meet or change jobs for more pay . . . to fit in with our peers and the glamorous girls of Hollywood (as if we have their genetics and their paychecks!)."

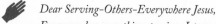

Dear Serving-Others-Everywhere Jesus,
Everyone has something to give. I pray that you show each of us what our individual gifts are. Help us to be faithful to administer those gifts to others in order to make this world a better place instead of chasing after the glamour of Hollywood. Amen.

Are you a giving person? Please visit www.faithbookofjesus.com and click on "Community" to share.

To Read Further: Romans 12; 1 Corinthians 12

YOUR REWARD

His master replied, "Well done, good and faithful servant! You have been faithful with a few things; I will put you in charge of many things. Come and share your master's happiness!"
— MATTHEW 25:23

If you were to count how many times you have been told "good job," what would the count be? Would it be high or low?

Some people are hard workers by nature. They enjoy finishing a job well. I don't know about you, but I like hearing "Good job!" Others enjoy assisting and facilitating work that needs to be done but don't thrive in the leader's position.

Yesterday we read that everyone has gifts and we are called to use them. Looking at Matthew 25:23, we see our reward.

In today's faltering economy the only things we can count on are higher gas prices and more job layoffs. And that's nothing to look forward to. I'd like to know that if I put in a hard day's work, I'm going to be rewarded; that if I take the time to make it through college, a job will be waiting for me.

The kingdom of God is set up with a reward system. Serving Jesus has its perks. There will be rewards that pay out in this lifetime and the next. Choosing holiness instead of worldliness will pay out in ways you could never imagine. At the end of your life, when you stand before God and he asks what you have to show for the life he gave you, what will you say to him? I hope and pray Jesus tells me, "Well done, good and faithful servant!"

66 99 Michael, 25, said, "What stresses me out about my family is that I will never be a success in their eyes, that I will never be able to find one [a significant other] whom I love who loves me back the same way."

 Dear Our-Reward Jesus,
Help us not to tire of doing what is good because we know that at just the right time we will reap a harvest of blessing if we don't give up. Amen.

Are you waiting for your reward? Please visit www.faithbookofjesus.com and click on "Community" to share.

To Read Further: Matthew 25:14-30

BORED-AGAIN CHRISTIAN

For everyone who exalts himself will be humbled, and he who humbles himself will be exalted.

— LUKE 14:11

Each of the four Gospels mentions at least once that if we want to be first, we must be last. For most of us, that is too difficult to fathom.

Every day I allow a little road rage, the corporate ladder, or my own insecurities to keep me from humbling myself before Jesus. It isn't until I read verses like Luke 14:11 that I even think about humility. I may be bored with my current circumstances, but that doesn't mean I'm humble and content. My favorite example on humility is found in Luke 14:8-11:

> When someone invites you to a wedding feast, do not take the place of honor, for a person more distinguished than you may have been invited. If so, the host who invited both of you will come and say to you, "Give this man your seat." Then, humiliated, you will have to take the least important place. But when you are invited, take the lowest place, so that when your host comes, he will say to you, "Friend, move up to a better place." Then you will be honored in the presence of all your fellow guests. For everyone who exalts himself will be humbled, and he who humbles himself will be exalted.

Giving up the bored-again Christian lifestyle is tough. But we can begin by praising God and being his guest of honor. Sometimes it just comes down to patience and being content with where you're at. Life doesn't start when you get the boyfriend or the job of your dreams. Life starts now.

 Erick, 22, said, "Sometimes trust is a factor. It's hard to trust when in the back of your mind you don't trust yourself."

 Dear Exalted Jesus,
Please forgive us when we get bored and don't put you and others first. Give us the trust we need to get past our own insecurities and serve others. Amen.

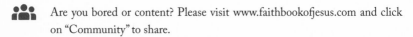 Are you bored or content? Please visit www.faithbookofjesus.com and click on "Community" to share.

To Read Further: Luke 14:8-11

YOUR WITNESS

On that day a great persecution broke out against the church at Jerusalem, and all except the apostles were scattered throughout Judea and Samaria.

— ACTS 8:1

The only way to put persecution into perspective is by understanding why Jesus allows persecution in the first place. Why did believers scatter after Stephen was stoned to death? (Hint: Read Week 27 // Wednesday • page 164.) The answer is pretty simple.

Everyone is a witness. Whether you are representing yourself or Jesus in you, you are a witness for him. In Acts 8:1, we find that the Jews did not want to leave their comfy town of Jerusalem. They were afraid and naive.

The Jews thought Jesus was coming back right away. Without even realizing it, the disciples were hoarding the most important gift that anyone could receive—the gift of salvation.

How could the believers—the ones who saw Jesus perform miracles, be crucified, and rise on the third day—get away with staying put in Jerusalem? They didn't. It says in Acts 1:8, "You will be my witnesses in Jerusalem, and in all Judea and Samaria, and to the ends of the earth." After the death of Jesus, the disciples needed to leave the upper room in order for the message of salvation to spread to Judea, Samaria, and the rest of the world.

Don't wait for persecution before taking your witness to the ends of the earth. Do it today!

66 99 Emanuel, 26, said, "I have no idea what my witness is. I have been trying to find out why I was given a second chance at life after an accident. All I can do is try not to make those same mistakes twice, even though I usually do."

Dear Can-I-Get-a-Witness? Jesus,
Some of us may not know how to be witnesses yet. We need your faith and courage to keep us moving even when life makes no sense and we'd rather stay put. Amen.

How are you using your witness? Please visit www.faithbookofjesus.com and click on "Community" to share.

To Read Further: Acts 8:1-3

KEEP YOUR MOUTH SHUT

Moses spoke to the people: "Don't be afraid. Stand firm and watch GOD do his work of salvation for you today. Take a good look at the Egyptians today for you're never going to see them again. GOD will fight the battle for you. And you? You keep your mouths shut!"

— EXODUS 14:13-14 (MSG)

When you face the impossible, do you start talkin' smack and say, "Game on!"? Or do you get out fast? Learning how to stand firm in faith requires effort because we're on a mission. The Israelites and Egyptians were in the midst of an impossible mission. The score was Egypt four hundred, Israel zero. Before Israel was about to score its first major points, the Egyptians upped their game and rolled out with chariots.

"Oh crap!" the Israelites probably said. They were freaked out. After living comfortably in Egypt as slaves (well, not quite *comfortably*), they were forced out into the open. "Was it because there were no graves in Egypt that you brought us to the desert to die? . . . It would have been better for us to serve the Egyptians than to die in the desert!" (Exodus 14:11-12).

Terrified, Moses told them to shut their mouths. Sometimes we need to shut ours, too. Drama happens when we start complaining instead of staying put. "Stand firm and you will see the deliverance the LORD will bring you today. The Egyptians you see today you will never see again. The LORD will fight for you; you need only to be still" (verses 13-14).

Today, as you go about your life, be careful how you respond. If you just keep your mouth shut and stay put, Jesus can come and deliver you.

66 99 Joshua, 24, said of his mission, "I am a U.S. Marine. It has its moments, but it is a good fit."

Dear Mouthful Jesus,
It's hard not to curse when we're trapped. Give us the faith to keep our mouths shut while you annihilate the competition. Forgive us for taking your name in vain.
Amen.

What did you say today when you should've kept your mouth shut? Please visit www.faithbookofjesus.com and click on "Community" to share.

To Read Further: Exodus 14

KEEP PRESSING ON

Let us acknowledge the Lord; let us press on to acknowledge him. As surely as the sun rises, he will appear; he will come to us like the winter rains, like the spring rains that water the earth.

— HOSEA 6:3

When a child falls, he or she usually runs crying to Mom or Dad, wanting someone to acknowledge the pain.

No one likes to fall, yet we all do it. It's nice to know that we have a heavenly Father who is waiting with open arms to catch us when we fall. But what happens when we're pushed down or jump? The fall from grace can be quite embarrassing and can sometimes cause major damage.

What we thought was a sure thing turned out to be misleading, or what we had hoped would fill us up has left us empty.

This is where pressing on and exercising faith are important. We can't quit after the first fall. We have to get back up again. The Enemy wants us to believe we are all failures, that Jesus can't use broken people. Well, I'm here to tell you he can and he does!

Keep pressing on. Press on toward all the things Jesus has for you. Press on even when you feel your fall from grace was just too far. Acknowledge Jesus in the midst of your pain, and he will meet you there.

66 99 David, 25, said, "When people try to live vicariously through you or direct your life without respect to your ability and beliefs, it causes me to stop pressing on."

Dear Pressing-On Jesus,
We're not perfect, and we need help sometimes. May we press into you each and every day — not just when we're stuck. Help us to forget the past and strain toward what is ahead. Amen.

Do you need help pressing on? Please visit www.faithbookofjesus.com and click on "Community" to share.

To Read Further: Philippians 3:12-14

HOLD ON

Let us hold unswervingly to the hope we profess, for he who promised is faithful.
— HEBREWS 10:23

I took my brother's dog for a walk tonight, and as I was holding on to the leash, I wondered what it is that I am really holding on to . . .

As a twentysomething, I usually hold on to work, relationships, body image, and the fact that I'm still single. I love my job. I love my friends. I hate my body. I wish I had a boyfriend. Forget a boyfriend—I want a husband.

What do you hold on to that keeps you from pressing on and staying in the game? What does it look like to actually hold on to faith? How do we hold on to something we can't see?

When you're not sure where Jesus is leading you (I hate this sometimes), keep holding on. Don't let go of the rope because you won't go anywhere at all.

I'm going to keep holding on to the rope that is Jesus, reach out to others while I'm waiting, and hope for the day when I finally get to say the famous words "I do." What will you hold on and wait for?

" Adam, 22, said, "I don't really know my specific purpose. I've always been good at reaching out to people. I've already done a devotional on priorities in life in high school, but I want to know more."

Dear Holding-On-to-Us Jesus,
Help me to never cut so much slack in the rope that I stop climbing. No matter if I fall or if someone pushes me, I choose to hold on to you today. Amen.

Do you need help holding on? Please visit www.faithbookofjesus.com and click on "Community" to share.

To Read Further: Hebrews 10:22-25

KEEP THE FAITH

He who is faithful in a very little thing is faithful also in much; and he who is unrighteous in a very little thing is unrighteous also in much.

— LUKE 16:10 (NASB)

It's hard for me to think of faithfulness as a small matter. Proverbs 29:18 says that if people lack vision, they perish. Solomon wrote that for us because we need vision and the faith to keep at it. Simply knowing that tomorrow is a new day isn't enough because we need vision.

We need to take responsibility with whatever visions Jesus puts on our hearts so when he calls us into greater faith, we'll be ready for greater responsibility. That could mean a new degree, a better job, a spouse, or money to pay off debt.

Luke 16:10 says that if you are faithful in small matters, you will be faithful with more. This translates for me as refusing to allow a lack of contentment in my singleness to knock me out of my spot in the kingdom. Or not eating that extra piece of cheesecake because I'm trying to love my body and watch my weight.

It's great that God has given us the freedom to have faith that can handle more responsibility, but if you're like me (human and fearful), it's easier to live in the moment. Instead of worrying that Jesus won't come through with our reward, keep the faith.

 Adrienne, 23, said, "I'm in school right now. I'm almost out, my last semester. And I'm about to get out in the real world. It's scary."

 Dear Keep-the-Faith Jesus,
Some of us are about to graduate, and others are still praying for a better job. Help us to keep the faith in the small matters so we can move on to bigger and better things when the time is right. Amen.

 Are you keeping the faith? Please visit www.faithbookofjesus.com and click on "Community" to share.

To Read Further: Luke 16:10-14

UNDER THE INFLUENCE

By their fruit you will recognize them. Do people pick grapes from thornbushes, or figs from thistles?

— MATTHEW 7:16

Most twentysomethings know what it means to be under the influence. How about under the influence of the Spirit? The Bible says that by our fruit people will recognize us. Yes, I said fruit. The Bible is very clear on what it looks like, and it has nothing to do with being drunk.

There are oranges and apples and lemons and pears. Well, actually it looks more like this: "But the fruit of the Spirit is love, joy, peace, patience, kindness, goodness, faithfulness, gentleness and self-control. Against such things there is no law" (Galatians 5:22-23).

When you are living under the influence of the Holy Spirit, your life will produce love, joy, and peace. You're not green with envy or drunk with impatience but are instead living the sugar-baby sweet life.

How do we become ripe? It's as simple as remaining in Jesus. John 15:5 says, "I am the vine; you are the branches. If a man remains in me and I in him, he will bear much fruit; apart from me you can do nothing."

I'd like to grow patience on my own, but it takes a trial to produce that. I can't love my friends and family without support. My faith doesn't grow unless I'm given a vision (see yesterday's devotional). And neither can yours.

Let's taste and see how sweet we can be today when we remain in Jesus.

66 99 Andy, 25, said, "I'd like the ability to forgive and be forgiven."

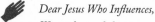 *Dear Jesus Who Influences,*
We need your help to remain close to you, to be under the influence of the Spirit.
Thank you for hearing and listening to our prayers today. Amen.

What are you under the influence of? Please visit www.faithbookofjesus.com and click on "Community" to share.

To Read Further: Galatians 5:22-25

I'VE GOT THE JOY!

Purify me from my sins, and I will be clean; wash me, and I will be whiter than snow. Oh, give me back my joy again; you have broken me—now let me rejoice.

— PSALM 51:7-8 (NLT)

I've got the joy, joy, joy, joy down in my heart. Where? The fruit of unspeakable joy doesn't even compare to the kind of happiness the world has to offer. Yesterday we read about the fruit of the Spirit and how it makes us seem like we're under the influence.

People sing under the influence. King David knew joy. He was the king of Israel and had waited a very long time to sit on the throne. But something happened one spring. Second Samuel 11:1 says, "In the spring, at the time when kings go off to war, David sent Joab out with the king's men and the whole Israelite army. They destroyed the Ammonites and besieged Rabbah. But David remained in Jerusalem."

David might have become too comfortable in his role as king, or maybe he was taking the summer off. I'm sure you can relate. After a semester of school and work, it's nice to take time off.

But it's what David saw on his break that ended his joy. There was a woman. (There always is.) He saw her bathing up on the roof. He saw, he wanted, and he slept with this woman named Bathsheba (see 2 Samuel 11:2-5). After the prophet Nathan confronted David, he begged for forgiveness and was set free. Maybe not everyone can relate to David, but we've all taken something or someone that didn't belong to us. David became a man after God's own heart because he came clean.

You don't have to be a perfect Christian to receive the kind of joy that only Jesus can offer.

I've got the joy. Do you?

66 99 Teresa, 20, said, "I feel my purpose is to help, bring joy, but mainly to listen. Not enough people listen."

Dear Joy-Bringing Jesus,
Confront me when I sin. Give me my joy back when I've stopped singing. Remind me of people from the Bible like David who were just like us. Amen.

Do you need more joy? Please visit www.faithbookofjesus.com and click on "Community" to share.

To Read Further: Psalm 51:7-10

DON'T BE PICKY

But Barnabas took him and brought him to the apostles. He told them how Saul on his journey had seen the Lord and that the Lord had spoken to him, and how in Damascus he had preached fearlessly in the name of Jesus.

— ACTS 9:27

Everyone is picky about something. The apostle Paul knew a little something about being picky. My pastor said Barnabas picked Paul to come to their meetings because God told him to (see Acts 9:27).

This would've been the modern-day equivalent of inviting Osama Bin Laden to speak at your church. Paul made murderous threats against the Christians until his conversion on the road to Damascus (see Acts 9:1). After Jesus confirmed to Barnabas that Paul was now the real deal, the two men became quite the team.

They traveled and spread the news about Jesus wherever they went—*until Paul became picky*. Paul said they couldn't bring Mark, a disciple, with them. Barnabas and Paul had such a sharp disagreement that the two parted ways (see Acts 15:39). Thankfully, the story doesn't end there.

Even though they went their separate ways, both of their ministries doubled. And eventually, Paul and Mark reconciled (see 2 Timothy 4:11). Sometimes the pain of not being picked can cause us to shut down and stop trying. But keep putting yourself out there. If Paul had stayed picky, Mark may not have written his gospel account. Can you imagine only having three gospels (Matthew, Luke, and John)? Seriously.

❝❞ Carl, 23, said, "Oftentimes we are so focused on our needs that we fail to understand the needs of those closest to us. Not only that, but we can't see the needs of society as a whole."

 Dear Not-So-Picky Jesus,
What an amazing story in the Bible about Paul and Barnabas disagreeing over who their travel buddy should be, the man who ended up writing one of the four Gospels of Jesus. If there is an area in my life where I'm being picky, please show me today. Amen.

Are you picky? Please visit www.faithbookofjesus.com and click on "Community" to share.

To Read Further: Acts 9:1-30; 15:36-40; 2 Timothy 4:11

A STRESS MESS!

Don't act thoughtlessly, but understand what the Lord wants you to do.
— EPHESIANS 5:17 (NLT)

If you're a single twentysomething, you may be growing impatient and looking to get married. If you're a thirtysomething, you may be looking for a reason to stay married.

We have a guide that shows us how to live our lives. It's the Bible. Every day that we read the Word and put our faith in Jesus, he shows up. If we pay close attention, we won't miss out or get into a mess.

Your issue may be singleness or staying faithful to the mate you already have. Maybe it's a job situation that you're not sure how to handle. Or maybe you're about to graduate and are unsure of the future.

Don't miss out on the opportunity to learn how to hear and understand Jesus through his Word. If you're struggling, consider joining a small group at your church. The Bible says if we don't neglect meeting together, we will find the encouragement we need.

66 99 Amy, 29, said, "I'm stressed out by the fact that I'm twenty-nine and not married. No kids. A lot of my Christian friends are married with one child and a second on the way. I feel pressured to be married and a success at marriage.... And the kicker is—I don't think getting married right now would be a great idea. I just want to have a place in church, so church has become stressful, and I don't want to go. Being out of regular Christian fellowship causes me more stress! It's a stress mess!"

 Dear No-Stress Jesus,
Paul, the writer of Hebrews, and Amy (above) said it best: We need each other to walk through life. Give us the kind of encouragement we need through the right kind of people in our lives. Amen.

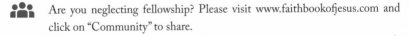 Are you neglecting fellowship? Please visit www.faithbookofjesus.com and click on "Community" to share.

To Read Further: Acts 2:42; Hebrews 3:13; James 5:16

OUT OF THE SHAKER

You are the salt of the earth. But if the salt loses its saltiness, how can it be made salty again? It is no longer good for anything, except to be thrown out and trampled by men.
— MATTHEW 5:13

How can salt be effective if it never leaves the shaker? I'm sure you've met Christians who have lost contact with the outside world. All they do is attend church (at least three times weekly), listen only to Christian music, and have only Christian friends. There's nothing wrong with those things, but avoiding contact with the world because of our own inadequacies is a sin.

That's how the early church started. It's nothing new, really. Sometimes we just get comfortable. The Jews were waiting for Jesus to come back. They weren't comfortable though; they were afraid. They had been filled with the Holy Spirit (see Acts 1:8), but they didn't have the motivation to get out there and change the world. God ended their plans to stay inside the holy huddle. He wanted them to be the salt.

Scattered Salt—"On that day a great persecution broke out against the church at Jerusalem, and all except the apostles were scattered throughout Judea and Samaria" (Acts 8:1).

Seasoned Salt—Jesus didn't want them to stay inside the shaker. He wanted his disciples to be seasoned Christians full of flavor who would go and preach the gospel to the ends of the earth.

Refined Salt—"Therefore go and make disciples of all nations, baptizing them in the name of the Father and of the Son and of the Holy Spirit" (Matthew 28:19). Jesus wanted his disciples to add flavor to the world, and he wants the same thing for us today.

Table Salt—Every day salt is used (as Matthew 5:13 suggests) in the way you talk, at the office, at the dinner table, and with your friends. Whether you feel comfortable or afraid, Jesus said we are the salt of the earth. Ask God how you can add flavor to the world as you go about your business today.

❝❞ Katy, 30, said, "Right now I am venturing [out of the shaker and] into the radio industry, and I love it."

 Dear Salt-Shaking Jesus,
There are people in our lives who need the flavor of Jesus to help preserve them from the drama of this world. Help us to be the kind of salt that is spilled out, seasoned, refined, and table-ready for the world. Amen.

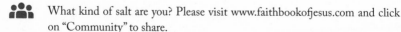 What kind of salt are you? Please visit www.faithbookofjesus.com and click on "Community" to share.

✄ To Read Further: Matthew 5:13-16

YOUR LIFE [REVEALED]

Then the eyes of both of them were opened, and they realized they were naked; so they sewed fig leaves together and made coverings for themselves.
— GENESIS 3:7

Do you know the real you? This is not a trick question. When Adam and Eve sinned, they changed the course of the world forever. We are no longer in paradise. Hiding is now our middle name. To uncover the real you, keep reading.

The First Mask—It all started with Adam and Eve in the Garden of Eden (see Genesis 3:7-11). When they became aware of their nakedness, they covered themselves. And now we cover ourselves with clothes.

I Wear One—Whenever we feel exposed, we wear a mask; it's that simple. You may view me as self-assured, outgoing, and full of life, but what you don't see are the past ten years of intense suffering that make me feel ugly and full of shame. What are you hiding?

Because It's Pretty—It's easier to hide well in our twenties. To fit into the drama of life (are we still in high school?), we cover ourselves with money and more responsibility. Want to learn how to be an authentic follower of Jesus? Take off your pretty mask, read the Word, pray, get into a small group—there's so much we can do.

It's Your Turn—To share your thoughts on the masks we wear, please visit www.faithbookofjesus.com and click on "Community."

66 99 Quimby, 31, said, "I wear three masks: money, drama, dishonesty."

  Dear Real Jesus,
It is my prayer that we could surrender our man-made masks. I'm tired of wearing a mask, but it's much easier than facing the real me. I'm not the only one wearing a mask. Please reveal the reasons why we try to hide and help us to toss our masks aside. Amen.

What mask are you wearing? Please visit www.faithbookofjesus.com and click on "Community" to share.

To Read Further: Genesis 3:7-11

DUMPSTER STORY

Therefore, get rid of all moral filth and the evil that is so prevalent and humbly accept the word planted in you, which can save you.
— JAMES 1:21

When I need to get rid of the bad in my life, I reread James 1:21. Moral filth, as James called it, looks like bitterness, rage, anger, brawling, slander, every form of malice, and filthy language (see Ephesians 4:31; Colossians 3:8).

Getting rid of all those things can be quite painful. Once my symptoms of bitterness over an ex-boyfriend became so painful that I literally drove to a Dumpster and threw away [got rid of] every physical reminder I had of him so I could finally let go. I had never felt so free in all my life. But it took me many years to get to that point.

Humbly accepting God's Word can cause symptoms of depression and anxiety. Doing the right thing often takes more courage than doing the wrong thing. "Above all else, guard your heart, for it is the wellspring of life" (Proverbs 4:23). I had stopped guarding my heart because my ex told me we were going to get married. But the weeks turned into months, which turned into years, and I finally had to say good-bye.

I'm still single and holding on to Jesus. At least I know I did my part. I got rid of the bad. That's my Dumpster story.

❝❞ Shiloh, 35, said, "I want to get rid of my shyness to finish writing my novel and take risks that would further my life, like a better job. Also, I want to find my future husband and have a family."

Dear No-Masking Jesus,
Help us to joyfully get rid of our bad masks instead of painfully surrendering them. May we be confident in your good promises today and every day while we wait. Amen.

Do you have a Dumpster story? Please visit www.faithbookofjesus.com and click on "Community" to share.

To Read Further: James 1:21-25

THE PERFECT MAN

And being found in appearance as a man, [Jesus] humbled himself and became obedient to death—even death on a cross!

— PHILIPPIANS 2:8

Jesus was the perfect man. He wore no masks and demanded no special attention. Instead, Jesus lived to serve others. He could see past the masks others wore and healed them all. Isn't that amazing?

Matthew 4:23 says, "Jesus went throughout Galilee, teaching in their synagogues, preaching the good news of the kingdom, and healing every disease and sickness among the people."

Verses like this make me want to rip off my mask and help others to be free as well. Seriously, right now, I can think of at least four people I said I'd pray for and three others who need my help.

When was the last time you served the needs of others? There are many hurting people wearing masks they don't want to wear. Masks that look like eating disorders; addictions to alcohol, pornography, and food; and depression, anxiety, loneliness, and despair.

Turn to your fellow neighbor who wears a mask and offer him or her the perfect solution. His name is Jesus.

❝❞ Kevin, 28, said, "I should be taking time to address important problems, trying to be intentional instead of just spending money on recreation."

🖐 *Dear Perfect-Man Jesus,*
You chose to wear a crown of thorns for all to see instead of a mask. When I believe I'm the only one who needs healing, remind me to look around and serve the needs of others today. Amen.

👥 What makes Jesus perfect in your life? Please visit www.faithbookofjesus.com and click on "Community" to share.

🐟 To Read Further: Philippians 2:5-8

TILL DEATH DO US PART

So then, since Christ suffered physical pain, you must arm yourselves with the same attitude he had, and be ready to suffer, too.

— 1 PETER 4:1 (NLT)

I'm afraid of dying. I'm afraid of hearing "no" one more time. Why would Jesus deny me, his child, healing when I'm in need?

A few years ago, I had my doctor emergency-paged because a rash (eczema) that started on my finger had spread to my hands and was spreading up my arms. There was absolutely nothing I could do to stop the eczema from destroying my flesh.

My doctor called me back within a few hours and told me, "Renee, there's nothing more I can do for you. We've already done everything possible. What happens when God says 'no'?"

The fear of death forced me to surrender. I got down on my knees with my mom and cried out to Jesus. I told him if he never healed me, I'd still believe in him. I also asked him to help me not be afraid.

Two weeks later, a miracle happened: The rash stopped spreading. The steroids started working (weeks after the dose was done and over with), and three years later I got my hands back, completely.

If you are facing death, Jesus can and will save you. Arm yourself with the same mentality as Jesus and be ready to suffer.

❝❞ Gigi, 28, said, "I guess I am not really afraid of failure. . . . We all fail from time to time, but it makes us who we are."

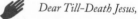 *Dear Till-Death Jesus,*
The road to contentment has a rest stop in the valley of death. Be with those who are on that road right now. Deliver them from evil and keep their foot from slipping. Amen.

What are you afraid of? Please visit www.faithbookofjesus.com and click on "Community" to share.

To Read Further: 1 Peter 4:1-2

REJECTED

He was despised and rejected by men, a man of sorrows, and familiar with suffering. Like one from whom men hide their faces he was despised, and we esteemed him not.

— ISAIAH 53:3

About a year ago, I was getting to know a guy. We had some great conversations, one of which lasted for six hours over the phone. We talked about Jesus, the Bible, ministry, sermons, weekly devotional series, changing the world, and what he was going to cook me for dinner when he flew out to California.

Then twenty-four hours later I found out he had a girlfriend. I felt like a freaking idiot.

This guy mentioned flying across the United States to see me, cooking chicken cordon bleu, and going to Disneyland with me. Being the outgoing person I am, I didn't think to ask, "Hey, do you have a girlfriend?"

Want to know how I found out? His MySpace status said "In a relationship." I was humiliated, and the next day one of the Bible verses in my e-mail was Isaiah 53:3. I felt as if Jesus were reaching his hands through my computer and giving me a hug.

Jesus said to me (and to all of us), "I've been rejected by men. I've been rejected in the worst way. Nothing you could ever experience will be out of the loving grasp of my hands."

❝❞ Josiah, 25, said, "I want to be the best husband, father, and friend I can be. If I feel like I am not measuring up, it really takes a toll on me."

 Dear Jesus Who Was Rejected,
Thank you for your death on the cross. If you hadn't endured this kind of punishment and torture, we wouldn't have direct access to the Father and Holy Spirit. Help us to overcome rejection just as you did by picking up our cross and following hard after you. Amen.

Are you feeling rejected? Please visit www.faithbookofjesus.com and click on "Community" to share.

To Read Further: Isaiah 53:4-5

JESUS, WHO IS HE?

In the beginning was the Word, and the Word was with God, and the Word was God. . . . The Word became flesh and made his dwelling among us. We have seen his glory, the glory of the One and Only, who came from the Father, full of grace and truth.

— JOHN 1:1,14

Jesus Christ is the most famous person in all of history but also the most misunderstood. Most people believe he was a good teacher, but he is more than that. *Jesus is the Son of God and God the Son!*

In the verse above, *Word* is capitalized because it refers to a person: Jesus Christ. In the beginning was *Jesus*, and *Jesus* was with God, and *Jesus* was God. And *Jesus* became flesh and made his dwelling among us. He is totally God and totally man. The primary reason Jesus came to earth was to die on the cross and rise from the dead to pay the penalty for our sins. Now he is in heaven preparing a place for us (see John 14:2).

Let's say there's a record book of our lives being kept in heaven. The front cover is our birth certificate, and the back cover is our death certificate. All the pages in between list everything we've done—the good, the bad, and the forgiven. If we were to be judged based only on the contents of this record book, we'd spend eternity in hell separated from God.

Jesus Christ took all of our sins and paid our debt in full.

❝❞ Travis, 25, said, "I want to show God's love [Jesus] to others."

 Dear Jesus, the Son of God,
Thanks for showing us more of you through your Word. May we go a step further and receive these words as our light and life today. By faith we believe in you. Amen.

 Who do you say Jesus is? Please visit www.faithbookofjesus.com and click on "Community" to share.

✵ To Read Further: 1 John 4:7-21

TWO KEYS

Believe in the Lord Jesus, and you will be saved—you and your household.
— ACTS 16:31

There is only one key that unlocks the door to heaven and eternal life. But before I tell you what that key is, I need to tell you what it's not. There are two false keys that people trust in, which they think will get them into heaven.

The first one is head knowledge—knowing facts about Jesus. Many people believe in Jesus Christ just as they believe in Santa Claus or George Washington. But they don't trust in them as we trust in Jesus.

Even demons believe that Jesus is the Son of God, but they aren't going to heaven. James 2:19 says, "You believe that there is one God. Good! Even the demons believe that—and shudder."

The second false key is temporal faith. Here are some examples: airplane (traveling faith), parent and child (health faith), and a money decision (financial faith). They all have something in common: They are all bound by space and time. They are temporary. Temporal faith will not unlock the door to heaven. *So what is the only key?*

The apostle Paul was asked by the Philippian jailer, "What must I do to be saved?" (Acts 16:30). Believe. Faith is trusting in Jesus Christ alone—and nothing else—for eternal life.

❝❞ Josiah, 25, said, "Trying to meet everyone's expectations and still have time to myself stresses me out."

Dear One-Key Jesus,
Just knowing you is not enough. We need to have faith that you are who you say you are. Thank you for being the key that unlocks the door to eternal life. We look forward to spending eternity with you someday. Amen.

Are you holding the right key? Please visit www.faithbookofjesus.com and click on "Community" to share.

To Read Further: Acts 16:25-40

IT'S YOUR BIRTHDAY

Here I am! I stand at the door and knock. If anyone hears my voice and opens the door, I will come in and eat with him, and he with me.

— REVELATION 3:20

Today we see Jesus standing at the door. He is waiting for us to open the door and receive him as our Lord. Dawson Trotman, the founder of The Navigators, said, "A person is born again when he receives Jesus Christ."[28]

We do this by repenting of our sins. Be willing to turn from anything that is not pleasing to Jesus. Right now he is standing at the door waiting. Accept his gift by praying this prayer today:

> Lord Jesus, I thank you that heaven is a free gift and that I cannot earn it or deserve it. I acknowledge that I am a sinner and cannot save myself. Thank you for coming here to earth to die on the cross for my sins: past, present, and future. I place my trust in you and ask you to come into my heart and life. I repent of all my sins. Please take control of my life and be my Savior and Lord. In Jesus' name I pray. Amen.

Congratulations! Your new life starts today. "If you confess with your mouth, 'Jesus is Lord,' and believe in your heart that God raised him from the dead, you will be saved. For it is with your heart that you believe and are justified, and it is with your mouth that you confess and are saved" (Romans 10:9-10).

66 99 Renee, 27, said, "I remember praying the prayer on my fifth birthday. Being welcomed into the family of God was amazing because I now had two birthdays."

Dear Birthday Jesus,
I know your feet must get so tired because I make you wait all the time. Show everyone how they can have a personal relationship with you by praying the prayer of faith. Amen.

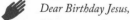 Do you know when your spiritual birthday is? Please visit www.faithbookofjesus.com and click on "Community" to share.

To Read Further: John 1:12-13

FROM DEATH TO LIFE

I tell you the truth, whoever hears my word and believes him who sent me has eternal life and will not be condemned; he has crossed over from death to life.

— JOHN 5:24

From death to life in one grand gesture, Jesus saved us while we were still sinners. He broke the power of death over sin and shame forever.

Whenever I'm afraid, I put my hope in the eternal Word and ask those closest to me to pray for me. Here are two passages I hope will encourage you to choose life today:

"This day I call heaven and earth as witnesses against you that I have set before you life and death, blessings and curses. *Now choose life*, so that you and your children may live and that you may love the LORD your God, listen to his voice, and hold fast to him. For the LORD is your life, and he will give you many years in the land he swore to give to your fathers, Abraham, Isaac and Jacob" (Deuteronomy 30:19-20, emphasis added).

"For I am convinced that neither *death nor life*, neither angels nor demons, neither the present nor the future, nor any powers, neither height nor depth, nor anything else in all creation, will be able to separate us from the love of God that is in Christ Jesus our Lord" (Romans 8:38-39, emphasis added).

❝❞ Matthew, 25, said, "I work at an auto emissions station driving cars all day. I have no idea what life is."

Dear Living Jesus,
Help us to choose life today, and every single day. Bring us out of the valley of the shadow of death so we can spread the good news of Jesus. Amen.

How do you choose life? Please visit www.faithbookofjesus.com and click on "Community" to share.

To Read Further: Deuteronomy 30:19-20; John 5:24; Romans 8:38-39

THE OPPOSITE SEX

Do not fret because of evil men or be envious of those who do wrong.
— PSALM 37:1

I first read this passage when I had the choice between two men. The first was pure evil and made my skin crawl, and the second was a bad boy (who also made my skin crawl, but in a different way).

I didn't listen to prudence when the *evil* man asked me to drinks after work. After one drink, he proceeded to take advantage of me. I wasn't used to attention from the opposite sex, so I went with it. I also never thought I'd have to tell a man "no." Aren't all men gentlemen? (Naive, right?)

That night became the most humiliating night of my life. I was blindsided. He went further physically than I expected him to, and after that night I never wanted to see him again. Unfortunately, I had to see him at work every day. He was the one who sat closest to me. Suddenly, the bad boy downstairs didn't seem so bad.

I charmed my way into his e-mail inbox and his embrace. I didn't want the last guy I had kissed to be a creep. This became the second-worst decision of my life.

I kissed temptation hello and my inhibitions good-bye. I was completely lost in him and didn't want any other man. I told my friends, parents, and church leadership that I needed to take a break from them because I couldn't stop spending time with him. Psalm 37 became a comfort for me in the process of self-discovery and recovery from the power of the opposite sex. If you're struggling with the opposite sex, don't fret about or envy him or her—let Jesus help you through.

66 99 Ryan, 26, wanted to know more on "how to deal and cope with the opposite sex."

 Dear Control-over-the-Opposite-Sex Jesus,
It's amazing the power that Scripture has over the opposite sex—or any problem, for that matter. Help us to realize the healing power that Scripture has over our lives. Amen.

What are your fears of the opposite sex? Please visit www.faithbookofjesus .com and click on "Community" to share.

To Read Further: Psalm 37:1-5

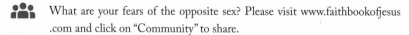

CHUMP CHANGE

Give, and it will be given to you. A good measure, pressed down, shaken together and running over.

— LUKE 6:38

If you're wondering, *How am I going to pay the bills?* or *Will I make it through the next set of layoffs?* read on. Here are three ways to manage your change:

1. **Do Not Worry**—"Therefore I tell you, do not worry about your life, what you will eat or drink; or about your body, what you will wear. Is not life more important than food, and the body more important than clothes? . . . Who of you by worrying can add a single hour to his life?" (Matthew 6:25,27).
2. **Do Not Steal**—"'Will a man rob God? Yet you rob me. But you ask, "How do we rob you?" In tithes and offerings. You are under a curse—the whole nation of you—because you are robbing me. Bring the whole tithe into the storehouse, that there may be food in my house. Test me in this,' says the LORD Almighty, 'and see if I will not throw open the floodgates of heaven and pour out so much blessing that you will not have room enough for it'" (Malachi 3:8-10).
3. **Do Not Reveal**—"But when you give to the needy, do not let your left hand know what your right hand is doing, so that your giving may be in secret. Then your Father, who sees what is done in secret, will reward you" (Matthew 6:3-4).

Today's economy isn't stable, but that doesn't mean our faith in God has to change. Ask God how to help you apply these three principles to your life.

66 99 Chad, 26, emphasized the importance of "learning how to tithe in your twenties, even if you're only making chump change as it seems. If you don't tithe now, you never will."

Dear Chump-Change Jesus,
Show us if there's anything we can do to increase our funds. Help us to be good stewards of our resources, even if we are making chump change. Thank you for always providing for our needs. Amen.

Do you need help with money? Please check out Matt Bell's book *Money, Purpose, Joy* or visit www.navpress.com and search *money* for great resources and helps.

To Read Further: Malachi 3:8-10; Matthew 6:3-4,25-27; Luke 5:24

MORE CREDIT, PLEASE!

May a creditor seize all he has; may strangers plunder the fruits of his labor.
— PSALM 109:11

I searched *creditors* in the Bible and found five references. I searched *money* and found 114 references. It's not surprising that the Bible is full of references relating to our finances. Here are a few verses to keep us in the black:

"'Blessed be God Most High, who delivered your enemies into your hand.' Then Abram gave him a tenth of everything" (Genesis 14:20).

"If you lend money to one of my people among you who is needy, do not be like a moneylender; charge him no interest" (Exodus 22:25).

"Dishonest money dwindles away, but he who gathers money little by little makes it grow" (Proverbs 13:11).

"Whoever loves money never has money enough; whoever loves wealth is never satisfied with his income. This too is meaningless" (Ecclesiastes 5:10).

"Why spend money on what is not bread, and your labor on what does not satisfy? Listen, listen to me, and eat what is good, and your soul will delight in the richest of fare" (Isaiah 55:2).

"No one can serve two masters. Either he will hate the one and love the other, or he will be devoted to the one and despise the other. You cannot serve both God and Money" (Matthew 6:24).

There will always be more bills than money coming in. We serve a God whose resources can never be depleted. Ask him today how to spend within your means so the creditors won't be knocking down your door.

66 99 Derrick, 33, said he fears "creditors becoming impatient with my current monthly payments and pursuing action."

Dear Resourceful Jesus,
What a blessing to learn how to manage our finances from the Bible. Show us, in light of today's economy, how to manage our money well. Amen.

Do you need help managing your money? Please visit www.faithbookofjesus .com and click on "Community" to share.

To Read Further: Matthew 25:14-30

HUMBLE PIE

It is not good to have zeal without knowledge, nor to be hasty and miss the way.

— PROVERBS 19:2

Jesus does not like pride. "Pride goes before destruction, and haughtiness before a fall" (Proverbs 16:18, NLT).

I struggle with pride. Sometimes I want to be the lone ranger, who does things on my own, because—let's face it—I work better alone. I get more work done that way. The only time I stop along the way is if I'm forced to surrender. Nobody likes to eat humble pie.

Thanks be to Jesus. He chose to lead the way and invite others into the process. In the Old Testament, God started by giving the Israelites the Law so they could detect if they were on course. The Law wasn't meant to make them perfect but to help them succeed. In the New Testament, God the Father allowed Jesus to be born on this earth to show us our need for a Savior.

Pride doesn't ask for help. That's why humble pie doesn't taste so good. It's hard to ask for help. But we aren't meant to figure out life alone. That's why Jesus gave us his Word, the Bible, to help us grow in our knowledge of him and not miss the way.

❝❞ Monica, 45, said, "I noticed young people think that the Bible has changed for today's problems. I will quote a Scripture, and they will say, 'Yeah, I know, but if Jesus were talking about that today, he would not feel that way or say that.'"

Dear Humble-Pie Jesus,
I'm so stubborn sometimes. I don't want to surrender my life unless I am forced to. Give me the courage to follow through on my convictions and enjoy my time with you today. Amen.

Is it difficult for you to ask for help? Please visit www.faithbookofjesus.com and click on "Community" to share.

To Read Further: Matthew 5:1-10

THE TRUTH SUCKS

Love does not delight in evil but rejoices with the truth.
— 1 CORINTHIANS 13:6

I'm a woman of action. To say that I'm not shy is an understatement. I never thought I was afraid of conflict until I moved out of my parents' house for good. I'm sure you can relate to roommates from hell.

My roommates were nothing like my family. They didn't keep the place clean, and they liked to come and go at all hours of the night. Since I liked a clean place, I did not tolerate anything out of order. I soon realized that life is not clean and orderly. No matter how much we tried, we couldn't say the truth in love and be considerate of each other. I wish I could've kept my mouth shut to preserve our friendship, but instead I moved out in haste. It took more than a year to repair the damage that had been done.

Streams in the Desert (my favorite devotional) says this: "There are times when doing nothing demands much greater strength than taking action. Maintaining composure is often the best evidence of power."[29]

If you are dealing with a roommate, co-worker, or family member who needs to hear the ugly truth, ask Jesus for help. After all, he is the one who gave us this command: "Love each other. Just as I have loved you" (John 13:34, NLT).

66 99 Dennis, 25, said, "While God's love is very important, I really feel God's truth is just as important. If we were to love others the way Jesus taught us to, that would also mean we would have to tell the truth—even if it sucks."

  Dear Truth-in-Love Jesus,
It's hard to speak the truth in love, especially when we're human, and it sucks some-times. Today if there is someone we haven't been completely honest with, help us to speak up (in love). Amen.

How do you speak the truth in love? Please visit www.faithbookofjesus.com and click on "Community" to share.

✝ To Read Further: Ephesians 4:14-16

PEACEFUL TILL THE END

And teaching them to obey everything I have commanded you. And surely I am with you always, to the very end of the age.
— MATTHEW 28:20

Reaching for my dreams is something I will do as long as I'm alive. How will I find the love of my life? When will I buy a house? Have a family? It seems as if I'm always waiting for something to happen. And always rushing to check each item off my list, only to find there's one more thing to check off.

The Bible says, "You will keep in perfect peace *all* who trust in you, all whose thoughts are fixed on you!" (Isaiah 26:3, NLT, emphasis added). I will be the first to admit how difficult it is to fix my thoughts on Jesus when all I see is a to-do list in front of me.

If Jesus is rest, how come I'm always so stressed? Striving to reach for my dreams keeps me alive, but choosing to focus solely on what I do instead of letting Jesus come through for me causes me anxiety.

I wonder if you're like me: running around trying to fulfill everyone's wishes and fantasies, including your own, so you don't have time to rest in Jesus. He loved us so much that he gave up his life for us so we could find forgiveness and rest from our sins. The least we can do is offer our lives as a sacrifice of praise.

66 99 Stephanie, 27, said, "My greatest fear is wasting my life—not spending it in a way that would honor Jesus."

 Dear Peaceful Jesus,
Today I choose not to feel like a broken record when I come to you with the same problem of unrest. Help me to realize it's okay to take some time out of my busy, fast-paced world to pray. Amen.

Do you have trouble resting in Jesus? Please visit www.faithbookofjesus.com and click on "Community" to share.

To Read Further: Matthew 28:16-20

WHY SO DOWNCAST?

Why are you downcast, O my soul? Why so disturbed within me? Put your hope in God, for I will yet praise him, my Savior and my God.

— PSALM 43:5

Do you feel there are valid reasons to be downcast? The Bible says there are only two reasons. First, if you haven't put your faith in Jesus. Ephesians 1:18 says, "I pray also that the eyes of your heart may be enlightened in order that you may know the hope to which he has called you, the riches of his glorious inheritance in the saints."

This book is meant to help you connect with Jesus every day—which brings me to the second reason: if you have faith in Jesus but continue to live in sin. I struggle with the second. As a single Christian girl, I feel like an outcast. I can no longer hang out with boys alone because I know where it will lead (or where I would like it to lead). This has led to much depression. But sacrificing my desires for the sake of the gospel is worth it.

You may feel that there are a lot more reasons to feel downcast and sorrowful. The loss of a parent, job, or spouse qualifies as a valid reason to be downcast. However, the two reasons listed above are the only true reasons to be downcast because everything else may be brought to Jesus "by prayer and petition, with thanksgiving" (Philippians 4:6).

66 99 Nicole, 28, said, "I am honestly not very religious."

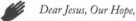 *Dear Jesus, Our Hope,*
I don't want to be downcast if I can help it. Vindicate me and anyone else who is living in sin today. May we be truly repentant and turn around and go the other way today. Amen.

Are you downcast? Please visit www.faithbookofjesus.com and click on "Community" to share.

To Read Further: Psalm 43

ON FOOT

He turned the sea into dry land, they passed through the waters on foot — come, let us rejoice in him.

— PSALM 66:6

I wish I could've been there when the Israelites passed through walls of water. That must have been quite the faith-builder on foot. I've personally experienced such great sorrow that it seems impossible to go any further. I'm sure you can relate to the kind of trembling, terror, anguish, and dismay that happen when you're forced to surrender.

I heard something interesting at church recently. At the point of surrender, Jesus is the only person who saves. If you like the History Channel as my pastor does, then you know that stories of war and surrender typically don't end well. When we surrender to Jesus, he leads us on foot. Isn't that amazing?

We are close to Jesus and his promises in our point of deepest need. We see numerous examples of this in the Bible: the Israelites crossing the Red Sea; Joshua leading the troops across the Jordan (at flood stage); Jacob at Jabbok wrestling with an angel for his life; John on the Isle of Patmos seeing visions of the end and what is to come.

Oh, weary traveler. Are you in need of a comfy sofa and padded shoes? Take comfort in the stories of those believers who have gone before you in faith.

❝❞ Chelsea, 19, said, "I fear people getting desperate and taking their lives as well as the lives of others because they have no hope. This is already happening more and more because people don't have the hope in Christ that he is in control."

 *Dear Jesus on Foot,*
We live in a desperate culture that is searching for hope. Help us to realize the hope that comes from surrendering our lives to you. Amen.

Do you need to surrender to Jesus today? Please visit www.faithbookofjesus .com and click on "Community" to share.

To Read Further: Joshua 3

TIME'S UP

Blessed is the man who perseveres under trial, because when he has stood the test, he will receive the crown of life that God has promised to those who love him.

— JAMES 1:12

I struggle with waiting patiently for Jesus. Sometimes I feel like Jesus is waiting until the very last second to answer my prayers. Or that he's going to let time run out and leave me without an answer.

We are blessed when we are under trial. At first glance, I totally disagree. I never feel blessed when I'm suffering. With Jesus holding the time clock, I usually anticipate how long and wonder "what if." I can't tell you how many anxiety attacks I've had while waiting for Jesus to help me pass the test.

We are blessed when we stand the test. As we persevere under trials, we pass the test. There may be an area where Jesus wants to see growth in our lives, so he temporarily allows suffering. You might be shaking your head right now. If that's you, ask Jesus to reveal your test to you.

The Bible gives us permission to ask Jesus anything. "If any of you lacks wisdom, he should ask God, who gives generously to all without finding fault, and it will be given to him" (James 1:5).

The time is now. Ask Jesus today.

66 99 Paul, 29, said, "My time is spent to glorify God first, be a godly husband, godly father. My purpose and gift in life is customer service and helping others."

Dear Time-Crunch Jesus,
Thank you that we are blessed as we persevere under trials. Help us have the strength to stand the test so that we may receive the crown of life that you have promised to us. Amen.

Do you struggle with waiting for Jesus? Please visit www.faithbookofjesus .com and click on "Community" to share.

To Read Further: James 1:5-12

WHISTLE WHILE YOU WAIT

Be joyful in hope, patient in affliction, faithful in prayer.
— ROMANS 12:12

It's not easy to live joyfully in the midst of hard times. That's when it's the hardest for me because I forget all the wonderful things Jesus has already done in my life.

Paul wrote in Hebrews, "So do not throw away your confidence; it will be richly rewarded. You need to persevere so that when you have done the will of God, you will receive what he has promised" (10:35-36).

I'm tempted the most when I'm waiting. It's a fact: The Enemy does not like me to be joyful in hope, patient in affliction, and faithful in prayer. He tempts my heart to turn to the left and the right (or to turn the clock in my favor).

Praise Jesus that he is the One who makes our path straight (see Proverbs 4:27). Therefore, let us choose to "fix our eyes on Jesus, the author and perfecter of our faith, who for the joy set before him endured the cross, scorning its shame, and sat down at the right hand of the throne of God" (Hebrews 12:2).

Jesus, teach us how to whistle while we wait.

66 99 Melissa, 32, said, "Being a single parent of two can get stressful, especially when the other parent is not involved at all. As a new believer, I had many questions [about] . . . what is right and what is wrong, but I always went to the Bible for answers."

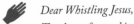
Dear Whistling Jesus,
Thank you for teaching me how to have joy while I wait. I also ask you for the peace of God, which transcends all my understanding, to guard my heart and mind while I wait on you. Amen.

Do you find it difficult to live joyfully in the midst of hard times? Please visit www.faithbookofjesus.com and click on "Community" to share.

To Read Further: Romans 12:9-12

SALVATION IS NEAR

In repentance and rest is your salvation, in quietness and trust is your strength, but you would have none of it.

— ISAIAH 30:15

Throughout the Old Testament we read about the Israelites rebelling against the Lord and then returning back to him.

Passages like this one are cornerstone: "If you return to the LORD, then your brothers and your children will be shown compassion by their captors and will come back to this land, for the LORD your God is gracious and compassionate. He will not turn his face from you if you return to him" (2 Chronicles 30:9).

Because of what Jesus did on the cross, I don't have to wait to repent. I can find rest and strength in the Lord today. That certainly doesn't mean that I don't wrestle with Jesus on a daily basis over my wants and needs (see Psalm 13:2), but it does mean that Jesus provides a way out when I do begin to struggle (see 1 Corinthians 10:13).

The biggest lie the Enemy wants us to believe is that we can't repent, that our lives are too busy. He tries to stop us from coming to the Father and asking for forgiveness. Passages like these remind me salvation is near.

❝❞ Brenna, 20, said, "I want to plant seeds in people's hearts to come to Jesus."

Dear Salvation-Is-Near Jesus,
Thank you that you live to revive the spirits of the lowly and the hearts of those who are contrite. Help me to turn around immediately when I know I'm going in the wrong direction, for the Word is near. Let me rest in your forgiveness today. Amen.

Do you struggle with asking for forgiveness? Please visit www.faithbookofjesus.com and click on "Community" to share.

To Read Further: Isaiah 30:15-18

STILL SINGLE

I will give them singleness of heart and action, so that they will always fear me for their own good and the good of their children after them . . . and I will inspire them to fear me, so that they will never turn away from me.

— JEREMIAH 32:39-40

One of the exhibitors at the True Woman Conference in Chicago asked me, "How it is possible that you're still single?" I thought I'd found my new best friend. I would love to find out the answer to that question.

It's not like I haven't tried meeting or dating people. I've gone to larger churches hoping to meet someone. I've tried blind dates, coffee dates, meeting handsome strangers online. I've tried eHarmony (more than once), Match.com, ChristianCafe .com, and others. But for whatever reason, *I am still single.*

The most ironic part is that every day at my job I take at least five calls from pastors who want to book Kirk Cameron at their churches. Since his latest movie *Fireproof,* I've had the pleasure of helping churches host marriage conferences, marriage seminars, and couples' date nights.

No matter if you're single or married, the Bible says we can have singleness of heart and action. If Jesus is inspiring us to stay faithful to him, how much more does he value our relationships? I hope one day I can look back and see how much Jesus inspired me to be faithful to him and my husband.

66 99 Zach, 35, said, "There are dangers of cohabitating prior to marriage (we do it *a lot*). I want to be a man of God in the area of sexual purity."

Dear Singleness Jesus,
Show us the power of Scripture by inspiring us to stay single in both our actions and in our hearts today. Give us the courage to say "yes" to sexual purity in all our relationships. Amen.

What does singleness of heart mean to you? Please visit www .faithbookofjesus.com and click on "Community" to share.

To Read Further: Jeremiah 32:37-41

PLANT IN TEARS

Those who plant in tears will harvest with shouts of joy.
— PSALM 126:5 (NLT)

Nothing is ever out of the reach of Jesus' grasp. No amount of sorrow, loss, sickness, pain, grief, or negative emotions will ever separate us from him. Why? Jesus is sovereign and *still* in control over all our circumstances.

Does this mean that we never ask "why" or "what if" when trials come? Or never soak our pillows in the night with our tears? No!

Whenever we face difficult times, we're sustained through reading the Bible. "The Sovereign LORD has given me an instructed tongue, to know the word that sustains the weary. He wakens me morning by morning, wakens my ear to listen like one being taught" (Isaiah 50:4).

Whenever we're up against an unmovable trial, we are sustained through fellowship with other believers. "Is any one of you in trouble? He should pray. Is anyone happy? Let him sing songs of praise. Is any one of you sick? He should call the elders of the church to pray over him and anoint him with oil in the name of the Lord" (James 5:13-14).

Whenever we've cried and can't cry anymore, we are sustained through prayer. "The prayer offered in faith will make the sick person well; the Lord will raise him up. If he has sinned, he will be forgiven. Therefore confess your sins to each other and pray for each other so that you may be healed. The prayer of a righteous man is powerful and effective" (James 5:15-16).

66 99   Nate, 29, said, "I fear that people will lose hope and stop trying."

Dear Tearful Jesus,
Some days I feel like the end of the world is near. Help me to cry out to you, knowing that those who plant in tears will reap with shouts of joy that come in the morning. Amen.

Are you planting in tears? Please visit www.faithbookofjesus.com and click on "Community" to share.

To Read Further: Psalm 126

RED LIGHT, GREEN LIGHT

The Lord is not slow in keeping his promise, as some understand slowness. He is patient with you, not wanting anyone to perish, but everyone to come to repentance.
— 2 PETER 3:9

Did you play Red Light, Green Light when you were a child? My favorite part was being able to tell everyone else when to go.

Sometimes I feel like Jesus is telling me "red light," and other times I feel him saying "green light." The worst is waiting at a red light and wondering if it's ever going to turn green. The Bible says that Jesus is not slow in keeping his promises.

Do you ever feel like you're waiting on Jesus? Life takes time. It took me ten years of intense physical suffering to heal, eight years to graduate college, and eight months to find the job of my dreams.

What green light are you waiting on today? A new job? A new relationship? Another roommate to help with bills? These are all valid things we're waiting on. However, Jesus wants us to see traffic from his perspective. All these red and green lights are part of the grid of eternity. Sometimes the reason Jesus is patient and slow with us is because he has something better in store.

❝❞ Nate, 29, said, "We have a wrecked view of Jesus because of the time we were born into, and we're all looking for his will when Jesus just wants us to experience the absolute freedom of making choices and taking big risks for the sake of his kingdom."

Dear Green-Light Jesus,
Wake us up to the freedom of choice today. Show us how many green lights we are experiencing and caution us when we need to slow down and stop at the red lights. Amen.

👥 What green light are you waiting on? Please visit www.faithbookofjesus.com and click on "Community" to share.

✠ To Read Further: 2 Peter 3:8-10

FOLLOW THE RULES

Athletes cannot win the prize unless they follow the rules.
— 2 TIMOTHY 2:5 (NLT)

If I were training for a marathon, do you think I'd be sitting on my couch eating potato chips every day? No way! I'd be outside running for miles and miles, training properly and getting in shape for the big day.

Paul was pretty serious about training. He said, "Run in such a way as to get the prize. Everyone who competes in the games goes into strict training" (1 Corinthians 9:24-25). Is there an area of your life that could use some discipline? Weak flesh produces weak Christians.

We have a reason to follow the rules. If you claim to be a Christian and your lifestyle does not match up with that, you will cause others to sin. Are you sleeping with your girlfriend? You're not living the life of a Christian.

We can't pick and choose which rules to follow. All marathon winners stay away from sweets until after the race. We are also in a race. All sins lead to the same destination: We miss the mark and lose the race.

Want to lead by godly example? Follow the rules Jesus laid out in his Word. Don't become part of the statistic of twentysomethings who don't go to church. Be the answer to why they do.

66 99 Nate, 29, said, "We need to realize there is no separation between sacred and secular. Jesus is in all of it. We need to make choices out of our passion and creativity, not out of our common sense and what the world tells us is smart."

Dear Rule-Book Jesus,
We need faith to make right choices so we don't discredit our Christian witness. Lead us to others who are hurting because of hypocrisy. May we be the real answer this world needs. Amen.

Do you follow the rules? Please visit www.faithbookofjesus.com and click on "Community" to share.

To Read Further: 1 Corinthians 6:19-20; 9:24-27

ON A MISSION

At the end of the time set by the king to bring them in, the chief official presented them to Nebuchadnezzar. The king talked with them, and he found none equal to Daniel, Hananiah, Mishael and Azariah; so they entered the king's service.

— DANIEL 1:18-19

King Nebuchadnezzar besieged Jerusalem, and Daniel and his friends (also known as Shadrach, Meshach, and Abednego) were taken to live in Babylon. Yet in the midst of a terrifying situation, these young men pleased the king.

Your mission, should you choose to accept it, could be overseas on the mission field or right in your own backyard. Culture has taught us to believe that we have to travel to go on a missions trip. Daniel did, but we don't have to. Some of you might be scared to travel to the next state while others might have been to Japan, India, or Australia already.

I was lucky enough to grow up in a home with loving parents who are still missionaries to this day. As a twentysomething, it's easy to find my identity in what I do. Therefore, I believe I'm worth something if I'm raising support and following in my family's footsteps. It wasn't until I had worked in the corporate world for more than three years that I learned a powerful lesson: I didn't have to travel. Showing up to work every day with a smile on my face did more for my co-workers than pretending all year except for the two weeks I went on a missions trip.

Daniel won over the foreign king because of his character. He and his friends were on a mission, and because of their witness, Jesus showed up (literally) and saved them. To read more of this fascinating story, read Daniel 3.

❝❞ Emily, 33, said, "I desire to be a Daniel—working in a secular environment and yet reflecting Jesus, *never* afraid to take a stand for my God in spite of what my world (family, work, friends, society) is saying or thinking."

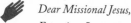 *Dear Missional Jesus,*
Ever since I can remember, I've always wanted to tell others about the good news of Jesus Christ. I pray you would give us the ability, as Daniel had, to represent Christ whether we're in a foreign land or in our backyard. Amen.

Where is your mission? Please visit www.faithbookofjesus.com and click on "Community" to share.

To Read Further: Daniel 1

STEP UP!

In his heart a man plans his course, but the LORD *determines his steps.*
— PROVERBS 16:9

Just imagine where you'd be right now if the Lord said "yes" to all your prayers. I'd have married at least twenty different guys, own houses all over the United States, and be a size 6 not 16.

Not every prayer is selfish, but I'm glad Jesus knows our hearts. Here are a few verses to inspire us today to step up to Jesus:

"To man belong the plans of the heart, but from the LORD comes the reply of the tongue" (Proverbs 16:1).

"Many are the plans in a man's heart, but it is the LORD's purpose that prevails" (Proverbs 19:21).

"A man's steps are directed by the LORD. How then can anyone understand his own way?" (Proverbs 20:24).

"If the LORD delights in a man's way, he makes his steps firm" (Psalm 37:23).

"I know, O LORD, that a man's life is not his own; it is not for man to direct his steps" (Jeremiah 10:23).

"Give discernment to me, your servant; then I will understand your laws" (Psalm 119:125, NLT).

66 99   Ani, 19, said she struggles with "trying to keep my prayers in balance and the age-old question: 'Who am I going to marry?'"

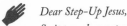   *Dear Step-Up Jesus,*
Scripture does not return void, and you keep all your promises. Therefore, we can step up and ask for help from you today. Give us the discernment to know where to go and what steps to take. Amen.

Do you need help stepping up to Jesus? Please visit www.faithbookofjesus .com and click on "Community" to share.

To Read Further: Psalm 37:23; Proverbs 20:24; Jeremiah 10:23

A STUDY IN MEEKNESS

Blessed are the meek, for they will inherit the earth.
— MATTHEW 5:5

You want me to be what? What does *meek* mean? *Merriam-Webster's Dictionary* defines it as "enduring injury with patience and without resentment: mild; deficient in spirit and courage: submissive; not violent or strong: moderate."[30]

Our normal reaction to something life-threatening is rarely ever mild, submissive, or moderate. There is something to be said of a meek person whose life is controlled by Jesus. He or she is not easily angered, doesn't have a temper, doesn't get drunk, doesn't envy, kill, or sleep around. He or she also respects authority. This list could go on and on.

There's no way we can be perfect on this earth, but the Bible says the meek will inherit the earth. If we know Jesus is in control of every circumstance, we should have the courage not to overreact or become proud (the opposite of meek).

"The high and lofty one who lives in eternity, the Holy One, says this: 'I live in the high and holy place with those whose spirits are contrite and humble. I restore the crushed spirit of the humble and revive the courage of those with repentant hearts" (Isaiah 57:15, NLT).

Remember the God who lifted you up is the same Jesus who can keep you up.

❝❞ Brad, 25, said what stresses him out are "the times when I feel ministry/work/life is creeping in and pulling me from [meekness] and what I believe God is really calling me to do."

 *Dear Meek Jesus,*
Don't let our pride overtake our ministry and our lives. Help us to come to you on bended knee whenever we feel the urge to be proud. Amen.

Do you know how to be meek? Please visit www.faithbookofjesus.com and click on "Community" to share.

To Read Further: Matthew 5:3-10

SHEEP ARE STUPID

If you see your brother's ox or sheep straying, do not ignore it but be sure to take it back to him.

— DEUTERONOMY 22:1

Sheep are notorious for wandering off. Whether they're continuously jumping over a fence in a dream or searching for the perfect blade of grass to eat, sheep don't stay still. People don't stay still either. The Bible is full of illustrations that compare people to sheep.

Jesus gave us the greatest example of how to rely on him: "I am the good shepherd. The good shepherd lays down his life for the sheep" (John 10:11). Jesus protects us as a shepherd protects his sheep.

Like sheep we, too, are stupid sometimes. We need constant care from our enemies, and even from ourselves (see 1 Samuel 17:24). David was a master shepherd who became king of Israel. He wrote that Jesus is the one who helps us through our stupidity. "Know that the LORD is God. It is he who made us, and we are his; we are his people, the sheep of his pasture" (Psalm 100:3).

According to Psalm 23, we shouldn't worry or want. Is there an area of your life where you need help? Ask the Good Shepherd. No matter how far you think you've wandered away from the flock, Jesus the Shepherd will come and find you (see Matthew 18:12). He will make you lie down in green pastures and sit you beside a still stream in the form of a new job, a new apartment, or a real friend. No matter what we are facing, we can trust Jesus to look after us and provide our daily needs.

66 99 Wilson, 26, said, "Too often we look around and think, *I will do that or be there eventually*, and limit our response to the vision Jesus has placed on our hearts because we listen to the lies that we are too young or inexperienced or broke to make a difference and wander further from him."

Dear Good-Shepherd Jesus,
Help us if we're lost today. Show us those around us who might need help finding you again. Thank you for being our Good Shepherd and for watching over us. Amen.

When was the last time you wandered off? Please visit www.faithbookofjesus .com and click on "Community" to share.

To Read Further: Matthew 18:10-14

A SHOUT-OUT

Enter his gates with thanksgiving and his courts with praise; give thanks to him and praise his name.

— PSALM 100:4

"In 1621, the Plymouth colonists and Wampanoag Indians shared an autumn harvest feast, which is acknowledged today as one of the first Thanksgiving celebrations in the colonies."[31]

I love how the Thanksgiving holiday fits perfectly into today's Bible verse. After planting a harvest of tears, it's time to reap a giant *shout-out* (see Psalm 126:5).

In the book of Psalms, David (the author) cried out to Jesus a lot. He had been promised the position of king of Israel because he was a man after God's own heart, but he had to wait. Not only did David have to wait, but his life was threatened by King Saul, who was the current king of Israel.

Everywhere David hid, Saul tried to find and kill him. If there is anyone we can learn from regarding planting in tears, it's David.

There have been times when, like David, I needed God to intervene on my behalf, but it wasn't until I started thanking God (like David) and letting go of control that he began to work.

Have you ever experienced a planting season in your life that didn't turn around until you began praising God?

66 99 Debbie, 27, said, "I am a wife, mom, quality management director (in that order); I'm very happy with all this."

Dear Shout-Out Jesus,
Some of us need help shouting out to you. Teach us to sing your praises whether we're looking for a job or just waiting for the clock to turn to five p.m. Amen.

What's your shout-out? Please visit www.faithbookofjesus.com and click on "Community" to share.

To Read Further: Psalm 100

HOT PURSUIT

The seventh time around, when the priests sounded the trumpet blast, Joshua commanded the people, "Shout! For the LORD has given you the city!"
— JOSHUA 6:16

In Joshua 6:1, the Israelites were up against the fortified city of Jericho in battle. No one entered or left the city. Even though Jericho was much more powerful and had enormous walls to protect it, Israel inspired fear in whomever it pursued. The stories of the parting of the Red Sea were circulating through enemy camps as the Israelites walked toward their Promised Land.

God commanded the Israelites to march around Jericho once a day for six days (see Joshua 6:3). I'm sure Joshua and the people felt a little silly. No battle plan, just walking. They were also commanded to stay silent. No shouting! But on the last day they marched around Jericho seven times. "Have all the people give a loud shout; then the wall of the city will collapse and the people will go up, every man straight in" (Joshua 6:5).

Jesus wasn't concerned about the Israelites' image or what the people of Jericho must have been shouting down at the men while they marched in silence.

What does this look like in your own life? Don't let Satan tempt, taunt, or tease you. He's already shaking in fear because he knows the outcome of the battle. We win—every time! Take your battles to the Lord. We might have to circle our problems seven times, but when Jesus gives us the signal to shout for victory, we will win that hot pursuit.

66 99 Catherine, 22, said, "I know my purpose is to serve God and to live a life that glorifies God. How that looks in my life . . . [I'm] not always sure."

 Dear Hot-Pursuit Jesus,
Thank you for great examples in Scripture that teach us how to run long and hard after you. Break the silence, the walls, and the attacks of the Enemy in our lives today. Amen.

Are you in hot pursuit? Please visit www.faithbookofjesus.com and click on "Community" to share.

To Read Further: Joshua 6:1-16,20

DONKEYS TALK?

When the donkey saw the angel of the LORD standing in the road with a drawn sword in his hand, she turned off the road into a field. Balaam beat her to get her back on the road.
— NUMBERS 22:23

Do you remember the story of the talking donkey in the Bible? Growing up, I heard it at church and in my family's devotional time. As a child, it was fun to hear about talking donkeys.

I recently reread the story of Balaam and realized I had missed something. Balaam was a prophet of God who spoke blessings and curses. But he was also a sorcerer. "Now when Balaam saw that it pleased the LORD to bless Israel, he did not resort to sorcery as at other times, but turned his face toward the desert" (Numbers 24:1).

How could I have missed that part in Sunday school? I was enamored with the talking donkey and didn't understand why Balak, the king of Moab, summoned Balaam.

Balak wanted Balaam to call down curses on God's people, the Israelites. It took a donkey to crush Balaam's foot, make a fool of him, and remind him of his loyalties (see 22:25).

What are the "donkeys" in your life? We sometimes don't see the work of God around us and impatiently take off. Wounds from a friend are better than many kisses from an enemy, or in Balaam's case, a crushed foot (see Proverbs 27:6). "Then the LORD opened the donkey's mouth, and she said to Balaam, 'What have I done to you to make you beat me these three times?' . . . Then the LORD opened Balaam's eyes, and he saw the angel of the LORD standing in the road with his sword drawn. So he bowed low and fell facedown (verses 28,31).

 Chris, 30, said, "How do I please everybody without compromising my own beliefs?"

 Dear Jesus Who Makes Donkeys Talk,
Open our eyes so we can see our divided hearts today. Show us the way we should walk so we don't have to learn the hard way as Balaam did. Amen.

 When has Jesus had to get your attention? Please visit www.faithbookofjesus .com and click on "Community" to share.

To Read Further: Numbers 22:21-41

HE'S JUST NOT THAT INTO YOU

He who watches over you will not slumber; indeed, he who watches over Israel will neither slumber nor sleep.

— PSALM 121:3-4

Your significant other may not be that into you, but Jesus is. As corny as that sounds, we are given a beautiful passage in the Bible written by King David.

Whenever the Israelites took their annual trip up to worship the Lord, they would sing a song of ascents. As they climbed, they sang praises to Jesus. I hope Psalm 121 shows you just how much Jesus is into you no matter if you're single, in a relationship, or it's complicated.

I lift up my eyes to the hills —
where does my help come from?
My help comes from the LORD,
the Maker of heaven and earth.

He will not let your foot slip —
he who watches over you will not slumber;
indeed, he who watches over Israel
will neither slumber nor sleep.

The LORD watches over you —
the LORD is your shade at your right hand;
the sun will not harm you by day,
nor the moon by night.

The LORD will keep you from all harm —
he will watch over your life;
the LORD will watch over your coming and going
both now and forevermore.

" DonNika, 21, said, "I want to have faith and reliance on the true God."

Dear You're-Just-That-into-Us Jesus,
As we head into the world today, show us how special we are. We have been bought with a price, and we can have fellowship with the one true God. We thank you for that. Amen.

Are you into Jesus? Please visit www.faithbookofjesus.com and click on "Community" to share.

To Read Further: Psalm 121

TANSTAAFL

Hey there! All who are thirsty, come to the water! Are you penniless?
Come anyway—buy and eat! Come, buy your drinks, buy wine and milk.
Buy without money—everything's free!
— ISAIAH 55:1 (MSG)

"There ain't no such thing as a free lunch" (or TANSTAAFL) originated from Robert A. Heinlein's book *The Moon Is a Harsh Mistress*, which now appears in most economics textbooks. Remember opportunity cost? You can't get "something for nothing."[32]

In my job I'm always asking speakers and comedians for favors so I can book more events for them. Sometimes it's coming up with a better marketing plan or sending a personal e-mail before an event is booked. The more I know my performers, the easier it is for me to sell them. The general manager of events tells me to "sell, sell, sell" all the time. How many events do I have pending? How many are going to be faxed back this week? The neverending cycle of "I'm only as good as my last month" can overwhelm me. Sales ain't easy.

One of my favorite Bible passages is also one of my favorite worship songs. Isaiah told the people of Israel not to worry where their money was coming from. There *was* such a thing as free food. "Why do you spend your money on junk food, your hard-earned cash on cotton candy? Listen to me, listen well: Eat only the best, fill yourself with only the finest" (Isaiah 55:2, MSG).

Even though we live in a country that promotes "self" and the idea that "you're only as good as your last sale," don't sell yourself short. Buy from Jesus for free.

66 99 Chad, 25, said, "Sell, sell, sell."

  Dear Free Jesus,
Some of us are dirt poor and don't have a penny to our name. It's hard to imagine that we must pay everything back in this life, but in your economy we can buy for free. Provide for our needs today as we put our faith in you. Amen.

 Are you penniless? Please visit www.faithbookofjesus.com and click on "Community" to share.

To Read Further: Isaiah 55:1-3 (MSG)

NEED A BACK RUB?

The King will reply, "I tell you the truth, whatever you did for one of the least of these brothers of mine, you did for me."
— MATTHEW 25:40

One day at work one of my co-workers was having a bad day. I walked over to his chair and gave him a shoulder rub to cheer him up. He groaned, and his limp arms let me know I was doing my job. He told me it was so good that I had to make it into a devotional and put it in my book. I laughed. What verse would be appropriate? Is there such a thing as "give your co-worker a back rub when he is having a bad day"? No. But there is a passage in Matthew that says everything we do is seen and remembered by Jesus.

> Then the King will say to those on his right, "Come, you who are blessed by my Father; take your inheritance, the kingdom prepared for you since the creation of the world. For I was hungry and you gave me something to eat, I was thirsty and you gave me something to drink, I was a stranger and you invited me in, I needed clothes and you clothed me, I was sick and you looked after me, I was in prison and you came to visit me." (25:34-36)

Do something nice for someone today, whether it's giving that person food, clothing, or a back rub.

66 99 Jennifer, 25, said, "I'm an only child, and [my family] babies me so much and feels the need to tell me how to do *everything* all of the time."

 Dear Backrub Jesus,
You train our hands to help others in need. Put others in our path today who are in need of a simple touch from you. Amen.

Are you in need of Jesus' touch today? Please visit www.faithbookofjesus.com and click on "Community" to share.

To Read Further: Matthew 25:31-46

EAT AND DIE

For the jar of flour was not used up and the jug of oil did not run dry, in keeping with the word of the LORD spoken by Elijah.
— 1 KINGS 17:16

The economy sucks. And I know California is not the only state in the United States that is experiencing skyrocketing layoffs, fluctuating gas prices, and financial uncertainty.

Until recently, I had never experienced such economic turmoil firsthand. Then, to top it all off, my health started failing me. I watched as more than half of my small group was laid off, fired, or unable to find a job . . . and then found myself in a similar situation, not knowing what to do with my life.

Because of the insta-community we share, we have pooled enough resources to help tide each other over. I recommended a friend for a seasonal job at the company where I work, helped my co-leader with his résumé, and encouraged another friend through her move, and that's just a drop in the bucket.

Elijah was faced with a similar financial situation. A widow had a son and no means of supporting herself. She told Elijah, "I don't have any bread—only a handful of flour in a jar and a little oil in a jug. I am gathering a few sticks to take home and make a meal for myself and my son, *that we may eat it—and die*" (1 Kings 17:12, emphasis added).

We need money to survive. Thankfully we serve a God who provides both community and finances. No matter the century, whether it's the woman Elijah helped thousands of years ago or the present-day reality of my twentysomethings group, God will provide. Bank on God!

66 99   Brandi, 29, said, "I'm unemployed, baby! But I want to be a full-time grad student."

 Dear Bank of Jesus,
Today's economy is tough, but it won't be this way forever. Help us to rely on you whether it's our last meal or we have enough to last us for a while. Amen.

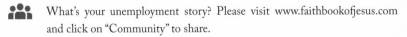 What's your unemployment story? Please visit www.faithbookofjesus.com and click on "Community" to share.

To Read Further: 1 Kings 17:7-24

THE GOLD SCEPTER

When he saw Queen Esther standing in the court, he was pleased with her and held out to her the gold scepter that was in his hand. So Esther approached and touched the tip of the scepter.

— ESTHER 5:2

Every once in a while we see glimpses of Jesus throughout the Old Testament that connect us with the New Testament. My best friend Monique showed me a connection between the books of Esther and Hebrews and the word *scepter*.

"When he saw Queen Esther standing in the court, he was pleased with her and held out to her the gold scepter that was in his hand. So Esther approached and touched the tip of the scepter" (Esther 5:2; see also 8:4). "Your throne, O God, will last for ever and ever, and righteousness will be the scepter of your kingdom" (Hebrews 1:8).

I found twenty-six references to the word *scepter* in the Bible, starting in Genesis 49:10. It says, "The scepter will not depart from Judah, nor the ruler's staff from between his feet, until he comes to whom it belongs and the obedience of the nations is his." Did you know that Jesus was from the line of Judah?

Jesus risked his life so that we don't have to risk our lives. We now have full access to the throne. If you are struggling with fear, loneliness, or unanswered questions about life, you can "approach the throne of grace with confidence, so that we may receive mercy and find grace to help us in our time of need" (Hebrews 4:16).

66 99 Alex, 23, said, "I want to learn about Old Testament law. It's great to hear about the life of Jesus, but I find comfort at the craziest times in the structure of obedience that our faith was built on."

Dear Scepter-Wielding Jesus,
Thank you for sightings of you throughout the Old and New Testaments. Help us to come boldly before your throne of grace today to find help where we need it most. Amen.

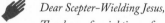 When was the last time you approached the throne of Jesus? Please visit www .faithbookofjesus.com and click on "Community" to share.

To Read Further: Esther 5:2; 8:4; Hebrews 1:8; 4:16

WHAT YOUR VOICE MAIL
SAYS ABOUT YOU

When we tell you these things, we do not use words that come from human wisdom.
Instead, we speak words given to us by the Spirit, using the Spirit's words to explain
spiritual truths.

— 1 CORINTHIANS 2:13 (NLT)

I come across some interesting people who call me at work asking to book a speaker or comedian. Sometimes it's their accent that makes me laugh, and other times it's their attitude that turns me off. I don't understand when they want to be called "Prophetess Divine" or "Reverend Brother."

I respect churches that use adjectives to describe their volunteers, but what I don't understand is why their actions sometimes don't match their words. For instance, one day I was leaving a message for a lady who was inquiring about one of my comedians. Her voice-mail message didn't make any sense. It was long-winded and mentioned something about how President Obama was the answer to all her prayers.

I thought, *If God truly answered such divine prayers, why couldn't she return a phone call?* Jesus said on the day of judgment there will be people who he "never knew" (Matthew 7:23). Some of us can sound so spiritual, yet our actions don't quite match up. Don't just say you're a Jesus follower; let your actions back up your words.

Want to know what's in the mind and heart of Jesus to encourage your "brothers and sisters" today? Read 1 Corinthians 2:6-16.

❝❞ Steve, 24, said, "I am stressed out when I don't know what is going on in the other person's head and whether I am doing something right."

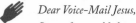 *Dear Voice-Mail Jesus,*
Some of us need help to stop talking the talk and start walking the walk. It could be in small matters, such as returning phone calls (I know I'm guilty of that), or larger matters. Give us an attitude of humility so we can encourage others today. Amen.

When was the last time you approached the throne of Jesus? Please visit www .faithbookofjesus.com and click on "Community" to share.

To Read Further: 1 Corinthians 2:6-16

BEDTIME STORIES

So the LORD sent Nathan the prophet to tell David this story.
— 2 SAMUEL 12:1 (NLT)

I love a good story. My favorite stories are written in books, made for television, or seen on the big screen. Everyone loves a great story.

Sometimes stories inspire us to be better people. In the movie *Bedtime Stories* Adam Sandler tells his nephew and niece stories before they go to bed, and when they wake up the next day, the stories come to life. The stories all weaved together to make an even better ending. Everyone loves a happy ending.

Stories can be a powerful tool to show us our sin. When I was reading through the *One Year Bible* in my personal quiet time last week, I found a great story. Nathan the prophet had been sent by God to tell David a story. If you skip to the end of the story found in 2 Samuel 12:9-12, you will see the Lord was furious with David. He had committed adultery, conspiracy, and murder (two of which were forbidden in the Ten Commandments). Yet the Lord gave David a second chance. Everyone loves redemption stories.

What bedtime stories do you need to read? Before you hit the pillow tonight, read the story found in 2 Samuel 12.

66 99 Teresa, 43, said, "My purpose in life is to guide my children to become honest, faithful, contributing members of society."

Dear Bedtime-Stories Jesus,
You are the ultimate storyteller. Thanks for using parables to speak to us and for the many stories compiled in the Bible to show us how to live and have a happy ending. Amen.

What's your happy ending? Please visit www.faithbookofjesus.com and click on "Community" to share.

To Read Further: 2 Samuel 12:1-12

RICH DAD, POOR DAD

For this reason I kneel before the Father, from whom his whole family in heaven and on earth derives its name. I pray that out of his glorious riches he may strengthen you with power through his Spirit in your inner being.

— EPHESIANS 3:14-16

Ephesians 3 describes our rich heritage as children of Jesus. Paul wrote of our legacy in his prayer found in verses 14-20. You may be familiar with verse 20: "Now to him who is able to do immeasurably more than all we ask or imagine." But do we know whom this is coming from? Christ our Savior is our Rich Dad.

Do you believe your heavenly Father can provide for your needs?

My response is to get down on my knees before the Father, this magnificent Father who parcels out all heaven and earth. I ask him to strengthen you by his Spirit—not a brute strength but a glorious inner strength—that Christ will live in you as you open the door and invite him in. And I ask him that with both feet planted firmly on love, you'll be able to take in with all followers of Jesus the extravagant dimensions of Christ's love. Reach out and experience the breadth! Test its length! Plumb the depths! Rise to the heights! Live full lives, full in the fullness of God.

God can do anything, you know—far more than you could ever imagine or guess or request in your wildest dreams! He does it not by pushing us around but by working within us, his Spirit deeply and gently within us. (Ephesians 3:14-20, MSG)

66 99 Amy, 25, said, "I am afraid of being homeless. No child support right now for me and my kids."

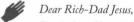 *Dear Rich-Dad Jesus,*
Remind us of how rich our heritage is in you today. Don't let us live as poor children, but rich in faith, hope, and love. Amen.

Do you know your Rich Dad? Please visit www.faithbookofjesus.com and click on "Community" to share.

To Read Further: Ephesians 3

WALK IN TRAFFIC

Thus says the LORD, "Stand by the ways and see and ask for the ancient paths, where the good way is, and walk in it; and you will find rest for your souls. But they said, 'We will not walk in it.'"

— JEREMIAH 6:16 (NASB)

Some of us need to walk in traffic. The world is full of hostility, angst, and fear. We're all speeding to find purpose. Sometimes in the process, we try to pass others to get there faster. What do I mean by that?

This Sunday, when I was driving to work, I cut someone off on my way *into* the church parking lot. What is wrong with me? Someone wasn't driving fast enough for me. By the time I was in the shoulder ready to pass the car, the bozo decided to put his blinker on two feet before the entrance—and then I cut him off to park. I know I'm a fast driver, but . . . seriously?

The Bible tells us that Jesus provides rest for us (see Isaiah 11:10; 30:15; 32:17; Jeremiah 6:16; Matthew 11:28-29)—but we ain't havin' it. Is it pride? Is it our rush to get that Mocha Frappuccino on our way to work, even though we are already fifteen minutes late? Let today's verse serve as a reminder along with your fresh cup of coffee.

When we walk in the path of the Lord's commands, we will be blessed, and our strength will be renewed; when we run, we will not stumble (see Proverbs 4:12; Isaiah 40:31).

66 99 Shanelle, 23, said, "I am my biggest problem. I seek accolades and confirmation and acceptance from my relationships."

 Dear Traffic-Control Jesus,
We are all seeking for purpose in this life. Help us to slow down and smell the roses along the path you have created instead of cutting someone off in traffic on our way to church as I did. Amen.

How do you deal with traffic? Please visit www.faithbookofjesus.com and click on "Community" to share.

To Read Further: Isaiah 11:10; Jeremiah 6:16; Matthew 11:28-29

DIAL 9-1-1

Call to me and I will answer you and tell you great and unsearchable things you do not know.

— JEREMIAH 33:3

Do you know how to pray? I realize this is a silly question because I'm asking it toward the end of the book. But let's get serious. Some of us don't know how to pray. We read the Bible, pray before meals, and cry out to God when we're stuck. But what do we say and how do we pray?

My favorite Bible verse on prayer is Jeremiah 33:3. It is the Bible's response to dialing 9-1-1. "Call to me and I will answer you." Need help with a pressing matter today? Start dialing by saying the name of Jesus. Not sure what to say? "I will . . . tell you great and unsearchable things you do not know." The Bible gives us the Holy Spirit. He prays on our behalf when we're too stunned or hurt to pray.

"In the same way, the Spirit helps us in our weakness. We do not know what we ought to pray for, but the Spirit himself intercedes for us with groans that words cannot express. And he who searches our hearts knows the mind of the Spirit, because the Spirit intercedes for the saints in accordance with God's will" (Romans 8:26-27).

Call on the Lord today. Don't be afraid to dial 9-1-1. Jesus is ready, waiting, and standing by to answer your prayers.

❝❞ Emily, 22, said, "Breaking through the 'prayer barrier' is where I want to be. I want to feel that not only am I reaching God, but that he is reaching me too."

Dear Emergency-Response Jesus,
We need to hear you loud and clear today. Be with us in the midst of great pain when we don't know what to pray for. Amen.

Do you need help learning how to pray? Please visit www.newlife.com.

To Read Further: James 1:5

TWENTYSOMETHING JESUS

Now Jesus himself was about thirty years old when he began his ministry.
— LUKE 3:23

Jesus was about thirty when he started his public ministry. Doesn't it feel like forever to wait until we're thirty to begin life? In our search for purpose, we worry too much. "Who of you by worrying can add a single hour to his life?" (Luke 12:25).

My friends know that I worry about the future. Who will I become? When will my career take off? It sounds exhausting because it is. I know I'm not the only one who is questioning when my life will begin.

Just tonight I was praying with my roommate for more personal requests. I believe Jesus puts others in our path to help us recognize his answers to prayer in our lives. As we looked at my prayer requests, we both saw how many prayers had turned into praises.

When Jesus was in his twenties, he didn't sit around sulking that his time had not yet come. Instead, he spent a lot of time at the temple (which he did since he was a little boy); he worked hard at his family's trade of carpentry; and he loved others.

Are you waiting for your ministry to begin? "See, the former things have taken place, and new things I declare; before they spring into being I announce them to you" (Isaiah 42:9). Follow Jesus' example today and ask him where to begin.

66 99   Kelsey, 32, said her worries include, "Am I too fat, am I toned, am I tan enough, am I 'hot' enough? Will my bills get paid on time? Will I ever be married? Will I ever have a comfortable savings account? Will I ever be a mother?"

Dear Twentysomething Jesus,
You see our hormones, empty bank accounts, and lonely hearts. Help us to stand strong in purity as we seek you daily for purpose. Amen.

Are you waiting for your ministry to take off? Check out Miles McPherson's book *Do Something!*

To Read Further: Luke 3:21-23

GENTLE RESPONSE

A gentle answer turns away wrath, but a harsh word stirs up anger.
— PROVERBS 15:1

I learned the lesson of gentleness the hard way. I sometimes say things out of anger that I don't mean. I even say things I do mean out of sheer frustration if someone's not tracking fast enough with me. Are you hot-blooded? If you're like the 5 percent that has been on reality television, then you've stirred up anger for bigger ratings.

I used to watch *The Hills* on MTV because I'm a fan of Lauren Conrad. When the feud between Heidi and Lauren heightened, I noticed how I was treating my roommates. Around the same time Lauren and Heidi stopped living together, I too was angry and upset with my roommates. I even paid double rent for a month.

Gentleness is an amazing friend. It goes everywhere with us and never grows tired of our antics. Yet, most of us never acknowledge it because it's too easy to sit in front of the television salivating on our potato chips and TV dramas. Scripted or not, real friendships are lost because of gossip, slander, and harsh words (see Proverbs 20:19; 26:22).

If you want to live a life that encourages other people, consider your tone. Watch your body language. Send the right signals. If you can't hide your anger, find a positive outlet, such as the gym or a best friend who is a great listener.

66 99 Chris, 19, said, "What stresses me out? Communication: miscommunication, lack of communication, etc."

 Dear Gentle-Response Jesus,
Where would we be today if you spoke to us the way we speak to others? Thank you for using restraint with us — and for teaching us how to use the same in our responses to others. Amen.

Do you need more gentleness? Please visit www.faithbookofjesus.com and click on "Community" to share.

To Read Further: Galatians 5:23; Colossians 3:12; 1 Peter 3:15

MISSIONARY DATING

You adulterous people, don't you know that friendship with the world is hatred toward God? Anyone who chooses to be a friend of the world becomes an enemy of God.

— JAMES 4:4

The phrase "missionary dating" applies when a Christian pursues a relationship with someone of a different faith. This is a hot topic today, just as it was in biblical times. Paul said that we are not the same as those who do not believe. So do not join yourselves to them. Good and bad do not belong together. Light and darkness cannot share the same space (see 2 Corinthians 6:14).

In the Old Testament, the Israelites were commanded not to intermarry with other nations (see Deuteronomy 7:3; Joshua 23:12-13; 1 Kings 11:2; Ezra 9:14). The main reason the Lord commanded them not to "missionary date" was because "they will surely turn your hearts after their gods" (1 Kings 11:2).

Missionaries are pure in heart. They have one purpose: to spread the good news that Jesus saves. Most missionaries also bring a skill or a trade to help the people group they are trying to reach. For instance, my parents are missionaries, and when they fly overseas, they assist in humanitarian aid to meet people's needs. Jesus didn't come just to save souls but to heal all diseases and set people free from the bondage they are in.

Missionary dating is a noble task, but not one that Jesus said was okay. Light and darkness do not go together. Flee from temptation, and don't try to change someone you shouldn't be with.

66 99 Julie, 26, said, "Fellowship with nonbelievers—what should our relationships with non-Christians look like?"

 Dear Missionary Jesus,
You want us to be happy. Don't let us believe the lie that you don't care about our relationships. Help us to let go of the preconceived notion that it's our responsibility to change someone's spiritual beliefs. Amen.

What are your thoughts on missionary dating? Please visit www .faithbookofjesus.com and click on "Community" to share.

To Read Further: 2 Corinthians 6:14-18

TODAY

Then he rolled up the scroll, gave it back to the attendant and sat down. The eyes of everyone in the synagogue were fastened on him, and he began by saying to them, "Today this scripture is fulfilled in your hearing."

— LUKE 4:20-21

When Jesus began his public ministry, two things happened. Jesus was immediately led into the desert to be tempted by the Devil. Then, as he returned victorious and full of the Spirit, he began preaching in the temple courts.

Do you ever feel that as we discover our purpose, life becomes increasingly more difficult? I know I do. Ever since I started writing this book, I've had nothing but struggles. I also remember that when I finally decided to go back to Biola University to finish my degree, bad things happened: My car broke down; I got sick multiple times; and my anxiety returned. This is nothing new. The Enemy has been after souls from the beginning of time. Don't consider it a blessing when the Enemy leaves you alone.

Today, if you are stumbling back from the desert of temptation, rest assured that the same Jesus who beat temptation can help you overcome. "And Jesus returned to Galilee in the power of the Spirit, and news about Him spread through all the surrounding district. And He began teaching in their synagogues and was praised by all" (Luke 4:14-15, NASB).

66 99 Stephanie, 26, said, "I really don't know about today. Right now I'm just going day by day."

 Dear Ta-Ta-Today Jesus,
Show us what it was like for you to begin your public ministry as a twentysome-thing. Give us the power and the strength of the Holy Spirit to tell others about you today. Amen.

Has life been increasingly difficult for you lately? Please visit www .faithbookofjesus.com and click on "Community" to share.

To Read Further: Luke 4:14-21

THE DREAM GIVER

Joseph stored up huge quantities of grain, like the sand of the sea; it was so much that he stopped keeping records because it was beyond measure.

— GENESIS 41:49

God places people right where he wants them. Remember the story of Joseph? Joseph was the favored child. His jealous brothers sold him into slavery for twenty shekels of silver.

"*Meanwhile*, the Midianites sold Joseph in Egypt to Potiphar, one of Pharaoh's officials, the captain of the guard" (Genesis 37:36, emphasis added). I love the word *meanwhile*. It should be circled in your Bible. Meanwhile Jesus had a plan. He knew Pharaoh would have dreams and Joseph, nicknamed "The Dreamer," would interpret them.

Jesus also knew it would be a while before this happened, so he made provisions for Joseph at the home of Potiphar. While in the home of his master, Joseph was tempted by the *witch*, also known as Potiphar's wife. After she set her trap, Joseph was sent to prison.

The cupbearer and baker had dreams that Joseph interpreted in prison. He begged and pleaded for them to remember him. The cupbearer forgot until Pharaoh himself had a dream. It was then that the Lord remembered his promise to Joseph.

Joseph told Pharaoh what his dream meant and was put into his charge as second in the kingdom. Years later when the dreams came true and the land of Israel was in a great famine, Joseph was reunited with his family in a way that only the real Dream Giver could make happen.

What dreams do you have? If you're waiting on Jesus, be encouraged and find strength for the journey today. Jesus sees you and won't forget you.

66 99 Olivia, 26, said, "In light of today's economy, I fear losing my job."

Dear Dream-Giver Jesus,
We praise you for life-giving dreams. Don't let us get stuck in a rut; we want to dream big—even if that means more changes around the corner until the dream is fulfilled. Amen.

Do you have a dream? Please visit www.faithbookofjesus.com and click on "Community" to share.

To Read Further: Genesis 41

YOUR CONFIDENCE

Blessed is the man who trusts in the LORD, whose confidence is in him.
— JEREMIAH 17:7

Did you know we are blessed for our confidence? As we trust Jesus with our lives, he blesses us and makes our paths straight (see Proverbs 4:25-27).

What are the perks of trusting in Jesus? The Bible says we "will be like a tree planted by the water that sends out its roots by the stream. It does not fear when heat comes; its leaves are always green. It has no worries in a year of drought and never fails to bear fruit" (Jeremiah 17:8).

Trees can withstand the fiercest of storms. We can, too. Although it doesn't feel like it at the time, Jesus blesses us to endure. "Perseverance must finish its work so that you may be mature and complete, not lacking anything" (James 1:4).

What about the trials that turn into tragedy? Jesus told his disciples in Mark 4:35 to "go over to the other side." He knew they would encounter a storm. "A furious squall came up, and the waves broke over the boat, so that it was nearly swamped. Jesus was in the stern, sleeping on a cushion. The disciples woke him and said to him, 'Teacher, don't you care if we drown?'" (Mark 4:37-38).

Jesus rebuked the storm and asked them where their confidence was. Was it in circumstances or in him? "Indeed, he who watches over Israel will neither slumber nor sleep" (Psalm 121:4). Put your confidence in Jesus. He will never fail you.

❝❞ Rach, 24, said, "My purpose is to show Christ's love and to serve women, children, and men who have been victims of domestic violence and sexual assault!"

 Dear Jesus Who Is Our Confidence,
Whether we are crossing over during a storm or stepping on dry ground, may we find our confidence in you today. Thank you for sustaining us by the power of your Word. Amen.

👥 Where is your confidence? Please visit www.faithbookofjesus.com and click on "Community" to share.

✝ To Read Further: Jeremiah 17:7-10

BLESSINGS AND CURSES

*If you fully obey the Lord your God and carefully follow all his commands I give you today,
the Lord your God will set you high above all the nations on earth.*
— DEUTERONOMY 28:1

What could happen if you don't spend time with the Lord? That's a question I set out to answer for my first big speaking engagement. I was invited to San Francisco for a women's conference where I taught two breakout sessions on how to have a *Wild Faith Devotional Life with God.*

When I asked for advice on how to set up my talk, my comedian friend Adam Christing told me to make sure women know why it's important to have a devotional life with the Lord. He said to name ten bad things that can happen if you don't.

Lust and adultery were the first two bad things that came to mind. A few others would be language, what we choose to watch on television, and how often we choose shopping over spending time with God (credit-card debt).

There are only two responses when we follow God: We are either blessed or cursed. Even King David, a man after God's heart, committed adultery. We are blessed if we obey Jesus; there's no question about that. We may not feel like it, because doing the right thing is tough. When we sin, we fall short. There are consequences for sin, although we may not see them right away. Jesus didn't set up a series of rules for us to fail but as a way for us to be blessed. What things come to your mind?

❝❞ Kimberly, 20, said, "My purpose is to spread the love of Jesus and live my life walking next to him!"

Dear Jesus Who Blesses,
We need your help to be obedient. Help us understand what it says in your Word so we can apply it directly to our lives. Amen.

Have you ever experienced bad things because you didn't spend time with Jesus? Please visit www.faithbookofjesus.com and click on "Community" to share.

To Read Further: Deuteronomy 28

BREAKTHROUGH!

When a man makes a vow to the LORD or takes an oath to obligate himself by a pledge, he must not break his word but must do everything he said.
— NUMBERS 30:2

What are some words commonly associated with *break*? You can break up, break out, and break through. John Maxwell said there are eight breakthroughs that build your dream. I will share only three.[33]

Groundbreakers encourage you to start. The original groundbreaker, God, created the world in six days. He "called the dry ground 'land'... And God saw that it was good" (Genesis 1:10). Do you need validation for all your groundbreaking hard work? Start by reading Genesis 1.

Tiebreakers encourage you to serve. Jesus was the ultimate servant. He put up with a lot from the crowds, his disciples, and the spiritual leaders of the day—the Pharisees. When Peter, his beloved disciple, denied him three times, Jesus could have given up or gotten angry. Instead, Jesus asked, "Simon son of John, do you truly love me?" (John 21:15). Three times he asked and three times he told Peter to serve others. If you want more of a servant's heart, read John 13.

Chart-breakers encourage you to soar. Ask the one who made the heavens and the earth to make sense of the storms of life. "You yourselves have seen what I did to Egypt, and how I carried you on eagles' wings and brought you to myself" (Exodus 19:4). When a storm is approaching, an eagle will fly directly into the wind, and instantly he soars. If you're having trouble keeping up, read Isaiah 40:30-31.

❝❞ Nicholle, 29, said, "I've been sick for a year and a half with woman problems, and I don't know whether or not I'm going to graduate."

Dear Breakthrough Jesus,
We need your help to break through all areas of life. Some of us make promises we can't keep, and others are struggling to get better. Amen.

Do you need a breakthrough? Please visit www.faithbookofjesus.com and click on "Community" to share.

To Read Further: John 21:15-19

AN INTERESTING REQUEST

Go, take to yourself an adulterous wife and children of unfaithfulness, because the land is guilty of the vilest adultery in departing from the LORD.

— HOSEA 1:2

The prophet Hosea's first request from the Lord was a strange one. Hosea was told by God to marry a prostitute. Why on earth would the Lord ask Hosea to do such a thing?

Jesus calls leaders to live on a higher level than followers.[34] We don't always understand the commands of the Lord. Nevertheless, Hosea was asked to go and reconcile with his wife who was involving herself in some very inappropriate relationships. She was a hooker! Like the Israelites, his wife Gomer was not accustomed to faithfulness.

When God told Hosea to pursue reconciliation, he told him to act with love rather than seeking revenge. That's a higher level of living than is required of followers. Followers tend to want to act out, create drama, be a victim, and get even.

Leaders are called to be examples and set the tone for followers, to take the high road, to stay focused on obedience to God, and to operate out of principle rather than reaction. Hosea showed mercy to his wayward wife.

It is a daily choice whether or not to follow the Lord's requests. Do you hold firm to integrity as a leader or stray from his commands? Who will you be today?

66 99   Traci, 23, said, "I feel I am to give words of prophecy to people — to help them better their lives, to tell the stories that should be told."

Dear Jesus Who Requests,
I want to know what you request of me today and every day. I might not understand it or like it, but every request is made with purpose and in mercy. Amen.

When has Jesus asked you to do something you didn't understand? Please visit www.faithbookofjesus.com and click on "Community" to share.

To Read Further: Hosea 1

YOUR GOALS

Let your eyes look straight ahead, fix your gaze directly before you. Make level paths for your feet and take only ways that are firm. Do not swerve to the right or the left; keep your foot from evil.
— PROVERBS 4:25-27

Have you ever met anyone who just wasn't able to prioritize?[35] Someone who gave more attention to the trivial than the important? I doubt you would define that kind of person as "successful." Today's verse is for that person.

We all need help to focus on one thing. In all likelihood, we all need help setting and accomplishing goals because goals matter.

Goals help you determine what's first, second, and third in life and responsibilities. Goals direct you and measure you. Mark it down: Successful people in any arena of life must have clear, attainable goals. No one fulfills their purpose, reaches their potential, or adds value to others without goals.

For instance, three years ago I wrote down a list of three things I wanted to accomplish: graduate college, move out of my parents' house, and find the career of my dreams. My dream of becoming a writer happened because I finished college.

Today, take some time to write a list of attainable goals.

66 99   Tyson, 20, said, "I need help with real issues such as drinking, drugs, partying, relationships, money."

   *Dear Goal-Setting Jesus,*
It is tough to set goals when we don't know what we want and where we're going. Help us with the issues we face on a daily basis and give us the courage to stick to the narrow path. Amen.

What are your goals? Please visit www.faithbookofjesus.com and click on "Community" to share.

To Read Further: Matthew 7:13-14

YOUR FAMILY WINS!

Similarly, if anyone competes as an athlete, he does not receive the victor's crown unless he competes according to the rules.
— 2 TIMOTHY 2:5

John Maxwell said, "To be a winner, you must allow God to work in your life."

Did you know most people secretly believe winners accomplish what they do because they have it easier than everyone else? Athletes aren't just lucky. They have more talent. In other words, their circumstances aren't better than ours. The Bible says an athlete plays by the rules to win the game.

John Maxwell also said,

People who succeed often do so because they are able to overcome terrible odds and miserable circumstances. If a leader faces a deck stacked against him or her, that leader has to start overcoming obstacles in his or her life.

In the Bible, King Josiah faced major obstacles. He was only eight years old when he became king. He came from a legacy of leaders during some of Israel's worst times. He didn't have a positive role model around him. And yet he ruled a nation with great leadership (2 Kings 21).[36]

No matter what the odds are against you, you can praise Jesus for the family he has given you and allow God to help you be the winner he knows you can be. It doesn't matter if you feel alone like Josiah, the eight-year-old king, or Angela (below), the twenty-four-year-old with a crazy family.

66 99 Angela, 24, said, "Family. Ah! They are crazy! I think God put me in the wrong family sometimes. Maybe there is a nonbeliever, 'knucklehead' kid about my age stuck in a Christian family wondering the same thing."

Dear Jesus Who Lets Us Win,
Give us the ability to play the game by the rules. If we have a great family or a hor-
rible background, show us how to be a winner despite our circumstances. No matter
what, may our lives be an encouragement to others. Amen.

Have you allowed God to work in your life? Please visit www
.faithbookofjesus.com and click on "Community" to share.

To Read Further: 2 Timothy 2:1-5

YOUR NEEDS

But a poor widow came and put in two very small copper coins,
worth only a fraction of a penny.
— MARK 12:42

The Bible is very clear. We help others by giving our time, money, and talents. The widow from today's verse was very poor. She gave everything she had. "If you see a need around you, do something about it!"[37] Don't let your busy job, small bank account, or age determine what you do for the kingdom.

"Perceiving a need in your community could become a catalyst of your leadership journey. Moses saw the need of liberating his people from slavery. Joseph saw the need to keep his constituency from starving, and Nehemiah saw the need to rebuild the walls of a defenseless city."[38]

What are the needs where you live? Mentoring? Caring for the elderly? Starting a reading program? Reaching out to expectant moms?

Leaders perceive a need and they take action in response to that need. What would happen if you took one step toward meeting a need in your community or your family today? We have no idea the kind of impact and the difference we can make when we serve the needs of others over ourselves daily.

66 99 Brea, 29, said, "I worry sometimes about my husband losing his job and not being able to provide for our family."

 Dear Jesus Who Provides for Our Needs,
You don't need our time or money. Your great and endless resources will meet our needs, but you often desire for us to reach out and help. Show us how to meet the needs of others today. Amen.

How can you help meet the needs of others? Please visit www .faithbookofjesus.com and click on "Community" to share.

To Read Further: Mark 12:41-44

POWER TO THE PEOPLE

But I have raised you up for this very purpose, that I might show you my power and that my name might be proclaimed in all the earth.

— EXODUS 9:16

Moses was a mighty man of God. Esther shone as queen. It is important for leaders to empower those around them. People become empowered when you provide them with three basic things: opportunity, freedom, and security.

John Maxwell said, "I want to create an empowering atmosphere for the leaders who work for me. Giving them opportunities to do new things within the organization, using their own creativity and initiative—and give them the security that I will back them up—even if things don't go as planned."[39]

Empowering others is tough. How do you balance your own needs with helping others' development? Today's verse (along with other biblical examples) shows us just how much we can empower others. Write down the names of three people you could encourage in your sphere of influence today. It might be a co-worker, a friend of the family, or your neighbor. Determine to do something to encourage them today—even if it's as simple as walking someone's dog or paying for lunch.

66 99 Annie, 28, said, "I am a small-group leader, and too often I have to have the conversation with my group that [empowers them to] obey God. . . . I don't want them to feel like I am judging them."

Dear Empowering Jesus,
We need the power of the Holy Spirit to empower others to be their best. Show us how to point others toward your sustaining power. Amen.

Is God using you to empower others to share? Please visit www.faithbookofjesus.com and click on "Community" to share.

To Read Further: Esther 4:14-16

WORRY WELL

Therefore I tell you, do not worry about your life, what you will eat or drink; or about your body, what you will wear. Is not life more important than food, and the body more important than clothes?

— MATTHEW 6:25

There is no such thing as a "worry-free" life because Jesus gave us emotions. Here are a few things we can learn from worry:

Worry helps us avoid going down the wrong path. If we are going too far or too fast off the path, the Lord allows us to experience fear and anxiety. But it's easy to get stuck in the trap of worry. Worry hinders us from moving forward. When the right path has been rediscovered and we're making steps toward restitution, the bad kind of worry disappears.

Jesus told us not to worry about things like food and clothing. When I struggle with worry, I find myself eating and shopping more. Most people have a favorite comfort food. Others hide behind their comfort clothes. Worry can keep us from doing what we know we shouldn't be doing, if you know what I mean. That's worrying well.

If you're not struggling with worry today, you can help out a friend who is. Galatians 6:1-2 says, "If someone is caught in a sin, you who are spiritual should restore him gently. But watch yourself, or you also may be tempted. Carry each other's burdens, and in this way you will fulfill the law of Christ."

66 99 Marie, 22, said, "Worry to me is not having enough money to stay at home with my kids when we have children, but I have to trust that Jesus wouldn't want me to work and that I would have more value at home with our children."

Dear Worry-Well Jesus,
It is our pleasure to give our worries and cares to you. Now whether or not we leave them there is another story. Help us worry well today. Amen.

Do you worry well? Please visit www.faithbookofjesus.com and click on "Community" to share.

To Read Further: Matthew 6:25-34

IT'S NEVER TOO LATE

"Lord," Martha said to Jesus, "if you had been here, my brother would not have died. But I know that even now God will give you whatever you ask."
— JOHN 11:21-22

The choices we make in our twenties will affect the rest of our lives. Some of us will decide to get married and have children. Some might end up in divorce or bankruptcy. In light of today's economy, nothing is certain except for the Word of God (see 1 Peter 1:25).

If you feel that it's too late, put yourself in Martha's shoes. When Jesus was told that Martha's brother, Lazarus, was sick, he stayed two more days. It was during those two days that Lazarus died, and on the third day Jesus brought him back to life. Martha was upset with Jesus.

Jesus didn't come to earth to make friends (although he made plenty, and Mary, Martha, and Lazarus were three of his closest friends). Jesus came to show us the way to the Father.

Maybe it was because Jesus wanted to give us more signs (which the people kept asking for). Maybe Jesus was listening to the Father, so he stayed put. Maybe he wanted us to have more faith. Whatever the reason, it certainly wasn't too late to save Lazarus, and it's never too late to trust Jesus.

❝❞ Katrina, 27, said, "I would like to have pursued a dance career, but I feel like it's too late now and wouldn't be logical with my other goals for family."

 Dear Never-Too-Late Jesus,
We might never know your reasons, but we can experience your resurrection power in our lives today. Show us how. Amen.

Do you feel it's too late for you? Please visit www.faithbookofjesus.com and click on "Community" to share.

To Read Further: John 11:17-37

DON'T JUDGE ME

Do not consider his appearance or his height, for I have rejected him. The LORD does not look at the things man looks at. Man looks at the outward appearance, but the LORD looks at the heart.

— 1 SAMUEL 16:7

The only person who can follow his heart is Jesus. He is the only one who can look through a person's thoughts and intentions and dig deep into the heart. We can only understand what is going on in our own brain before making a judgment or an accusation.

Today's verse is one of my favorite verses in the Bible. It gives me hope not to trust in my own abilities but to rely on the Lord to show me a person's heart. It's too easy to judge. Samuel was sent by God to anoint the next king of Israel. He judged too quickly.

When David's father, Jesse, brought out his seven sons, Samuel thought for sure the first son was it. Jesus had a thing about the firstborn son. But when he passed in front of Samuel, the Lord said "no." Then he said "no" again and again and . . . I think you get the point.

You might be praying about your future mate. When will I recognize him or her? How will I hear the Lord's voice as he or she passes in front of me? I hope you understand why this verse has quickly become one of my favorites. Don't judge too quickly. You will know because Jesus will tell you.

 Brock, 26, said, "How do I recognize when something is of Jesus?"

 Dear Judge Jesus,
How we need your ability to judge correctly. Help us see past our own faults and the faults of others before we snap to judgment today. Amen.

 Do you judge too quickly? Please visit www.faithbookofjesus.com and click on "Community" to share.

To Read Further: 1 Samuel 16:1-13

PARENTHESES

(It takes eleven days to go from Horeb to Kadesh Barnea by the Mount Seir road.)
— DEUTERONOMY 1:2

In writing, the use of parentheses is meant to add extra information (like this). If you don't pay close attention, you could miss something. In Deuteronomy 1:1-5 it states the preamble and gives the historical setting for the entire book and introductions for Moses — stuff we typically gloss over.

In Deuteronomy 1:2 we see a parentheses. What it is really saying is that the trip out of Egypt into the Promised Land should have taken *eleven days* but instead it took *forty years*. Oops. (What did we miss?)

The Israelites departure out of Egypt into the desert turned into a disaster. They grumbled. They complained. They tried to kill Moses. They angered Jesus so badly that he took them on the scenic route. "The LORD's anger burned against Israel and he made them wander in the desert forty years, until the whole generation of those who had done evil in his sight was gone" (Numbers 32:13).

Do you need help being obedient? Today's verse is a great reminder not to miss the parentheses because we all sin and fall short. But take heart "for it is God who works in you to will and to act according to his good purpose" (Philippians 2:13).

66 99 Loli, 29, said, "I try to be obedient to the calling God has on my life, reaching little girls to let them know that their worth is far greater that what this world can offer; it's hard but that's my purpose."

Dear (Jesus),
It's not an understatement to say that we need your help to be obedient. The Israelites sinned, and we still sin today. Show us the grace and mercy we need to continue on. Help us not to miss anything we should've seen (like you in our lives). Amen.

What are you missing (in life)? Please visit www.faithbookofjesus.com and click on "Community" to share.

To Read Further: Deuteronomy 1:1-3

LET'S TALK ABOUT SEX

Marriage should be honored by all, and the marriage bed kept pure, for God will judge the adulterer and all the sexually immoral.

— HEBREWS 13:4

Is premarital sex a sin? Yes. The Bible is black and white when it comes to sexual immorality. The world unfortunately is not. Instead of letting the media dictate your sex life, here are five verses from the Bible about sex:

"Flee from sexual immorality. All other sins a man commits are outside his body, but he who sins sexually sins against his own body. Do you not know that your body is a temple of the Holy Spirit, who is in you, whom you have received from God? You are not your own; you were bought at a price. Therefore honor God with your body" (1 Corinthians 6:18-20).

"But among you there must not be even a hint of sexual immorality, or of any kind of impurity, or of greed, because these are improper for God's holy people" (Ephesians 5:3).

"Do you not know that the wicked will not inherit the kingdom of God? Do not be deceived: Neither the sexually immoral nor idolaters nor adulterers nor male prostitutes nor homosexual offenders nor thieves nor the greedy nor drunkards nor slanderers nor swindlers will inherit the kingdom of God" (1 Corinthians 6:9-10).

"We should not commit sexual immorality, as some of them did—and in one day twenty-three thousand of them died" (1 Corinthians 10:8).

"But the cowardly, the unbelieving, the vile, the murderers, the sexually immoral, those who practice magic arts, the idolaters and all liars—their place will be in the fiery lake of burning sulfur. This is the second death" (Revelation 21:8).

❝❞ Becky, 26, said, "We need to address issues of premarital sex."

 Dear Jesus Who Created Sexuality,
Today's society accepts sex as a natural part of loving someone, yet your Word says differently. May we see and understand that sex is meant for the marriage bed. Help us remain pure until marriage. Amen.

How can you stay pure before marriage? Please visit www .faithbookofjesus.com and click on "Community" to share.

To Read Further: 1 Corinthians 6:9-10; Ephesians 5:3; Hebrews 13:4

ARE YOU A NEW BELIEVER?

Whoever believes and is baptized will be saved, but whoever does not believe will be condemned.

— MARK 16:16

If you are a new believer, you might be wondering how to live. Don't let your faith or your relationship with Jesus Christ scare you. Instead, take your laundry list of things you feel you would have to change and throw it away.

Come as you are. That's the best way to describe your next step. Jesus knows your heart. He sees your thoughts and intentions and will help guide you. If you don't know how to read the Bible, start by reading one page at a time. Grab a Bible (consider *The Message* translation in today's contemporary language) at a local bookstore and ask Jesus to reveal himself through his Word. Join a small group at a church and get involved with other people your age.

Consider getting baptized. The Bible is quite clear on baptism. It is an outward sign of the inward change of becoming a new believer. It is also a choice that you make, not a decision made for you. When Jesus started his public ministry at age thirty, he was baptized by John the Baptist. You can read more about this in the "Your Faith" section below.

On your new faith journey, the best piece of advice I can give you is to keep short accounts with yourself and the Lord. Romans 3:23 says, "All have sinned and fall short of the glory of God." Confess your sins to the Lord through prayer on a daily basis.

" " Thy, 20, said of his new faith, "I don't exactly have a favorite Bible verse yet because I just started going to service two weeks ago."

Dear Jesus Who Saves,
We all struggle with our faith sometimes. I pray for your blessing on those of us who believe in you today, whether we have known you for two days or twenty years. Amen.

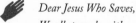 Where are you at in your faith journey? Please visit www.faithbookofjesus .com and click on "Community" to share.

To Read Further: Matthew 3:13-17

OVERFLOW

The good man brings good things out of the good stored up in his heart, and the evil man brings evil things out of the evil stored up in his heart. For out of the overflow of his heart his mouth speaks.

— LUKE 6:45

Christians are great at pretending. Just because we believe in Jesus doesn't mean we don't experience hurt like everyone else. Do we let out a stream of curse words or do we praise Jesus when life doesn't go our way? It says in the Bible that out of the overflow of our hearts, our mouths speak. Sarah (quoted below) wrote a beautiful overflow:

> I feel that I am being judged for not being right with the Lord, yet life is hard. And so we should be there to comfort each other. But I believe there are so many Christians who go through life alone who never share their real hurts and pains for fear of judgment. Or people will look down on us, so we always have to feel perfect. Maybe they have serious past hurts and have a hard time sharing what they have endured. Do others care about our wounds, or will they cast them off and not really see our true pain that we are dealing with? We turn ourselves into a pretender to be perfect, to be loved.

Don't let the label of "Christian" stop you from expressing yourself. But watch your overflow when words turn from needing help to gossip, slander, or cursing Jesus.

“ ” Sarah, 23, said, "I think there is a lot of pain in Christians' lives, and they always have to put up a front that they can't be sad or miserable."

Dear Overflow Jesus,
What an amazing God we serve! You give us mouths to speak freely. Help us to understand how to express our needs in a way that honors and glorifies you. Amen.

What does the overflow of your heart look like? Please visit www .faithbookofjesus.com and click on "Community" to share.

To Read Further: Matthew 12:33-35; Luke 6:43-45

MO' MONEY, MO' PROBLEMS

Didn't it belong to you before it was sold? And after it was sold, wasn't the money at your disposal? What made you think of doing such a thing? You have not lied to men but to God.
— ACTS 5:4

Ananias sold a field and conspired with his wife to give *some* of the profit to the apostles but make it seem as if they were giving *all* of the profit. They should have known Peter was a man filled with the Holy Spirit. Peter said, "Ananias, how is it that Satan has so filled your heart that you have lied to the Holy Spirit and have kept for yourself some of the money you received for the land?" (Acts 5:3). Then Ananias dropped dead. Sounds like a scene from an *E! True Hollywood Story*!

Three hours later his wife, Sapphira, came to the apostles. She hadn't seen or heard what had happened to her husband. They didn't have Twitter back then. Peter gave her a chance to speak. He asked her if the amount Ananias had brought was the full price, and she said "yes." "Peter said to her, 'How could you agree to test the Spirit of the Lord? Look! The feet of the men who buried your husband are at the door, and they will carry you out also'" (verse 9).

Don't let mo' money (or the lack of it) create more problems for you. As believers, we should be asking, "Am I living within my means?"

66 99 Matt, 28, said, "I am not worried about money because we're military, but I fear for my family and friends who don't have that job security."

 Dear Mo'-Money Jesus,
Some of us don't know how we're going to pay rent next month, and others are deep in credit-card debt. Show us how we can live within our means and honor you with what we have. Amen.

Have you ever lied about money? Please visit www.faithbookofjesus.com and click on "Community" to share.

To Read Further: Acts 5:1-10

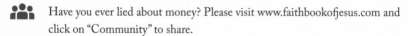

LEAVE THE DOOR OPEN

So you see, the Lord knows how to rescue godly people from their trials, even while keeping the wicked under punishment until the day of final judgment.

— 2 PETER 2:9 (NLT)

Living with roommates has taught me many things. Some of the fun things include different ways of cooking, new gadgets, and improved ways of dating. I mentioned in an earlier devotional that both of my previous roommates have gotten married because of me. I am great at connecting my friends, and whenever I plan a get-together, I invite everyone (including your mom).

My last roommate, Sara, married my friend Joshua. This was her second boyfriend, but her first serious relationship. It was interesting to watch them date, especially the first time Joshua came over. I came home to find the door open while it was forty degrees outside. I thought they were both nuts and shut the door. But I found their reasons valid. They wanted to live above reproach because at any moment someone could walk through the door. Were they being pure?

Temptation is no joke. I know this because it infiltrated the bubble I was living in. As a sheltered homeschooled girl who had lots of health issues, I never thought any boy would like me. Wrong! I have experienced a world of heartache too many times to count. I didn't know what "leaving the door open" meant.

I have since asked my friends and family to keep me accountable. If I spend time alone with a boy, I now leave the door open, too.

66 99 Martin, 25, asked for a devotional on "dating topics and premarital courtship."

 Dear Way-Out Jesus,
The Bible says we will not be tempted beyond what we can bear but that you will provide us a way out. Show us the open door so we don't fall today or any day. Amen.

Do you need a way out? Please visit www.faithbookofjesus.com and click on "Community" to share.

To Read Further: 1 Corinthians 10:12-13

BE RECONCILED

Therefore, if you are offering your gift at the altar and there remember that your brother has something against you, leave your gift there in front of the altar. First go and be reconciled to your brother; then come and offer your gift.

— MATTHEW 5:23-24

If a relationship bothers us, there are certain emotions we may feel: hate, anger, bitterness, resentment, envy, or lust. It says in the Bible that if we continue to fuel these emotions, we are living in sin (see Ephesians 4:31). The best and quickest thing to do is go and be reconciled with that person.

How do we reconcile with someone we truly dislike? The first place to start is praying and reading the Word daily. The Holy Spirit will bring the Scriptures to light in the dark places of our lives. Ephesians 4:27 says not to give the Devil a foothold. When we choose bitterness over forgiveness, we are actually sinning and allowing the Devil to win.

Matthew said to keep short accounts with others. If we're in church or reading the Bible and Jesus brings someone to mind that we have a problem with, we are literally to go and be reconciled.

Friendships and families have been torn apart due to sin. Grudges that started out as resentment turned into full-blown excommunication. I know because I once told my mother that I would rather be homeless than live with her. It took years of therapy to get over some deep hurts that we shared, but once I asked for her forgiveness, we were able to begin the healing process.

66 99 Tamryn, 20, said, "I feel like my family doesn't understand me. How do I fellowship with other believers?"

Dear Jesus Who Reconciles,
Don't let us wait, but help us to settle matters quickly so we do not fall into sin. Keep our relationships with family and friends free from blame. Amen.

Is there someone you need to make amends with? Please visit www .faithbookofjesus.com and click on "Community" to share.

To Read Further: Matthew 5:23-26

PLANS FOR HOPE

"For I know the plans I have for you," declares the LORD, "plans to prosper you and not to harm you, plans to give you hope and a future."
— JEREMIAH 29:11

Have you experienced a time in your life when you had to start over? My name Renee means "born again" or "new life." I can't tell you how many times I've had to start over or felt like starting over. I don't always get things on the first try, and sometimes I make huge mistakes. Either way I always find comfort when I read my Bible.

The Old Testament is a great place to start reading if you're not familiar with the Bible. Genesis begins with the first sinners, Adam and Eve, along with the first dysfunctional family, where the firstborn son kills the second son. If you think your family has problems . . .

How do we hope for a future when we have obstacles in our way? I know people who have experienced job loss, cancer, bankruptcy, and divorce at a young age. Some of the things were out of their control while others were a direct result of poor choices.

"We know that in all things God works for the good of those who love him, who have been called according to his purpose" (Romans 8:28). As a step of faith, offer Jesus your life today and watch him give you plans for hope. I've never seen a life that can't be fixed by Jesus.

66 99 Cameron, 22, said, "I feel my purpose in life is to create and share my music with the world."

  Dear Plans-for-Hope Jesus,
It says in your Word that when we seek you, we will find you if we seek with all our heart. So here we are asking, seeking, and knocking. Let us in, Jesus. Amen.

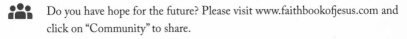 Do you have hope for the future? Please visit www.faithbookofjesus.com and click on "Community" to share.

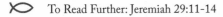 To Read Further: Jeremiah 29:11-14

WORKING CLASS

For it is God who works in you to will and to act according to his good purpose.
— PHILIPPIANS 2:13

When I speak at conferences or workshops, my favorite subject is devotional time. I have faithfully spent time with Jesus daily for the past twelve years. Ever since that day in the hospital when I didn't have any skin on my face and feet because of severe eczema, I vowed to be close to him.

I truly felt like I had made a promise I could keep. I needed time with Jesus. I didn't know him as well as I had thought. Growing up in a Christian home only taught me the way to Jesus, but the personal relationship was lacking. Do you ever feel that way?

I use today's verse when speaking on how to have a consistent devotional time with Jesus. All of us who are believers are in Jesus' working class. Thankfully, it's not up to us to live the Christian life by ourselves because we have help when we encounter problems. Are you struggling today? Write down today's verse and place it in your cubicle or on your bathroom mirror. Be encouraged; God is working in you.

66 99 Michelle, 34, said, "I need help with money as a single mom not being able to provide for my three kids."

 Dear Working-in-Us Jesus,
We need your help in life and work to stay consistent. Meet us every day as we read your Word, and help us to rise above each difficult situation we face. Amen.

How is God at work in your life? Please visit www.faithbookofjesus.com and click on "Community" to share.

To Read Further: Philippians 2:12-18

BODY IMAGE

Do you not know that your body is a temple of the Holy Spirit, who is in you, whom you have received from God? You are not your own; you were bought at a price. Therefore honor God with your body.

— 1 CORINTHIANS 6:19-20

I searched "body image" on Google and found more than 145 million hits. I found articles on celebs such as Jessica Simpson and Jennifer Love Hewitt, who have been criticized for gaining ten pounds.

It is astronomical the number of times we struggle with body image. It used to be the norm that kids in high school felt the pressure to be thin or in shape, but now I know elementary school kids who are facing eating disorders.

Body image and self-esteem are linked. If you struggle with low self-esteem, it is because you also struggle with poor body image. But did you know that your body is a temple of the Holy Spirit? When we say we hate our bodies, we're actually saying we hate Jesus, the one who made us.

We were bought with a price. Jesus "made himself nothing, taking the very nature of a servant, being made in human likeness. And being found in appearance as a man, he humbled himself and became obedient to death—even death on a cross!" (Philippians 2:7-8).

The way you view your body is your choice. You have the freedom to choose how you take care of your body. Before you make a decision that you might regret, remember to honor Jesus first.

66 99 Megan, 23, said, "I struggle with poor self-image. This has always stuck with me, and I believe it has made a huge impact on how I see myself."

Dear Jesus Who Lives in Us,
Thank you that you do not impose your will on us but allow us to use our bodies however we see fit. Be with those of us who might still be struggling with poor body image due to the choices we've made. Amen.

Do you struggle with body image? Please visit www.faithbookofjesus.com and click on "Community" to share.

To Read Further: 1 Corinthians 6:12-20

NOTHING GOOD HAPPENS AFTER 9 P.M.

Above all else, guard your heart, for it is the wellspring of life.
— PROVERBS 4:23

When you're tired, your guard isn't as effective. The Bible says to guard your heart, which controls your thoughts and emotions. If you're anything like me, I'm more susceptible to temptation when it's dark outside. I want to get comfortable, so I let my inhabitions go. I'll sometimes have my PJs on when a boy stops by, and we might happen to eat dessert and watch a movie together.

I've never been held more accountable than while writing this book. If my book includes topics like sexual purity, am I making sure to set an example myself? It took the stomach flu to wake me from my slumber. My mentor Marcia told me to make sure my message matched the messenger.

As Christians, we are to set examples for our non-Christian friends. I remember getting into many arguments with one of my classmates at Biola University; he was living with his girlfriend—breaking an unwritten rule in Christian circles.

More than 80 percent of twentysomethings say they are Christians, according to the Barna Group.[40] But if you look at the lifestyles of these so-called Christians, they look and act just like everyone else. Ask yourself today, "What am I doing after 9 p.m.?"

❝❞ Shawna, 24, said, "People portray Christians as 'no fun,' and it's important to remind young Christians that they can have way more fun then their non-Christian friends because they have Jesus planning their life."

 Dear Good and Fun Jesus,
Living the Christian life is not meant to harm us but to save us from the dangers of this world. Show us how we can have good, clean fun today in the power of your name. Amen.

What's your idea of fun? Please visit www.faithbookofjesus.com and click on "Community" to share.

To Read Further: 1 Corinthians 10:6-13

WINNING SOULS

He who wins souls is wise.
— PROVERBS 11:30

Earlier in the year we learned how to share our faith (see Week 29 // Friday • page 178 through Week 30 // Thursday • page 183). But what about the person who is sharing his or her faith? In other words, what's in it for you? Here are a few things the Bible tells us about those who share their faith:

He who wins souls is a lifesaver. Proverbs 14:25 says, "A truthful witness saves lives, but a false witness is deceitful." Do you know people in your life who need rescuing? Show them the truth by pointing them toward Jesus.

He who wins souls is a shining star. Daniel 12:3 says, "Those who are wise will shine like the brightness of the heavens, and those who lead many to righteousness, like the stars for ever and ever." Feeling a bit dull lately? Let the light of Jesus penetrate your heart and mind in Christ Jesus to win others over.

He who wins souls is a slave. First Corinthians 9:19 says, "Though I am free and belong to no man, I make myself a slave to everyone, to win as many as possible." Paul became like a Jew to win the Jews who were still under the law, and to the Gentiles he became like a free man. Want to blend into your surroundings? Learn how to be all things to all men so that by all possible means you might save some (see 1 Corinthians 9:22).

The richest and smartest man in the whole world (King Solomon) wrote, "He who wins souls is wise," and he was right.

❝❞ Mary, 25, when asked if she could do anything, said, "I would want to visit a village or a town in a third-world country and help build that village to make it more comfortable living for people."

Dear Jesus Who Makes Us Wise,
Help us to be lifesavers, shining stars, and slaves to become all things to all people today. Others need to know they can put their faith in you, just as we have. Amen.

Are you winning souls? Please visit www.faithbookofjesus.com and click on "Community" to share.

To Read Further: Proverbs 11:30; 14:25; Daniel 12:3; 1 Corinthians 9:19-22

FORGIVE MUCH, FORGIVE LITTLE

Therefore, I tell you, her many sins have been forgiven—for she loved much. But he who has been forgiven little loves little.

— LUKE 7:47

Your faith has saved you. Jesus has been telling us these words since he came to rid the world of sin. He also put them into action when he ate with prostitutes, tax collectors, and sinners (see Matthew 21:32).

Today we have a choice: We can sin and get into all kinds of evil, or we can try to live the Christian life. Either way we're still sinners. The good news is that Jesus came to save sinners (see 1 Timothy 1:15-16).

Some of us have been forgiven much. The churches that draw me back each Sunday are usually filled with former drug addicts, prostitutes, and drunks who knew how to party. They are the least judgmental and forgive much easier. The openness and vibrancy in their spirits, not to mention real authenticity, are amazing. I want friends like that in my life.

Jesus told his disciples a story. He said if two men owed money to a creditor (one's debt was way more than the other's) and their debts were suddenly canceled, which of the two would be happier? Of course, the one who owed more money.

If you're holding on to past regret, experience forgiveness in Jesus today. "Your faith has saved you; go in peace" (Luke 7:50).

66 99 Tanya, 32, said, "I am saddened by how many judgmental Christians there are out there who have a holier-than-thou attitude."

Dear Jesus Who Forgives Much,
Show us the joy of a lost soul who has been brought into repentance and forgiveness in your name. Amen.

Are you forgiven much or little? Please visit www.faithbookofjesus.com and click on "Community" to share.

To Read Further: Luke 7:36-50

DESIGNER CLOTHES

Your clothes did not wear out and your feet did not swell during these forty years.
— DEUTERONOMY 8:4

The Israelites were able to walk for miles and miles, for weeks, months, and even years in perfect clothing. What a wonderful blessing it was that their clothing never wore out.

Some of us are lucky enough to own name-brand clothing while others are too poor to afford food. It's an interesting country we live in. Yet if we study the Israelites' story a little more closely, we see their plight. They were desperate. They had been slaves to the Egyptians for more than four hundred years.

One day the Lord heard their cries for help and sent Moses and Aaron to deliver them. Even though God had designed a plan that took years to execute, it didn't mean that he was absent or didn't care (which some of you may feel right now).

The Master Designer and Creator designed the perfect rescue and executed his perfect plan. After the parting of the Red Sea, the Israelites rebelled and were severely punished. What should have taken eleven days took forty years. But Jesus in his sovereignty knew they weren't ready for the Promised Land just yet. So he designed their clothing and shoes to last forty years; they didn't fade or wear out. God knows where you're at, and he's designed a plan to get you through. You can trust him today.

66 99   Loli, 29, said, "I am a senior artist [makeup artist] for MAC cosmetics. I love it."

 Dear Master-Designer Jesus,
Thank you for designing a master plan that includes daring rescues and clothing provisions. Help us to be faithful to you and not rebel against you just because we feel like it. Amen.

What has Jesus given you? Please visit www.faithbookofjesus.com and click on "Community" to share.

To Read Further: Deuteronomy 8:1-5

WONDER WOMAN

Deborah, a prophetess, the wife of Lappidoth, was leading Israel at that time.
— JUDGES 4:4

The Bible has a few wonder women. Deborah the prophetess is one of the only women mentioned in the Bible as leading the people of Israel. What happened to the male-dominated society? The Israelites were in the heat of battle (what else is new?), and Barak asked Deborah to help him fight his battle. He told her, "If you go with me, I will go; but if you don't go with me, I won't go" (Judges 4:8).

Deborah's response is classic: "Very well . . . I will go with you. But because of the way you are going about this, the honor will not be yours, for the LORD will hand Sisera over to a woman" (verse 9). Go wonder woman!

At first glance it seems like the war's outcome will belong to Deborah. Instead, they kill all the troops of Sisera except for the king himself. King Sisera runs away on foot and ends up in the tent of Jael (another wonder woman). Jael invites him in, and Sisera takes a nap. In the middle of his slumber Jael pops him in the face with a tent peg. Go, Jael!

Superhero stories never grow old. I don't know about you, but I'd like to have that kind of strength to face my enemies and save the day. Ask God to help you fight your battles and turn you into the superman or wonder woman he knows you can be today.

66 99 Tiffany, 27, said, "I get stressed when my family or best friend tells me what to do because I think I already know. . . . It's a power/control issue."

Dear Superman Jesus,
Make us into wonder women and supermen of Jesus today. Fight our battles for us so we too can sing a song of victory at the end. Amen.

Do you know any wonder women or supermen? Please visit www .faithbookofjesus.com and click on "Community" to share.

To Read Further: Judges 4

YOUR BFF

After David had finished talking with Saul, Jonathan became one in spirit with David,
and he loved him as himself.
— 1 SAMUEL 18:1

Have you ever had a best friend forever? The relationship between David and Jonathan is the Bible's example of a BFF. In the course of their friendship, they made three covenants to establish, confirm, and reconfirm their special bond of love (see 1 Samuel 18:3; 20:16; 23:18).

Jesus has always been and will always be our Counselor and Best Friend Forever. Having a lifelong friend doesn't carry the same importance as it did in Jonathan and David's time. Jonathan's father King Saul was hunting David. Jonathan's friendship to David kept him alive.

Have you had a friend put his or her neck on the line for you? Jonathan's love for David was so strong that he gave up the throne for David. "Jonathan took off the robe he was wearing and gave it to David, along with his tunic, and even his sword, his bow and his belt" (1 Samuel 18:4).

Make a special covenant with the ones you love today. Give them a token of appreciation. Commemorate the special occasion for when tough times come (and they will).

"And Jonathan made a covenant with David because he loved him as himself" (1 Samuel 18:3).

66 99 Andrew, 26, said, "I know my purpose it to serve Jesus [like my brothers/sisters in Christ] but specifically, I still don't know. . . ."

Dear BFF Jesus,
You put your neck on the line when you died on the cross for us so we could be reunited in fellowship with you in heaven for eternity. Thanks for being our BFF. Help us love others as Jonathan loved David. Amen.

 Who's your BFF? Please visit www.faithbookofjesus.com and click on "Community" to share.

To Read Further: 1 Samuel 18:1-4; 20:16; 23:18

A PRIESTLY BLESSING

The LORD bless you and keep you; the LORD make his face shine upon you and be gracious to you; the LORD turn his face toward you and give you peace.
— NUMBERS 6:24-26

In Bible times, one could make a special vow of separation to the Lord. In particular, a Nazirite vow included abstinence from wine, fermented drinks, grapes, raisins, or anything that came from the grapevine and not eating anything unclean. Also, no razor was allowed to touch his head.

What does taking a Nazirite vow have to do with being blessed? Priests had direct access to God during this time, and taking this special vow put them in the same category.

Do you want to be blessed? Let's look at the stories of two people mentioned in the Bible who took the Nazirite vow: Samson and Paul (see Judges 13:5-7; Acts 18:18). I believe Paul chose to take the vow to continue the blessing of the Holy Spirit in the midst of sin.

Different pastors and commentaries explain that living a godly life in the city of Corinth would be equivalent to living godly on the Las Vegas strip. Temptation was everywhere, and messing up the first true witness of Christ was a fear that Paul refused to believe.

That's kind of where we're at today. Some of us may choose to abstain from alcohol to avoid making stupid decisions. Others may decide to dress differently.

Instead of stressing yourself out by trying to figure out God's blessing, know that you already have it—so you can keep going and be blessed.

66 99 Shawn, 25, said he is stressed by "trying to find time to make everyone happy and accommodate everyone. It is impossible to make everyone happy, and until I learn this . . . I will continue to stress myself out trying."

Dear Priestly Blessings Jesus,
Bless us and keep us today. Make your face shine upon us and be gracious to us. Turn your face toward us and give us peace. Amen.

How do you bless others? Please visit www.faithbookofjesus.com and click on "Community" to share.

To Read Further: Numbers 6:22-26

VIRTUOUS WOMAN

Charm is deceptive, and beauty is fleeting; but a woman who fears the LORD is to be praised.

— PROVERBS 31:30

There is a famous passage in the Bible that talks about the virtuous woman. It is found in the last chapter of Proverbs. Some of you may be familiar with it, while others of you may have never read it.

A virtuous woman has much character. Solomon said, "She is worth far more than rubies" (Proverbs 31:10). Who is this woman, and where can I meet her?

The Proverbs 31 woman has the attention and full confidence of her man. Her husband lacks nothing, and she brings him only good the rest of their days.

She is a hard worker. Her trade makes the family extra money, and she is able to provide food for her family and her maids. She even buys a plot of land for the family, and from the money she earns, she plants a vineyard (see verses 13-19). Again, I want to meet this woman.

The virtuous woman is a servant. She gives to the poor with open arms. She also serves her household and makes sure no one is lacking anything. Her husband is rich and well respected in the community. The Proverbs 31 woman dresses in designer clothing and is faithful to her family. Her children love her, and she fears the Lord. She is well praised wherever she goes.

If you want to learn more about this amazing woman and her husband, read Proverbs 31:10-31.

66 99 Stephanie, 26, said, "I would love to read more about becoming a virtuous woman."

Dear Virtuous Jesus,
We praise you for developing character in us and showing us how to use it. Teach us how to be more like the virtuous woman and her husband, who was highly praised at the city gate. Amen.

Are you virtuous? Please visit www.faithbookofjesus.com and click on "Community" to share.

To Read Further: Proverbs 31:10-31

LEAVING A LEGACY

I will establish my covenant as an everlasting covenant between me and you and your descendants after you for the generations to come, to be your God and the God of your descendants after you.

— GENESIS 17:7

Leaving a legacy for your family and friends is important. How do you want to be remembered? The last words Jesus said to his disciples as he ascended into heaven were to go and spread the good news of the gospel. Why?

John Maxwell wrote that "the gospel was His [Jesus'] message, but legacy was His method. Everything depended on the job He did with those twelve men."[41] It is through Jesus' disciples that we have heard about all the wonderful miracles and teachings. The Bible is another part of his legacy that we use to encourage others.

It is my hope that *Faithbook of Jesus* will be passed down through generations because the Word of the Lord stands forever (see 1 Peter 1:25). The stories of the Bible come to life through devotionals. There will always be new and improved ways to explain the Scriptures, but the Holy Scriptures never grow old and neither does our legacy.

Leave a legacy of faith, hope, and love. Allow your relationship with Jesus to make you a better person so you can leave the world a much better place.

❝❞ Tashawni, 25, said, "I work in insurance. I'm very grateful. I am in school and desire to be a nurse before I'm thirty. Lord willing, I want to leave a legacy."

 Dear Legacy-Leaving Jesus,
Some of us don't know what we're doing with our lives, while others know exactly who they want to be. As we carry on, give us the determination to leave a legacy that encourages the masses. Amen.

 What's your legacy? Please visit www.faithbookofjesus.com and click on "Community" to share.

To Read Further: 1 Corinthians 13:13

INTEGRITY

I know, my God, that you examine our hearts and rejoice when you find integrity there.
— 1 CHRONICLES 29:17 (NLT)

Integrity is something that happens when no one is looking. I believe integrity comes true when we practice it at all times. I'm most embarrassed about the way I spend time online or what movies or television shows I watch when I'm bored and emotional. Men are not the only ones who struggle with visual images. Did you know that Matthew McConaughey takes his shirt off in every movie he's in?[42]

Dr. Henry Cloud said integrity is the courage to meet the demands of reality.[43] Your life may be the only Bible some people read (the author of this saying is unknown). King David said our secret sins will ultimately be brought into the light of Jesus and his presence (see Psalm 90:8).

What do we do with the gap between who we want to be and who we are? Dr. Henry Cloud said there is always an opportunity for growth. The gap is also the place where dysfunction occurs. We get interrupted. Why? We get sidetracked. Sometimes we sin and make wrong choices in our pursuits of goals and relationships. Remember, character equals the ability to meet the demands of reality. To reach our goals and deliver in our relationships, we have to be able to negotiate those realities or else they will crush us, stop us, hurt us, or thwart us.

Work on growing your integrity today.

❝❞ Teresa, 27, said, "How do you make the right choices when temptation is sitting right in front of you and no one is looking?"

Dear Integrity Jesus,
Help us to remain in fellowship with you so that when you return, we will be full of courage and not shrink back from you in shame. Amen.

👥 Do you have integrity? Please visit www.faithbookofjesus.com and click on "Community" to share.

✝ To Read Further: 1 John 2:28

CELEBRATE!

While they were there, the time came for the baby to be born, and she gave birth to her firstborn, a son. She wrapped him in cloths and placed him in a manger, because there was no room for them in the inn.

— LUKE 2:6-7

I love Christmastime. It's a time to celebrate with family and friends and to learn more about the ultimate gift, Jesus. We also endure full shopping malls, present-buying frenzies, travel plans, and million-calorie foods. In the hustle and bustle of the season, it's important not to forget the reason we celebrate.

Christmas started with a teenage girl named Mary. She was a virgin and pledged to marry Joseph (see Luke 1:27). An angel greeted her and told her not to be afraid. She could easily have become an outcast because at that time unwed women who got pregnant were killed or ostracized from society.

Mary went to visit her friend Elizabeth, who was also pregnant with a special boy—John the Baptist. It was a musical time together. Mary sang, and later Zechariah, Elizabeth's husband, sang when John was born. I wish I could have been there (and I don't even like musicals).

When Mary and Joseph reunited, they were required to travel to Bethlehem, the town of David, to register. Jesus was born and fulfilled the Old Testament prophecies. That is why we worship him today and every day.

66 99 Jerry, 29, said, "I want to learn more about Jesus on my own and study more."

Dear Baby Jesus,
What an incredible sight it must have been to be born of a young teenage girl who had no clue the angel's words would come true. Just as you were with Mary, be with us today and show us more of you. Amen.

Do you know the true meaning of Christmas? Please visit www .faithbookofjesus.com and click on "Community" to share.

To Read Further: Luke 1:26–2:20

THE HEART JESUS REVIVES

The sacrifices of God are a broken spirit; a broken and contrite heart, O God,
you will not despise.
— PSALM 51:17

I grew up listening to Nancy Leigh DeMoss on the radio. She has a daily show called *Revive Our Hearts*. I most remember her shows on how to be the kind of woman God uses. Nancy spoke at a conference my family attended in 1995. A revival broke out, and people prayed and openly confessed their sins.

The revival spread like wildfire across the tens of thousands of people who were gathered that summer. I remember, as a twelve-year-old, getting up in front of my peers and participating by confessing my sins. Since that day I have never quite experienced that kind of godly brokenness.

Nancy made a list of "The Heart God Revives," including characteristics of proud, unbroken people who are resistant to the call of God on their lives compared with the qualities of broken, humble people who have experienced God's revival.[44]

Proud people focus on the failures of others. They are self-righteous and look down on others. They are independent and have a self-sufficient spirit. They have to prove they are right. They claim rights and have a demanding spirit. They desire to be served and to be a success. They have a drive to be recognized and appreciated. Shall I continue?

Broken people are overwhelmed with a sense of their own spiritual need. They receive criticism with a humble, open spirit. They are quick to admit failure and to seek forgiveness when necessary. They are able to acknowledge specifics when confessing their sin. They realize they need to have a continual heart attitude of repentance.

What kind of person do you want to be?

66 99 Bree, 20, said, "I am overcoming addictions."

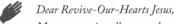 *Dear Revive-Our-Hearts Jesus,*
May we continually sense the need for a fresh encounter with you. Fill us today with your Holy Spirit so we may be used by you. Amen.

Does your heart need revival? Please visit www.faithbookofjesus.com and click on "Community" to share.

To Read Further: Psalm 34:18; 51:1-17

SHOW ME A SIGN

Gideon said to God, "If you will save Israel by my hand as you have promised — look, I will place a wool fleece on the threshing floor. If there is dew only on the fleece and all the ground is dry, then I will know that you will save Israel by my hand, as you said."

— JUDGES 6:36-37

Whenever I am looking for a sign, I read Judges 6. Gideon was a man handpicked by God to lead the people of Israel into battle. When an angel showed up, Gideon was hiding wheat inside a winepress to keep it from the enemy.

The angel said, "The Lord is with you, mighty warrior" (verse 12). But Gideon argued with the angel. He said, "Sir . . . if the Lord is with us, why has all this happened to us? . . . How can I save Israel? My clan is the weakest in Manasseh, and I am the least in my family" (verses 13,15).

Do you ever feel that way? Jesus shows up and asks you to do something that you don't feel qualified to do. So, you (like Gideon) ask for a sign. It sounds silly, but I ask Jesus for confirmation daily. "What boy should I date?" "Where should I eat lunch?" "How can I pay for rent *and* a big-screen TV?" "How do I witness to my neighbors?"

However big or small, ask Jesus to show you a sign.

66 99 Ketric, 26, said, "I believe Jesus is going to take care of my needs, and what isn't a need, it needs to go away anyway."

 Dear Show-Me Jesus,
Show me a sign! I need you to speak to me. I have needs that could be just wants, and I get confused sometimes. Help me to distinguish between the two by sending me a sign today. Amen.

Do you need a sign? Please visit www.faithbookofjesus.com and click on "Community" to share.

To Read Further: Judges 6

IT IS FINISHED

It is finished! I am the Alpha and the Omega—the Beginning and the End. To all who are thirsty I will give freely from the springs of the water of life.
— REVELATION 21:6 (NLT)

The first time I read today's verse, I had been out of the hospital for almost one year. I had made a vow to myself and to Jesus that I would read through the entire Bible that year.

On December 28, 1998, I read this verse with two days left to go in the year. My initial reaction was, "It's about time!" It's over. I can stop suffering now. It took the eczema on my feet and my face another few years to heal, but I was never the same after reading this verse.

I wonder what trials you are currently facing. Isn't it comforting to know that

he who was seated on the throne said, "*I am making everything new!*" Then he said, "Write this down, for these words are trustworthy and true."

He said to me: "It is done. I am the Alpha and the Omega, the Beginning and the End. To him who is thirsty I will give to drink without cost from the spring of the water of life. He who overcomes will inherit all this, and I will be his God and he will be my son." (Revelation 21:5-7, emphasis added)

It is finished—right now!

❝❞ Burke, 27, said he already graduated and is "now going back to school to make a career change."

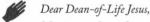 *Dear Dean-of-Life Jesus,*
May we graduate this year in thankfulness of heart knowing how far we've come and all the trials we've overcome. Thank you for not giving up on us and for finishing what you started. Amen.

What are you waiting to finish? Please visit www.faithbookofjesus.com and click on "Community" to share.

To Read Further: Revelation 21:5-8

INVITE A TERRORIST TO CHURCH

As he neared Damascus on his journey, suddenly a light from heaven flashed around him.
— ACTS 9:3

Jesus is in the business of changing lives, especially the really bad ones. The "baddest" person in the Bible was Saul (or Paul). He was a Jew, born in Tarsus of Cilicia. He was a zealot for God. He persecuted anyone who called himself a follower of Christ. He arrested men and women and threw them into prison, and he traveled to arrest more so they, too, could be punished and murdered (see Acts 22:3-5). Saul gave approval for the death of the first martyr, Stephen (see 8:1).

While Saul was still "breathing out murderous threats against the Lord's disciples," he encountered a light from heaven (9:1). He fell to the ground, blinded, as Jesus spoke to him for the first time. Not only did Jesus change his name from Saul to Paul, but he also became a messenger of "the Way."

We owe our salvation to Jesus, who saved the heart of a terrorist named Saul. He took the message of Christ into Rome and throughout the ends of the earth. Next time you're wondering how to invite that "bad" person to church, remember that Jesus is in the business of changing lives.

66 99 Marta, 21, said, "We are not really as great as we thought we were, and we need Jesus to cleanse and change us after getting out of denial."

Dear Changing-Lives Jesus,
Bring to mind that "bad" girl or boy we can be praying for. Change and transform them so they, too, can become followers of the Way. Amen.

Who can you invite to small group or church? Please visit www .faithbookofjesus.com and click on "Community" to share.

To Read Further: Acts 9:1-19

THE CURVEBALL

I have learned the secret of being content in any and every situation, whether well fed or hungry, whether living in plenty or in want. I can do everything through him who gives me strength.

— PHILIPPIANS 4:12-13

What's the point of a curveball? Pitchers use this throw in baseball to confuse the hitter and win the game. Isn't that like what the Enemy does to us? The curveball comes, and it's over. Done. Finished.

I can try so hard to make it work. I fake myself out. I pray. I seek wise council. I do everything in my power to win the game and make it work. The pitches that were once easy fastballs turn into something fierce.

Yet sometimes a new beginning is disguised as failure because the outcome of the game belongs to the Lord. Times of failure do not catch God by surprise. Nothing catches God by surprise. He does not panic or worry. But we do. Why wouldn't we when we experience a broken relationship, a job change, or, worse yet, losing our health?

Somehow the hardest lessons are learned while waiting on God. Contentment isn't easy. Curveballs aren't allowed unless they serve a purpose. You might feel like it's the end, but it might be the beginning of answered prayer. This curveball that you've been crying about just might bring the freedom you need to win the game.

66 99 Kyle, 25, said what he fears most about the game of life is not "knowing whether I'm fully in Jesus' will."

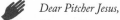 *Dear Pitcher Jesus,*
I keep striking out. Help me to realize that no matter how hard I play, I'm not out; I'm just moving on. You just might be helping me hit my home run into the next chapter of my life. Amen.

Do you have a curveball story? Please visit www.faithbookofjesus.com and click on "Community" to share.

To Read Further: Philippians 4:12-16

NOTES

1. http://www.youtube.com/watch?v=MWaRulZbIEQ.
2. http://thinkexist.com/quotes/hannah_moore.
3. L. B. Cowman, *Streams in the Desert* (Grand Rapids, MI: Zondervan, 1997), February 18 entry, 79–80.
4. D. James Kennedy, *Evangelism Explosion* (Carol Stream, IL: Tyndale, 1996).
5. Larry Crabb, *Soul Talk* (Brentwood, TN: Integrity, 2003), 65.
6. Neil T. Anderson, *Steps to Freedom in Christ* (Ventura, CA: Regal, 1993).
7. http://en.wikipedia.org/wiki/Sabbath.
8. *Merriam-Webster's Collegiate Dictionary*, 11th ed., s.v. "harbor."
9. *Merriam-Webster's Collegiate Dictionary*, 11th ed., s.v. "star."
10. John Eldredge, *Wild at Heart* (Nashville: Thomas Nelson, 2001), 137.
11. *Merriam-Webster's Collegiate Dictionary*, 11th ed., s.v. "idolatry."
12. Jerry Bridges, *The Discipline of Grace* (Colorado Springs, CO: NavPress, 2006), 12.
13. Joshua Harris, *I Kissed Dating Goodbye* (Sisters, OR: Multnomah, 2003), 31.
14. L. B. Cowman, *Streams in the Desert*, September 8 entry, 342.
15. Anjana Ahuja, "Every 7 seconds? That's a fantasy," *The Times*, February 1, 2006, http://www.timesonline.co.uk/tol/life_and_style/article723673.ece.
16. http://en.wikipedia.org/wiki/Heart_rate.
17. L. B. Cowman, *Streams in the Desert*, April 10 entry, 149.
18. http://www.coolquotes.com/despair.html.
19. http://en.wikipedia.org/wiki/Rachel_Scott.
20. Beth Nimmo and Darrell Scott, *Rachel's Tears* (Nashville: Thomas Nelson, 2000), excerpt from Rachel's journal on back cover of book.
21. Kay Arthur, *Lord, Heal My Hurts* (Colorado Springs, CO: WaterBrook, 2000), 250.
22. Arthur, 223–224.
23. http://www.divorcerate.org.
24. These questions have been adapted from Evangelism Explosion International and are part of its comprehensive training for personal witness. You can find out more about EE by visiting www.eeinternational.org. All rights reserved, including translations. Content used by permission.
25. Alex Leo, "Carrie Prejean, Miss California, Likes 'Opposite Marriage' Better Than Gay Marriage," *Huffington Post*, April 21, 2009, http://www.huffingtonpost.com/2009/04/20/carrie-prejean-miss-calif_n_188897.html.